Cultural Pessimism

To Rosemary and Catherine

Cultural Pessimism

Narratives of Decline
in the Postmodern World

Oliver Bennett

Edinburgh University Press

Edinburgh University Press Ltd
22 George Square, Edinburgh

Typeset in New Baskerville
by Hewer Text Ltd, Edinburgh, and
printed and bound in Great Britain by
MPG Books Ltd, Bodmin

A CIP Record for this book is
available from the British Library

ISBN 0 7486 0936 9 (paperback)

Contents

List of figures and tables

Acknowledgements

I WOULD LIKE TO THANK Peter Bendixen, Rosemary Bennett, Chris Bilton, David Fisher, Bill Greenslade, Adrian Heathfield, Karen Jones, Nobuko Kawashima, Philip MacGregor and Jonathan Milton for reading the drafts of various chapters and for their helpful comments, advice and encouragement. Thanks also to Jeremy Ahearne and Jim McGuigan who gave freely of their time at critical stages of the book's development. I would like to acknowledge the help given to me in different ways by Andy Edgar, Andy Feist, John Golesworthy, Anne Kelly, Pat Mayhew and Adrian Palka. I owe a particular debt of gratitude to Richard Perkins at the University of Warwick library for his help and success in tracking down vital sources of information. I would also like to thank postgraduate students at the Centre for Cultural Policy Studies at Warwick both for putting up with my preoccupation with pessimism and for the many interesting discussions we have had on the subject. Finally, I would like to thank Jackie Jones of Edinburgh University Press for her incisive comments, patience and support.

Introduction

C ULTURAL PESSIMISM ARISES WITH the conviction that the culture
of a nation, a civilisation or of humanity itself is in an irreversible
process of decline. In its severest form, it goes beyond the idea of
culture as a set of intellectual and artistic practices, or even culture as
a 'signifying system', and attaches itself to culture as a whole way of
life.[1] It is this form of pessimism with which this book is primarily
concerned.[2] It proposes: that in the era of postmodernity, that is, the
last few decades of the twentieth century, narratives of decline
emerged throughout the West in widely disparate fields; that these
narratives were deeply pessimistic in their implications; and that,
taken together, they produced a representation of decline which
could be seen as cultural in its broadest sense. The book explores how
this representation was constituted and considers its relationship to
the formation of cultural pessimism at both a cognitive and affective
level.

Of course, neither cultural pessimism nor its associated theories of
decline are new. The twentieth century, as Francis Fukuyama pointed
out, had 'made us all into deep historical pessimists', and we did not
have to wait until its last quarter for its exponents of despair to
appear.[3] In the United States, the historian Henry Adams was
denouncing the culture of America and the West, almost as soon
as the new century had begun. Adams believed that the age in which
he lived was decadent to the core and foresaw in the next hundred
years 'an ultimate, colossal, cosmic collapse'. His brother and fellow
historian Brooks Adams agreed, anticipating Oswald Spengler by
some years in both his cyclical theories of history and in his conviction

1

that Western civilisation was nearing the end of its own cycle. 'How can we hope to see a new world order, a new civilization or life?' he wrote to Henry Adams. 'To my mind we are at an end; and the one thing I thank God for is that we have no children.'[4] Spengler himself, whose *Decline of the West* was published in German in 1918 and translated into English in the 1920s, suggested that each civilisation had a life cycle of around 1000 years, moving from growth to decay in much the same way as a biological organism. His dark vision of the West approaching its final phase, expressed with Wagnerian intensity, was highly influential amongst a generation that had seen industrial progress applied to the relentless slaughter of millions during the First World War.[5] In England at around the same time, the very idea of progress, despite J. B. Bury's well-known attempt to celebrate it, had been condemned by W. R. Inge, the Dean of St Paul's, as a 'pernicious superstition'; and by Austin Freeman who, in *Social Decay and Regeneration*, suggested that the West was regressing at an accelerating rate due to the degenerative effects of industrialism on both the environment and the human psyche.[6]

Sigmund Freud's view of history was equally pessimistic. Indeed, his entire system of ideas was shot through with pessimism, from his account of the individual ego, attempting to steer its precarious course through the irreconcilable demands of the 'pleasure principle' and the 'reality principle' to the vision of civilisation itself turned neurotic by the repressions required to ensure its survival. His version of cultural decline, set out in *Civilization and Its Discontents* (1929), was not so much of a steady deterioration but of an accumulation of cultural frustration that threatened at any point to explode into aggression and self-destruction. As the technological capabilities of civilisations increased – to the extent that, long before the atomic bomb, Freud believed humanity already had the means to wipe itself out – the potential consequences of such a breakdown became catastrophic. This had the effect of strengthening the socio-psychological mechanisms through which societies kept control of themselves ('the cultural super-ego'), creating further repressions and setting up an even more powerful mood of collective anxiety. For Freud, there was no way out of this dilemma, and the evolution of civilisation was a perpetual struggle 'between Eros and Death, between the instinct of life and the instinct of destruction, as it works itself out in the human species'.[7] The British historian H. A. L. Fisher could find no meaning or pattern of *any* kind in the unfolding of history. 'These harmonies are concealed from me', he wrote in 1934.

'I can see only one emergency following upon another as wave follows upon wave.'[8]

For Max Horkheimer and Theodor Adorno, leading members of the Frankfurt School of sociology, the Enlightenment 'project' of liberating humanity from servitude and superstition had not only failed in its aims but had actually produced more powerful myths and even more absolute forms of domination. In *Dialectic of Enlightenment* (1944), they argued that enlightened reason had degenerated into 'instrumental rationality', a mode of abstraction which elevated the means of existence to the status of ends, denying and closing off the prospects of real freedom which the Enlightenment was supposed to bring.[9] The economic organisation of modern capitalist society was the final realisation of this process, leading to the increasing commodification of all human relations. It had even become difficult to find a form of language that escaped the imperatives of 'instrumental rationality', a dilemma which Adorno and Horkheimer tried to resolve by using 'fragmentary' writing to break with 'normal' modes of linguistic expression. Their vision of the future remained starkly pessimistic. 'After the catastrophes that have happened', wrote Adorno some years later,

> and in view of the catastrophes to come, it would be cynical to say that a plan for a better world is manifested in history and unites it . . . No universal history leads from savagery to humanitarianism, but there is one leading from the slingshot to the megaton bomb.[10]

Walter Benjamin, an associate of Adorno's at the Frankfurt School, believed that he saw in Paul Klee's painting *Angelus Novus* a visual representation of this 'catastrophic' view of history. According to Benjamin, Klee's painting shows an angel transfixed by his vision of the past:

> His eyes are staring, his mouth is open, his wings are spread. This is how one pictures the angel of history. His face is turned towards the past. Where we perceive a chain of events, he sees one single catastrophe which keeps piling wreckage upon wreckage and hurls it in front of his feet . . . a storm is blowing from Paradise; it has got caught in his wings with such violence that the angel can no longer close them. This storm irresistibly propels him into the future to which his back is turned, while the pile of debris before him grows skyward. This storm is what we call progress.[11]

Klee's painting, as read by Benjamin, could stand as a comment upon a significant proportion of early to mid-twentieth-century artistic and literary modernism. From the Berlin Dadaists to the Surrealists in Paris, from T. S. Eliot's *Wasteland* to Franz Kafka's *Trial,* from the dystopias of Aldous Huxley and George Orwell to the bleak landscapes of Samuel Beckett, writers and artists repeatedly denounced or despaired of the societies they inhabited. Their denunciations were delivered from radically differing positions and, politically, they could be seen to divide in extreme and polarised ways; but they shared a profound disillusion with the kind of world that philosophies of 'progress' had bequeathed.[12]

These narratives of decline, and the pessimism they generated, can in part be explained by the peculiarly terrible events of the first half of the twentieth century: the introduction of killing on an industrial scale during the First World War; the relapse into barbarism, mass murder and genocide during the Second; the development of 'total war', involving the mass destruction of civilian populations; the collapse of socialist idealism after Stalin had turned the Soviet Union into a murderous tyranny; and the fear which took root once the full implications of the bombing of Hiroshima had begun to sink in. In many cases, those who articulated a sense of decline had themselves experienced persecution and suffering. But this did not mean that the idea of cultural decline itself was an invention of these terrible years. If we go back into the nineteenth century, the century which perhaps produced more prophets of progress than any other, we still continue to find strongly expressed convictions of a culture in decline. Indeed, in his *History of the Idea of Progress,* Robert Nisbet suggests that, as far as intellectual content is concerned, there is very little in twentieth-century ideas of decline that does not draw on those of the nineteenth.[13]

Nisbet overstates his case and his history of ideas pays too little attention to the specific historical contexts in which these ideas were produced. Nevertheless, there were clear connections and these often centred around a shared scepticism to what Jürgen Habermas has called the 'project of modernity'. The term 'modern', of course, has a long history, and with varying content has been used again and again to distinguish one epoch from another in terms of a transition from the old to the new. But in Habermas's conception the 'project of modernity' stemmed from the eighteenth century and began with the efforts of Enlightenment philosophers 'to develop objective science, universal morality and law, and autonomous art according to their inner logic'.[14] Their expectations were extravagant, with those such as Condorcet believing that the accumulation of scientific and artistic knowledge would lead not only to the control of nature but also to moral progress, institutional exactitude and greater human happiness. As we have seen, it did not take long for the twentieth century to shatter this optimism. But there were those in the nineteenth who did not share this optimism in the first place.

Max Weber, whose work straddled both centuries, had already argued that the hopes and expectations of Enlightenment thinkers were a cruel illusion. Anticipating Adorno and Horkheimer, Weber argued that Enlightenment rationality had not only failed to deliver universal human freedom but had also actually promoted even more intractable forms of oppression. The rationality of the Enlightenment had turned out to be what Weber called 'purposive-instrumental rationality', a mode of thinking that was colonising all aspects of social and institutional life. This was Weber's 'iron cage', a kind of bureaucratisation of the human spirit, from which there would be no escape. 'Not summer's bloom lies ahead of us', he wrote, 'but rather a polar night of icy darkness and hardship'.[15] Friedrich Nietzsche had attacked *all* forms of rationality, with his ferocious repudiation of everything that the Enlightenment had stood for. Doctrines of progress were to him no more than a feeble charade, powerless against the wild and anarchistic forces that lay beneath the surface of modern life. In his 'tragic vision', he looked forward to the complete destruction of an effete and corrupt civilisation which had reduced human existence to a form of slow suicide. In promoting this vision, Nietzsche produced not so much a philosophy but, as John Carey has pointed out, more a form of rhetoric that licensed a way of feeling.[16] But it was a rhetoric which proved highly influential, inspiring both an important strand of modernist art and literature and a generation of Fascist leaders.[17] The influence of Nietzsche can also be seen in Freud, whose notion of primary and secondary processes closely resembles Nietzsche's Dionysian and Apollinian.[18] Nietzsche even invented the term 'id', which Freud was later to popularise.

Moving further back into the nineteenth century, we encounter Arthur Schopenhauer. Although Nietzsche and Freud were both clearly indebted to him, Schopenhauer stood alone in having constructed an entire philosophy of pessimism. This philosophy was not obviously related to a specific culture but connected to what Schopenhauer saw as fundamental and universal attributes of the human condition. His idea of decline, therefore, was conceived not in terms of civilisations, societies or historical periods but in terms of the inevitable journey towards suffering that each and every human being faced. In *Parerga and Paralipomena* (1851), he invited us to consider the difference between our beginnings and our end:

> We begin in the madness of carnal desire and the transport of voluptuousness, we end in the dissolution of all our parts and the musty stench of corpses. And the road from the one to the other too goes, in regard to our well-being and enjoyment of life, steadily downhill: happily dreaming childhood, exultant youth, toil-filled years of manhood, infirm and often wretched old age, the torment of the last illness and finally the throes of death – does it not look as if existence were an error the consequences of which gradually grow more and more manifest?[19]

In the same volume, Schopenhauer repeatedly referred to life as a form of punishment, describing the world as 'a place of atonement, a sort of penal colony'. Children could seem like 'innocent delinquents, sentenced not to death but to life, who have not yet discovered what their punishment will consist of'. It was possible, of course, to experience momentary pleasure, but, in Schopenhauer's vision, life was overwhelmingly skewed towards the experience of pain. Indeed, if one tried to imagine 'the sum total of distress, pain and suffering of every kind' experienced by human beings, then it was impossible not to conclude that it would have been better had the earth remained as devoid of life as the moon.[20] But for Schopenhauer, deeply influenced by Buddhism, there was no escape from life, not even in death: only the endless cycle of birth, death and rebirth, until, perhaps, one could at last achieve a state of death-in-life through the final annihilation of the will.

At a less metaphysical level, the entire capitalist world, with its system of 'naked, shameless, direct, brutal exploitation', was represented by Karl Marx as a culture in terminal decline; although, of course, in Marx's scheme, humanity would eventually be redeemed by the utopia which would arise from the ashes of capitalism's final collapse. William Morris, who through a different route came to share much of Marx's vision a couple of decades later, likened 'competitive commerce' to a system of war which brought waste and destruction. 'Our civilization is passing like a blight', he wrote in 1884, 'daily growing heavier and more poisonous, over the whole face of the country'.[21] Although Marx had a more ambivalent relationship to the phenomenon of 'industry' per se, recognising the emancipatory possibilities of its enormous productive powers, for both Marx and Morris, the development of 'industrialism' as a capitalist enterprise produced for the majority of people an impoverished form of existence. This was due not only to economic exploitation but also to the nature of industrial work itself. The new manufacturing processes relied on a greater and greater division of labour, which demanded the endless repetition of mind-numbing tasks. As Marx put it in *Capital*, this served to 'mutilate the labourer into a fragment of a man, degrade him to the level of an appendage of a machine, destroy every remnant of charm in his work and turn it into a hated toil'.[22]

Whilst these accounts of industrialism went further in their political and economic analysis than anything that had gone before, the idea that it represented a form of cultural decline was not in itself new.[23] The term 'industrialism' was, in fact, coined by Thomas Carlyle, who, in 'Signs of the times' (1829), suggested that if one epithet were to be chosen to characterise the age in which he lived it would be the 'Mechanical Age'. Carlyle recognised the extraordinary results that 'Mechanism' had achieved in the external world. 'We remove mountains', he wrote, 'and make seas our smooth highways; nothing can resist us'.[24] But for Carlyle a healthy culture depended upon advances not only in the external world but also in the inner world; and while we had excelled in the former, the latter had been seriously neglected. Indeed, so predominant had the 'mechanical' mode of thinking become that even the idea of an 'inner world', which could not be understood or investigated 'mechanically', was becoming increasingly difficult to grasp. 'Mechanism' had also taken over political discourse, which was concerned not with ends but almost exclusively with means. The issue of 'freedom', for example, was reduced to 'arrangements, institutions and constitutions'; the question of what freedom was for was barely even asked. 'Mechanism' had produced enormous power and wealth; but for Carlyle, 'in whatever respects the pure moral nature, in true dignity of soul and character, we are perhaps inferior to most civilised ages'.[25]

In arriving at this position, Carlyle was drawing on both English Romanticism and the theories of culture developed in Weimar during the last quarter of the eighteenth century. The Romantic revolt in England was, in part, a response to the development of an industrialism built, as William Blake had put it, upon the 'single vision' of science. The 'dark satanic mills' were only the most obvious symbol of a culture that was seen to promote a limited and mechanistic conception of human potentiality.[26] For Percy Bysshe Shelley, it was striking that there had been extraordinary advances in scientific, political and economic knowledge, yet this had resulted not in a more equitable world, but had only added to the general weight of human misery.[27] The explanation for this was the excessive development of the 'calculating principle', which had not been matched by a commensurate development of the 'creative faculty'. 'The great instrument of moral good is the imagination', Shelley had argued, and it was only through the strengthening of the imagination that humanity could advance. This opposition of the 'creative' to the 'calculating', with the rise of the latter and the eclipse of the former, was a central theme in the Romantic notion of decline.

In late eighteenth-century Weimar, industrialism was still to develop; yet, here also we find the idea of a culture in decline. 'The character of the age', wrote Friedrich Schiller in 1795, 'must first lift itself out of its deep degradation'.[28] Schiller was, to some extent, reacting to the terrible and violent aftermath of the French Revolution, which he believed had plunged 'a considerable part of Europe and a whole century, back into barbarism and slavery'.[29] In particular, he was exercised by the failure of 'reason' to maintain moral and ethical standards in the processes of political reform. Indeed, far from resisting corruption, the 'Enlightenment of the mind . . . had tended rather to bolster up depravity by providing it with the support of precepts'.[30] This distrust of 'reason', or rather an acute sense of its limitations, could also be found in Jean-Jacques Rousseau, to whom Schiller was openly indebted. In the early 1750s, Rousseau had delivered a powerful denunciation of the idea of progress, contending in two 'discourses' that modern civilisation displayed a level of corruption that was unknown in primitive societies.[31] In these 'discourses', which contained the seeds of almost every important element of his later philosophy, Rousseau argued that societies became more corrupt in direct proportion to the development of their intellectual culture. Intellectual 'progress' did not bring with it a moral advancement, but, on the contrary, provided the means of either concealing or legitimising corruption. Manners became a substitute for morals and inequality was 'naturalised' through the establishment of properties and laws. Anyone could see this, suggested Rousseau, for it was quite obviously 'contrary to the law of nature, however defined, that children should command old men, fools wise men, and that the privileged few should gorge themselves with superfluities, while the starving multitude are in want of the bare necessities of life'.[32]

These eighteenth- and nineteenth-century exponents of decline were, for the most part, swimming against the tide. During this period, faith in the opposite doctrine of progress, whether based

8

on biological, economic, technological or even religious principles, was far more common. But once we move out of this period, the position is reversed and it is the notion that humanity might be 'progressing' that becomes the challenge to intellectual orthodoxy. Indeed, according to J. P. Bury, who produced the first systematic study of 'progress', the idea only took root in the eighteenth century and was virtually unheard of before the seventeenth. This has been disputed by Robert Nisbet, who sees the development of rudimentary theories of progress in the post-Reformation world, during the Middle Ages and in the classical period as well; but, nevertheless, Nisbet acknowledges that it was not until the eighteenth century that the idea of progress became dominant.[33] Fundamental to the idea was the notion of historical continuity, of an unbroken and progressive advance either in knowledge or in mankind's moral or spiritual condition. Without this sense of continuity, there could, at best, only be temporary advances, to be followed by periods of decline in accordance with either the random movements of history or some underlying cyclical pattern. As we move further back in time, beyond the eighteenth century and out of Habermas's 'modern' period, the idea of history as unbroken progress recedes: narratives of decline are no longer the province of marginal voices but begin to take on a normative character.

During the Renaissance, for example, it was difficult to hold a progressive view of history when the entire span of the medieval world was dismissed by contemporary scholars as a barbaric period of ignorance and superstition, vastly inferior to the ancient civilisations of Greece and Rome. Desiderius Erasmus was influential in this respect, articulating a powerful sense of cultural regression which he extended not only to the medieval past but to his own period as well. Another Renaissance luminary, Niccolò Machiavelli, saw nothing in history but endless sequences of ups and downs (*ricorsi*): countries moved from order to disorder and vice versa, the fate of their political leaders subject only to the laws of chance. As Nisbet has pointed out, the vast majority of Renaissance thinkers, from the fifteenth-century Italian humanists to the English polymath Francis Bacon, 'tended overwhelmingly to see history not as something unilinear in its flow, as continuous and cumulative, but as a multiplicity of recurrences.'[34] This was not only a result of their need to adopt a theory of history which would accommodate their contempt for medieval culture; it was also a reflection of the ubiquity of cyclical or degenerative views of history amongst the Greek and Roman writers from whom they drew so much of their intellectual inspiration. For example, the first-century philosopher, Seneca, particularly in his early writings, had contrasted the pervading moral decay of Rome with the crime-free world of a primal and more innocent golden age. With a very modern appreciation of the increasingly destructive effects of military technology, Seneca looked forward with Stoic fatalism to the complete annihilation of his world and everything in it. The didactic Greek poet, Hesiod, writing in the late eighth century BC, had traced the history of the world through five stages, the 'age of gold' being the first and the 'age of iron' the last. Each was inferior to that which preceded it, and each ended in catastrophe. Preoccupied, like Seneca was to be, with the idea of moral decay, Hesiod believed he was living through the final and most degenerate historical phase, at the conclusion of which the whole cycle would begin again.[35]

It was not, however, only to the classical world that cultural pessimism, and the associated ideas of decline, could be traced; they were also central to Judaeo-Christian traditions. The fall from Paradise is inextricably bound up with the idea of decline; and, in visions of the apocalypse, man's prospects in this world (though not, of course, in the next) appear in an undeniably pessimistic light. With the expulsion from Eden and the eschatological prophecies of Daniel, the Jewish Bible gives us both the Fall and the apocalypse; and in the Christian Bible, the vision of a cataclysmic end to the world, where only the righteous are saved, is reinforced by the book of Revelation, which predicts a titanic struggle between the forces of Good and Evil. At the height of this violent and bloody conflict, Christ reappears in the world, leading his armies to eventual victory and the annihilation of his enemies. Christ and his saints rule for one thousand years (the Millennium), after which the world ends, to be replaced by the eternity of 'New Jerusalem'.

The prophecies of Daniel and Revelation were almost certainly written as a response to the persecution experienced by Jews and Christians during the second century BC and first century AD respectively: such persecution could be better endured if it was possible to believe in a better world to come and the prospect of retribution for one's persecutors. But despite the specific historical circumstances which surrounded these writings, the sequence of decline, destruction and salvation for the righteous took on an archetypal form and proved remarkably resilient as a template for both Christian and secular interpretations of history. Throughout the Middle Ages, the inevitability of the apocalypse was barely questioned, though there was, of course, endless dispute and speculation about where and when it would take place and precisely how the 'final' events would unfold. Apocalyptic thinking might not have outlasted the medieval period, however, had it not been for the crucial adjustment made by a twelfth-century abbott, Joachim of Fiore, who advanced the idea that a post-apocalyptic golden age might be possible within history, that is to say, in this world rather than the next. This prepared the ground for an association between apocalyptic change and political reconstruction, which lasted right up until our own time. For example, Marx's vision of a corrupt and declining world, destroyed by the proletariat after a titanic struggle with the bourgeoisie, and transformed into a communist utopia which solves 'the riddle of history', had recognisably apocalyptic resonances.[36] Whilst apocalypticism, in both its religious and secular manifestations, could be seen as an ultimately optimistic doctrine, in that it promised salvation to the faithful, it was based upon the complete destruction of the existing order which was viewed as irredeemably corrupt. This idea of decline was deeply embedded in Judaeo-Christian teleology, leaving its mark on the culture of the West.

It would be misleading, however, to suggest that the Judaeo-Christian world invented either the paradise myth or the apocalypse; even more that they had a monopoly on them. Variations of these ideas, as we have seen, were common in the classical world; they could also be found in earlier civilisations and in many of the world's historic religions. Norman Cohn maintains that the idea of the apocalypse first appeared in the teachings of Zoroaster, a prophet from central Asia who probably lived around 1400 BC.[37] Zoroaster's eschatological faith became the official religion of the Persian Empire, from which it was later 'borrowed' by the Jews. Belief in an original paradise was near universal across all religions, with the earliest surviving description coming from the Sumerians, who around 4000 BC described a magical land called 'Dilmin'. According to some scholars, the name of the Hebrew Garden of Eden is taken from the Sumerians, although no other connection has been discovered. Indeed, as Damian Thompson has pointed out, all the ancient paradise stories appear to be independent of one another. 'If they have a common ancestor', he has suggested,

it may well lie so far back in prehistory that it also gave birth to African, Aboriginal, Australian and American Indian myths . . The primitive belief in the moral superiority of ancestors may have its roots in a single preliterate tradition.[38]

We can see from this brief and far from exhaustive survey that the idea of cultural decline, conceptualised in a variety of different ways, has been a recurrent feature of the history of the West. There is therefore nothing new, per se, in the representation of the post-modern world as yet one more such period. But it is not the idea of decline as a generic form that is in itself significant; what is important is the content given to the form by specific historical conditions. This is so often missed in the genealogical approach to intellectual history, where the relationship between ideas can assume greater importance than the relationship of those ideas to the historical conditions from which they arise. As Raymond Williams once warned, 'the history of ideas is a dead study if it proceeds solely in terms of the abstraction of influences'.[39] Whilst the matter of influences is not ignored in this book – indeed, many of those cited in the preceding pages will be referred to again – the main focus is on narratives of decline as a response to the material realities of the postmodern world. What constitutes 'material reality' is, of course, problematic, and some theorists would argue that distinctions between 'representation' and 'reality' simply cannot be drawn.[40] However, in the narratives presented in the chapters that follow, whose concerns range from food shortages to the incidence of genocide, these epistemological uncertainties do not feature as a major preoccupation.

The book attempts to answer a number of key questions. First, what are these narratives and what are the conditions to which they refer? Secondly, to what extent are those conditions historically unprecedented? In other words, although the form of the narrative may be an old one, is there anything significantly new about its content? With regard to the natural environment, for example (the subject of Chapter 1), narratives of decline have been produced in England since the early years of the industrial revolution. What is it, if anything, about recent versions that distinguishes them from their predecessors? Thirdly, to which cultures do these narratives relate? By and large, they have originated, as we shall see, in the West, but do they refer exclusively to the West or do they have a broader reach? Fourthly, what political or cultural values are embedded in them? For example, in the representation of crime as a narrative of moral decline (see Chapter 2), whose interests are being served? Finally, to what extent are the identified processes of decline seen to be irreversible? As noted earlier, the perception of irreversibility is central to the formation of pessimism.

Before we can answer these questions, however, we must first of all clarify what we mean by the postmodern world. If we are using 'postmodern' as a periodising concept, to what period does it refer and what is the rationale for the periodising? Why base a study of cultural pessimism on this period in particular? And what world are we talking about? Does 'postmodernity' imply a universal condition or does it have specific geo-cultural boundaries? The idea of the 'postmodern' is, of course, subject to a multiplicity of often contradictory meanings, with one writer suggesting that there might even be 'an unconscious agreement to withhold a definition, partly because everyone's definition will expose the confusion the word is designed to cover'.[41] In particular, the relationship of the postmodern to the modern has been subject to very different formulations, with academic opinion divided between those who see the former as a continuation of the tendencies of the latter, and those who see it as a radical break with the past. There are further divisions around the relationship of modern*ity*/postmodern*ity* to modern*ism*/postmodern*ism* with some, such as David Harvey and Frederic Jameson, seeing a clear distinction between the former, as a configuration of political and economic arrangements, and the latter as a set of intellectual and aesthetic practices.[42] Conversely, others such as Jean Baudrillard have suggested that the two have collapsed into each other and that it is, in fact, this 'disappearance of the real' that is the defining characteristic of the postmodern.[43] However, despite these differences, there is, I think, a broad acceptance that the last few decades of the twentieth century represented some kind of epochal change, involving, if we want to preserve this distinction, both the 'base' and the 'superstructure'. Changes in the 'base', characterised by the transition from 'Fordism' to more aggressive forms of capital accumulation, produced a distinctive new phase of global capitalism; and changes in the 'superstructure' included radical new forms of epistemological uncertainty, further challenges to Enlightenment rationality and a massive collapse in intellectual and aesthetic hierarchies. As Andreas Huyssens observed in 1984, 'the nature and depth of that transformation are debatable, but transformation it is'.[44] The precise beginnings of the transformation are also debatable, although, as Hal Foster suggests, the late 1950s and early 1960s are 'the moment often cited as the postmodernist break',[45] with those inclined to a more materialist view, such as Harvey, seeing the early 1970s, and 1973 in particular, as the decisive 'moment'.

For the purposes of this book, then, 'postmodern' is used to signify the period inaugurated by this transformation, beginning in the

1960s and continuing up until the present day. There is no sign that this period is approaching its end and, indeed, as we shall see in the following chapters, the forces which gave rise to its emergence are still very much with us. There has, at the same time, been an escalation in the theorising of the postmodern, the influence of which can be seen in most areas of the humanities and the social sciences. It is inevitable, therefore, that many of the narratives discussed in the book should exhibit a direct relationship, antagonistic or affirmative, to the ideas which have emerged from this theorising. For example, in the narratives relating to aesthetic and critical practices (see Chapter 3), the postmodern 'turn' itself is identified as one of the primary manifestations of decline. In contrast, in those relating to the global economy (Chapter 4), there is a substantial body of shared ideas. However, this connection with theories of the postmodern has not been a determining factor in deciding which narratives should appear in the book; rather, it is the period which has been decisive, allowing us to include narratives, such as those relating to ecology, human rights and crime, which have had little connection with defining the postmodern, but which have nevertheless appeared around the same time. This does not, of course, mean that they will necessarily remain apart in the future: like some kind of conceptual black hole, the postmodern continues to draw more and more into its gravitational field.

Despite the characteristics of 'epochal change' that the postmodern world displays, the extent of the transformation needs to be kept in perspective. In most Western nations, evidence of such change could probably be deduced from any forty year period since the beginning of the nineteenth century. It would be difficult, for example, to claim that the Europe of 1910 to 1950 was any the less 'transformed' than the Europe of 1960 to 2000. We should also be careful of claiming a special status for the pessimism which our own period exhibits, for this is to indulge in a kind of inverted historical hubris. Nevertheless, as the following chapters show, the postmodern world has produced narratives of decline across a very wide range of fields which raise deeply disturbing questions. These cannot easily be dismissed, as they have been by some writers, with the casual and ahistorical assurance that they reflect no more than 'the ageless mythology of decline'; still less with the suggestion, much employed in the media, that they have in some mysterious and unexplained way been generated by 'millennial angst'. The pessimism of postmodernity may only be the most recent manifestation of a recurring historical phenomenon; but it is deeply rooted in the specific conditions of the world that has produced it.

The geo-cultural boundaries of the 'postmodern world', as conceived in the book, are much harder to draw than the temporal ones. It is in the advanced industrialised world and mainly, though not exclusively, in the anglophone part of it, that the narratives we discuss have been produced; and they therefore inevitably reflect, in some way, an anglo-american perspective. However, such a perspective is both so heterogeneous and so fluid that it is virtually impossible to define; furthermore, the world to which these narratives refer cannot easily be confined to specific geo-cultural formations. For example, the narrative of environmental decline (Chapter 1) is a global narrative, which relates to every human being on the planet. Alternatively, the narrative of moral decline (Chapter 2), which encompasses warfare, human rights abuse and crime, has many different geo-cultural reference points. The narratives around political economy (Chapter 4) refer primarily to the United States and the United Kingdom, but they also signal tendencies which have global implications. The boundaries are thus constantly shifting.

The narratives of decline themselves have been brought together under four main themes: the environmental, the moral, the intellectual and the political. These themes are closely connected and, indeed, it is possible to argue that they cannot be meaningfully separated. The issue of environmental decline is, at the same time, both a moral and a political question; the idea of intellectual decline has profound moral implications; and so on. However, the thematising of decline in this way does not preclude connections being made; and it has the advantage of giving a clear and distinctive focus to each of the four central chapters. What has been more problematic has been deciding which narratives to include and which to exclude. Not only are the four themes extremely broad in scope, encompassing a vast number of fields, but the idea of decline is also widely used as a rhetorical device, deployed to give weight to a huge array of critical positions. Indeed, it is often implicit in the very act of criticism itself. The idea of decline, therefore, rarely acquires the status of objective fact – or at least, only under very specific and tightly defined conditions – but gets hauled in to serve widely different and frequently competing ideological purposes.

On what basis, then, have these narratives been assembled? First, as suggested above, if cultural pessimism is to be understood as a pessimism which attaches itself to culture as 'a whole way of life', then the narratives which inform it will, in their totality, go some way towards reflecting 'a whole way of life'. Our configuration of the environmental, the moral, the intellectual and the political provides a kind of matrix through which 'a whole way of life' might be viewed. It enables us to draw on narratives from a broad range of discursive fields, bringing together that which the whole thrust of the division of intellectual labour tends to keep apart. These fields include ecology, human rights, military history, international relations, criminology, history of science, cultural criticism and political economy. Of course, this is not exhaustive, nor could any attempt to classify 'a whole way of life' ever be anything other than reductive. In the final analysis, as T. S. Eliot pointed out, the knowledge of a 'way of life' is in any case an epistemological impossibility: we are either on the outside, in which case the essence eludes us; or we are on the inside where we are too close to see.[46] Nevertheless, if we are to gain any insight into the cultural in this broad sense, the effort has to be made, despite the intellectual risks, or we confine ourselves to the tunnel vision that is so often an occupational hazard of disciplinary specialisation.

In deciding which narratives to examine within our four main themes, the chapter on environmental decline has posed the least problems. Although the significance of the decline has been contested, the agenda around which the debate has focused has at least been fairly well established: the direct effects of pollution on human health and wildlife; the indirect effects through impacts on the ozone layer and global warming; threats to biodiversity; the prospects of food and water shortages; the population explosion; and how all these factors interconnect. The chapter on moral decline, in contrast, has been far more problematic, in that it is within the sphere of the moral that the idea of decline has appeared in its most rhetorical, relative and narrowly ideological forms. From sexual behaviour to consumer culture, from street violence to political apathy, narratives of moral decline have been variously attached to a diverse range of ideological positions. I do not, of course, suggest that the ideological can ever be removed from the moral, but I have in this chapter tried to withstand the centrifugal pressures of moral relativism and focus on narratives which, if not aspiring to a universal status, have at least been pitched on some widely shared moral ground. These relate: to the morality of nuclear and post-nuclear warfare; to the incidence of torture, genocide and political murder; and to the crime explosion which has manifested itself more or less throughout the Western world since the 1960s.

The chapter on intellectual decline focuses on science and art. Science has occupied a paradoxical position, in that it has been unquestionably successful, both as a mode of cognition and as a transforming power; yet at the same time no other form of intellectual endeavour has been subject to so much opprobrium. The narratives around science have also been a comment on the decline of the religious, although this is by no means the only grounds on which science has been attacked. An investigation of these narratives leads directly on to the world of art, which has historically been seen as a repository of those values which science is either incapable of representing or which it actively destroys. However, art itself has been at the centre of another narrative of decline, in which it is seen as historically exhausted and its condition symptomatic of a 'dumbing down' of intellectual life in general.

The chapter on political decline draws on accounts of what many economic historians have seen as an aggressive new phase of capitalism, involving unprecedented organisational, economic and political changes. These are seen to have had growing impacts around the world, to have been the controlling movement of 'postmodernity', and to offer insights into what Robert Heilbroner has called the failure in 'our collective capacity for response'.[47] This narrative clearly also has a bearing on the pessimism which emerges elsewhere in the book.

From this brief account we can see the rationale behind both our thematising of decline and the selection of narratives for discussion under each theme. Nevertheless, given that the idea of cultural decline lends itself to any number of thematic configurations, and that, within any one configuration, many approaches could be taken to it, it has to be recognised that there is always going to be a contingent element to a study of this kind; and that the selection of these narratives creates a narrative of its own. The use of the word 'narrative', both in the title of the book and in the discussions within it, is an acknowledgement of this contingency.[48] The idea of the narrative also determines the discursive approach of the book, which is concerned not so much with challenging truth claims, or even with arbitrating between them, but with understanding how and why specific narratives have been constructed.[49] Whether or not we become attached to these narratives will ultimately be as much a matter of psychological or biological disposition as of intellectual judgement. This is the subject of the concluding chapter, which explores the nature of this disposition and its role in the formation of cultural pessimism at both a cognitive and affective level.

Notes

1. For an account of the history of the word 'culture' and its various meanings and connotations, see Williams, *Keywords*, pp. 76–82 and Williams, *Culture*, pp. 10–14.
2. For a discussion of cultural pessimism in its narrower sense, see Cowen, *In Praise of Commercial Culture*, pp. 181–210.
3. Fukuyama, *The End of History and the Last Man*, p. 1. Although Fukuyama could understand the historical pessimism that had been engendered by the first half of the twentieth century, he thought the events of the second of half of the century demanded that this pessimism be re-thought. I discuss this further in Chapter 4.
4. Nisbet, *History of the Idea of Progress*, p. 321.
5. Spengler, *The Decline of the West*, Vol. 1, *Form and Actuality*, pp. 3–50.
6. Nisbet, *History of the Idea of Progress*, p. 321.
7. Freud, 'Civilization and its discontents'.
8. Quoted in Fukuyama, *The End of History and the Last Man*, p. 5.
9. Adorno and Horkheimer, *Dialectic of Enlightenment*.
10. Adorno, *Negative Dialectics*, p. 320.
11. Benjamin, 'Theses on the philosophy of history', p. 259.
12. See Williams, *The Politics of Modernism*.
13. Nisbet, *History of the Idea of Progress*, pp. 318–19
14. Habermas, 'Modernity – an incomplete project', p. 9.
15. Quoted in Nisbet, *History of the Idea of Progress*, p. 320.
16. Carey, *The Intellectuals and the Masses*, p. 74.
17. Carey argues that Nietzsche's sense of decline arose from a revulsion towards common humanity. This same revulsion could be found in the many modernist writers whom Nietzsche influenced, such as D. H. Lawrence, Ezra Pound and Wyndham Lewis. Carey concludes that Hitler's *Mein Kampf*, far from being a deviant work, was in many respects rooted in European intellectual orthodoxy.
18. Anthony Storr makes this connection in *Freud*, p. 120.
19. Schopenhauer, *Essays and Aphorisms*, p. 54.
20. Ibid. pp. 47–9.
21. Morris, 'Art under plutocracy', p. 64.
22. Marx, *Selected Writings*, p. 482.
23. For a full discussion of this, see Williams, *Culture and Society*, pp. 23–161.
24. Carlyle, 'Signs of the times', p. 64.
25. Ibid. p. 77.
26. See Blake, 'Milton', p. 481, and 'Letter to Thomas Butts', p. 818.
27. Shelley, 'A defence of poetry', p. 293.
28. Schiller, *On the Aesthetic Education of Man*, p. 47.
29. Letter to the Duke of Augustenburg, 17 July 1793, quoted in Schiller, *On the Aesthetic Education of Man*, p. xvii.

30. Schiller, *On the Aesthetic Education of Man*, p. 27.
31. Rousseau, 'Discourse on the moral effects of the arts and sciences' and 'Discourse on the origin of inequality'.
32. Rousseau, 'Discourse on the origin of inequality', p. 105.
33. Nisbet, *History of the Idea of Progress*, p. 171.
34. Ibid. pp. 103–4.
35. Whilst Nisbet concedes that cyclical and degenerative views of history are common in the Classical world, he also sees embryonic theories of 'progress'. Furthermore, he sees in this respect an ambiguity in both Seneca and Hesiod, whose pessimism he considers to be by no means unqualified.
36. Damian Thompson, *The End of Time*, pp. 90–4.
37. Ibid. p. 15.
38. Ibid. p. 10.
39. Williams, *Culture and Society*, p. 85.
40. Gross and Levitt argue that 'the peculiarly quixotic view of the antagonism between "representation" and "reality" that is so thematic in postmodernist thought vouchsafes its practitioners an eerie absolution from having to measure their theories against the unyielding matrix of social fact'. See Gross and Levitt, *Higher Superstition*, pp. 73–4.
41. Brian O'Doherty, quoted in Wakefield, *Postmodernism*, p. 20.
42. See Harvey, *The Condition of Postmodernity*, and Jameson, *Postmodernism*.
43. Baudrillard, *Selected Writings*, pp. 166–84.
44. Quoted in Harvey, *The Condition of Postmodernity*, p. 39.
45. Hal Foster, 'Postmodernism: A Preface', p. xi.
46. Eliot, *Notes towards the Definition of Culture*, p. 41.
47. Heilbroner, *An Enquiry into the Human Prospect*, p. 62.
48. Gross and Levitt associate the term 'narrative' with those 'radical new forms of epistemological uncertainty', which were identified in this introduction as being part of the postmodern transformation. In their account of what they describe as the 'doctrine of postmodernism', they tell us that under this doctrine 'there is no knowledge . . . there are merely stories, "narratives", devised to satisfy the human need to make some sense of the world' (p. 72). In using the word 'narrative', as I hope I have made clear, I do not wish to deny the existence of Gross and Levitt's 'unyielding matrix of social fact' (see note 39) only to acknowledge that many different narratives could be constructed around this 'matrix' – even narratives of progress.
49. For a more polemical approach to the study of pessimism, see Tallis's sustained assault on 'the process by which contemporary humanity is talking itself into a terminal state of despair, self-disgust and impotence', in *Enemies of Hope: A Critique of Contemporary Pessimism*, p. xiv. Tallis sees contemporary pessimism as a product of counter-Enlight-

enment hostility towards 'the idea of a human being as a conscious, rational agent and of human society as susceptible to progressive improvement as a result of the efforts of conscious rational individuals'. He associates this with the systematic marginalising of consciousness, for which Marx, Durkheim, Freud and the Post-Saussureans (Derrida, Foucault, Lacan, etc.) are held collectively responsible.

1

Environmental Decline

Postmodernism is what you have when the modernization process is
complete and nature is gone for good.
(Fredric Jameson, *Postmodernism,
or The Cultural Logic of Late Capitalism*)

Introduction

I N THE NARRATIVES OF decline set out in this chapter, the human
species, growing to unprecedented numbers, was destroying the
environment, threatening future generations and extinguishing
other forms of life. The pollution generated, particularly in the
advanced industrialised world, was poisoning the planet, depleting
the ozone layer and changing the world's climate. Reckless consumption, the irresponsible deployment of productive powers and a
massively-expanding population was exhausting non-renewable resources, water and food-producing land. Many species of plants and
wildlife were rapidly becoming extinct. An environment which had
taken millions of years to evolve was being radically altered within the
space of a generation.

These narratives could be related to older intellectual traditions,
which combined a veneration of Nature with critiques of scientific
industrialism and capitalist values. Whilst the narratives continued
to reflect these traditions, they also exhibited an environmental
pessimism which was quite new. It was a pessimism that arose largely
in the advanced industrialised world, but was global in scope. It was
derived from three key factors: first, the sheer scale and pace of

21

decline, which was unprecedented in the history of the human species; secondly, the consequences of this decline and the anticipation of further but as yet unknown consequences; and thirdly, our collective inability to respond adequately to the scale of problems which confronted us. In the view of some analysts, a chain of events had now been set in motion which was already impossible to reverse.

Pollution

In 1962, Rachel Carson published her now-classic *Silent Spring*, in which she claimed that humanity was in the process of poisoning the entire planet. The focus of her concern was the indiscriminate use of synthetic pesticides, and their toxic effect on wildlife and humans. Rising up the food chain in increasing concentrations, pesticides such as dichlorodiphenyltrichloroethane (DDT) had poisoned thousands of fish, birds and mammals, threatening some species with extinction. There was also accumulating evidence of the dangers to human beings. 'We were', she suggested, 'in little better position than guests of the Borgias'.[1] Carson showed how such pesticides had been created in the course of developing agents of chemical warfare during the Second World War, and how a vast industry had subsequently been built up around them. Due to their widespread use, these pesticides, many of which were resistant to degradation and able to remain in the environment for a very long time, were bringing human beings into contact with dangerous chemicals right from the moment of conception through to death. This was unprecedented in the history of the species, and Carson had become alarmed at the scale of both scientific and public ignorance as to what the effects might be. If we were going to live so intimately with these chemicals, she argued, 'eating and drinking them, taking them into the very marrow of our bones', then it would make sense to know a little more about them.[2]

The evidence which Carson presented of both the extent of environmental contamination and of the dangers presented by what she referred to as 'elixirs of death' was disturbing. Toxic rivers and lakes, the elimination of fish populations, the destruction of birds and other forms of wildlife – all these were recorded in unsettling detail. Equally disturbing was the catalogue of symptoms, linked to pesticidal poisoning, which were now appearing in human beings. These included damage to the central nervous system, liver disease, muscular weakness, chromosomal abnormalities and cancers. Carson had also noted the long time lag that often existed between the deployment of new chemicals and the appearance of symptoms within humans. This suggested that the story was by no means over and that there were other problems still to present themselves. A final irony was that the 'project' of eliminating unwanted pests and insects by chemical means might actually have been failing in its main objective. Carson had noted that, as early as 1959, over one hundred major insect species had developed resistances to the major pesticides in use. In some instances, pesticides had succeeded only in killing off the natural predators of the insects to be eliminated, with the result that those insects had been able to exist in greater security and actually increase their population.[3]

Carson's analysis was initially criticised for being unscientific, but by 1970 her findings had been broadly accepted.[4] DDT and many other synthetic pesticides were eventually banned from use in both Britain and the United States, largely as a result of her work, although they continued to be manufactured in these countries and exported widely, mostly to the developing world. In 1991, for example, the United States exported at least 4.1m pounds of pesticides which had been suspended from use at home, including 96 tons of DDT.[5] After DDT had been banned from use in Britain, exports rose by seven times.[6] *Silent Spring*, in retrospect, could be seen as a seminal narrative of environmental decline, and a major contribution to what subsequently became an extensive literature.

A later example was *Our Stolen Future*, by Theo Colborn, Dianne Dumanoski and John Peterson Myers (1996), which concerned itself with many of the issues raised by Carson, and which Al Gore, the then Vice-President of the US, who wrote an introduction to the book, saw in some respects as a sequel to her work. At the time the book was published, the United States alone was using thirty times more pesticides than it had done in 1945, the killing power per pound of chemicals having risen tenfold. However, while Carson had focused primarily on the use and impact of pesticides, Colborn *et al* had extended their enquiry to the full range of synthetic chemicals which, they noted, were now proliferating at a rate of 1,000 new chemicals a year, adding to the 100,000 already in existence. Only a fraction of these were adequately tested. Moreover, by the time some chemicals had subsequently been identified as dangerous and prohibited from further use, vast quantities had already been released into the environment. This had been true of the group known as polychlorinated biphenyls (PCBs), which had been widely used in paints, varnishes, lubricating oils, plastics and electrical insulation. By the time they were banned in the United States in 1976, an estimated 3.4b tons had been produced around the world. A striking feature of PCBs, as of the early generation of pesticides which Carson had discussed, was that they were 'persistent'. This meant that they remained indestructible for many years (centuries in some cases), and, having got into the air, water or soil, could travel very long distances and accumulate in greater and greater concentrations as they rose up the food chain. Colborn *et al* recorded that synthetic chemicals had become so pervasive in the environment and in our bodies that it was no longer possible to define a normal, unaltered human physiology – not even in the remote communities of the Arctic. 'There is no clean, uncontaminated place', the authors observed, '. . . No children today are born chemical-free'.[7]

As to the long-term impact on humans of this kind of environmental contamination, while Carson had been largely pre-occupied with carcinogenic effects, Colborn *et al* turned their attention to the growing evidence of hormonal disruption. Reviewing research studies from around the world, the authors showed how hormonally active synthetic chemicals had affected animals, birds and fish, damaging their reproductive, nervous and immune systems, producing deformities (particularly in their reproductive organs) and causing aberrant behaviour. These chemicals, being 'persistent', had accumulated in the fat tissues of wildlife, but while they had appeared to have had little effect on the generation which had ingested them, they had had a devastating effect on their offspring, acting on the endocrinal system (which releases hormones and regulates vital metabolic processes) at critical pre-natal stages. The 'hand-me-down poisons', as Colborn *et al* termed them, even in infinitesimally small quantities, attacked the unborn and the very young.[8]

There was a growing suspicion that these chemicals had had, and would continue to have, an impact on humans as well as wildlife. This was consistent with what was known about the evolution of the endocrinal system, which arose early in the evolutionary history of vertebrates and which showed remarkably similar characteristics across a wide range of species. If animals could be so affected, then it was logical to assume that humans could be as well. Colborn *et al* cited the evidence of falling sperm counts, growing infertility, hormonally-triggered human cancers and neurological damage in children – all of which had been linked by researchers to hormone-disrupting synthetic chemicals.[9] At the time of writing, fifty-one such chemicals had been identified, many of which were 'persistent' and would be with us for years. There were almost certainly many more.

The attribution of endocrinal disorders in humans to hormone-disrupting chemicals was treated with scepticism in much of the medical community. This was to some extent due to the fact that it was difficult to prove conclusively that a particular contaminant had been responsible for a specific disorder, particularly when it was suspected that the contamination had taken place during the pre-natal phase. Although it was known in the 1990s that during the last fifty years every mother had carried within her a cocktail of synthetic chemicals to which her child would have been exposed in the womb, it was impossible to know precisely what the child might have been exposed to, in what concentrations and whether or not he or she had been affected at a critical stage of pre-natal development. Furthermore, given that everyone was contaminated in one way or another, it was not possible to find a control group of unexposed individuals for the purposes of comparative scientific study. Colborn *et al* argued that, under these circumstances, it was simply inappropriate to apply scientific ideals of proof and that it was necessary to make judgements on a 'weight of evidence' basis.[10]

Synthetic chemicals were used in agricultural, industrial and domestic activities and, as we have seen, could pollute water, soil and air. But they were not, of course, the only source of pollution. The burning of fossil fuels, for example, in electric power plants, industrial boilers and furnaces, was a major source of air pollution, along with emissions from the massively increased number of motor vehicles. The combustion of these fuels produced sulphur and nitrogen oxides which affected the quality of the air we breathed, particularly in cities, causing respiratory and other illnesses. In some cities (such as Osaka), slot machines had been installed where customers could buy their own oxygen. When sulphur and nitrogen oxides interacted with sunlight, moisture and oxidants, they formed acids which circulated through the atmosphere and then returned to earth in rain and snow. 'Acid rain', as it became known as, respected no frontiers and had become a global problem. With an acidity in some cases equivalent to vinegar, it destroyed vegetation, injured forests, killed fish populations, corroded metal and weathered stone buildings and monuments.

Another form of industrial pollution arose from mining. In a sobering assessment of risks which the human species faced, John Leslie noted in *The End of the World: The Science and Ethics of Human Extinction* (1996) that 2b tons of non-mineral fuels were being mined every year, during which process toxic metals were widely scattered. These included lead (also pumped into the atmosphere by cars), which was entering the environment at eighteen times the natural rate; cadmium, which was entering it at five times the natural rate; and mercury, which was entering it at twice the natural rate.[11] Lead poisoning caused anaemia, colic and general debilitation. In children, it could cause permanent mental retardation. Cadmium damaged the kidneys and the central nervous system, and, in large doses, resulted in complete loss of fertility or sexual potency. Mercury caused irreversible brain, liver and kidney damage.

The processes of industrial and agricultural production also spawned vast quantities of waste. As a general rule, resource extraction in mining, logging and farming generated around twenty tons of waste for every ton of final product manufactured, whilst the manufacturing process itself generated a further five tons. In the United States, factories produced around one ton of hazardous waste per person per year, of which about ten million tons were reckoned to be toxic chemicals. Much of this ended up in leaking dumps.[12] Waste produced by the nuclear industry was particularly hazardous, in that it could remain highly radioactive for anything from seven hundred to a million years. The problems of storing nuclear waste on this kind of timescale were formidable, given the virtual impossibility of anticipating all contingencies. Leaving aside the question of nuclear terrorism (which will be discussed in Chapter 2), there was also the continuing risk of nuclear accidents, which had the potential to cause both environmental and human devastation. It was estimated that anything from 40,000 to 500,000 people living within the vicinity of Chernobyl would die prematurely from leukaemia and other illnesses as a result of the reactor which had exploded in 1986. Following this accident, radiation had spread across Northern Europe and had been detected as far away as Great Britain.

Agricultural and industrial pollution of the kind outlined above was compounded by consumption at the domestic level which, in the industrialised world, was producing around half a ton of garbage per person in each year.[13] This was either incinerated in ways which could add pollutants to the air, or it was disposed of in landfill sites from which it could seep through into groundwaters.

In these accounts of pollution, the emphasis was mainly on the direct effects on humans and other life-forms. However, there were also indirect effects to be considered, namely those arising from impacts on the stratosphere and the global climate.

Destruction of the ozone layer

Formed naturally by the action of sunlight on oxygen, ozone is created continuously in the upper atmosphere, lying between fifteen and fifty kilometres above the earth's surface. It is also destroyed continuously by naturally occurring compounds, in a process which has maintained an ozone equilibrium for many millions of years.

During the 1970s, scientists discovered that this equilibrium was breaking down. The most likely cause was the destructive effect on ozone of chlorinated fluorocarbons (CFCs), which were being released into the atmosphere in vast quantities. Around a million tons of CFCs were being manufactured every year, for use in refrigerators, aerosol cans, industrial solvents and blowing agents for industrial foam. Once in the atmosphere, CFCs were broken down by sunlight, whereupon the chlorine reacted with and destroyed ozone molecules. The chlorine was unaffected by this process, so that just one molecule of chlorine could destroy thousands of ozone molecules.

CFCs were not the only substances found to destroy ozone. Others included halons, widely used in firefighting systems, and hydrochlorofluorocarbons (HCFCs), used in air-conditioning. According to some estimates, the vapour trails of aircraft, and particularly those flying at high altitudes, were reckoned to cause around 10 per cent of all ozone depletion; the use of nitrogen oxides in, for instance, fertilisers, another 10 per cent; and the use of methyl bromide, a crop fumigant, a further 10 per cent. The burning of forests, scrubs and grasslands also destroyed ozone through the generation of massive amounts of methyl chloride.[14]

In 1985, the British Antarctic Survey reported that since the late 1970s the amount of ozone above the Antarctic had fallen dramatically in each Southern Spring (October), returning nearer to normal some weeks later. The Antarctic conditions at this time of year increased ozone depletion, due to the presence of both sunlight and very low temperatures, the combination of which accelerated the destructive effect of CFCs. The low temperatures were caused by the presence of ice clouds, which in recent years had become more common as a result of the cooling of the stratosphere. This could have been due to the 'greenhouse effect' (see below) which caused incoming solar heat to be retained in the lower atmosphere, or it could have been a consequence of the thinning of the ozone layer itself. These 'knock-on' and 'feed-back' effects were, as we shall see, a distinctive feature of the dynamics of environmental degradation.

Following the discovery of the 'hole' in 1985, the situation in the Antarctic deteriorated. Ozone depletion became steadily more severe, extending over a wider area (sometimes equalling the size of the United States) and lasting for longer. In 1994, Antarctic ozone levels declined to 30 per cent of normal (that is, 70 per cent depletion). From the late 1980s on, ozone damage was also detected in the Arctic, spreading out over a wide area from Greenland to Western Siberia, where depletion levels reached 45 per cent in 1996, and extending into North America, Scandinavia and Northern Europe, where they were recorded at between 20 per cent and 30 per cent.[15]

As so often with the announcement of new threats to the environment, the evidence was not at first taken seriously. However, by 1987 the threat was sufficiently widely recognised for international agreement to be reached on the reduction of the manufacture and use of CFCs and halons. The Montreal Protocol to the Vienna Convention was initially signed by 27 countries, but the provisions were soon seen to be inadequate and were later strengthened. By 1997, the Protocol had been ratified by 161 countries, including all industrialised nations.

Some commentators saw in the Montreal Protocol and its later revisions evidence of the international community's ability to take co-ordinated action against a global environmental threat.[16] Others were not so sanguine, pointing to the fact that developing countries, including India and China, were allowed to continue to produce CFCs until 2010 and HCFCs until 2015. In China alone this would put CFCs into 50m new refrigerators. Some governments had failed to ratify the Protocol, and CFC manufacturers (including those who advertised their commitment to the environment) were all too ready to off-load their stocks on countries which had not yet signed. In India, for example, the amount of halons sold in 1990 had been eight times greater than in 1987.[17] The London-based Environmental Investigation Agency presented evidence in 1997 of a massive black market in CFCs, with between 6000 and 20,000 tonnes worth up to £90m being smuggled into Europe each year from Russia and China.[18]

As noted above, CFCs are stable compounds, which typically survive for up to 100 years in the atmosphere, diffusing only slowly into the stratosphere. Even with the strict implementation of the Montreal Protocol, ozone depletion was expected to increase in the early years of the twenty-first century and to improve only slowly thereafter. Some estimates suggested that ozone depletion in the year 2050 would be at least as much as it had been in 1990.[19]

The ozone layer is important because it absorbs most of the damaging ultra-violet radiation (UV-B) from the sun before it reaches ground level: the thinner the ozone layer, the more ultraviolet radiation gets through. Ozone depletion thus has a number of consequences. First, it leads to a significant increase in the rate of skin cancer. Secondly, UV radiation damages human eyes, causing cataracts and blindness. According to a UN Advisory Panel, 100,000 more people will go blind with each 1 per cent decline in strato- spheric ozone.[20] Thirdly, it can suppress human immune systems, making people more vulnerable to diseases, including cancers. Fourthly, it attacks plants, trees and crops, increasing their suscept- ibility to pests and diseases. Finally, it threatens the growth of phytoplankton, which is at the base of oceanic food chains, and which plays a crucial role in removing carbon dioxide from the atmosphere. This is another instance of where the consequences of one kind of pollution (ozone depletion) affect the consequences of another (global warming).

Global warming

Global warming arises from the 'greenhouse effect'. It is caused by the existence of certain gases in the atmosphere which permit sun- light to reach the surface of the earth but at the same time prevent heat escaping back into space. The existence of the 'greenhouse' is essential for maintaining a life-sustaining environment on earth, and without it the world would be frozen and inhospitable to human life. What caused concern was the increasing build-up of these gases and the resulting possibility of an intensification of the 'greenhouse effect'.

Although water vapour is the main 'greenhouse' gas, it was four other gases, mostly produced by human agency, which were respon- sible for 'greenhouse enhancement'. These were, carbon dioxide, methane, nitrous oxides, and chlorinated fluorocarbons.

By the mid-1990s, carbon dioxide (CO_2) was believed by many scientists to have had the greatest impact on global warming. Produced by the burning of fossil fuels, the clearing of forests and the burning of grasslands, its concentration in the atmosphere was 26 per cent higher than it had been 100 years ago. We were burning four times as much fossil fuel as we had been in 1950, and over thirty times as much since 1900. Consumption of coal in power stations had gone up from 2.3b tons in 1970 to 5.2b in 1990. The number of automobiles had increased from 244m in 1970 to 605m in 1996. The acreage of the earth's forests had dropped from thirteen to ten billion between 1950 and 1990, and it was predicted that tropical forests, disappearing at the rate of a million acres a week, would all be gone by the year 2040, if not earlier.[21] As James Lovelock reminded us, it was green plants, including trees, which had made the air contain so much more oxygen than CO_2 and, had green plants never appeared on earth, CO_2 would have made up about 98 per cent of the atmosphere.[22] As it was, the actual level was 0.036 per cent, and having risen gradually since 1850, was higher than it had been for 160,000 years.[23]

Methane (CH_4) was also at a higher level than it had been for 160,000 years, but its concentration in the atmosphere was rising three times as fast as CO_2 and had doubled since 1900. It was arising from many different sources, mainly cattle and sheep, forest fires, coal mining, gas pipe line leaks, refuse dumps and rice growing. By the 1990s, CH_4 was responsible for around 20 per cent of global warming, and predicted by some scientists eventually to become its most potent cause.

Nitrous oxides were the third group of 'greenhouse gases', produced in vast quantities by the use of fertilisers, internal combustion engines, aircraft and the burning of just about anything. As we have seen, they were also a cause of ozone depletion and acid rain. Finally, CFCs, the primary ozone destroyers, were estimated by some experts to contribute around 16 per cent of global warming.

There was a great deal of controversy over both the likely extent of global warming and its impact on the planet, with predictions ranging from the dire to the dismissive. Leslie noted that on the one hand, Irving Mintzer, from the World Resources Institute, had predicted that average temperatures would be higher in 2075 by a massive 16 C, while, on the other hand, Kenneth Watts, Professor of Environmental Studies at the University of California, Davis, had dismissed greenhouse fears as 'the laugh of the century'. The Soviet climatologist, Mikhail Budyko, had accepted the evidence of global warming, but had pointed to the fact that its effects would not be evenly distributed. While many regions of the world would become hotter and dryer, he had argued, others would become colder and wetter, thus creating a 'greenhouse paradise', with cattle grazing in the Sahara and crops growing in the present-day deserts of central Asia.[24]

What was not at issue as the century drew to a close was the fact that globally averaged air temperatures had risen by about 0.5 °C over the previous 100 years. In addition, the Intergovernmental Panel on Climate Change (IPCC) pointed to data which suggested that climatic changes had been more rapid than at any time over the previous 10,000 years, with 1995 being the hottest year since historical records had begun. Although these climactic changes might still be attributable to natural variability, an increasing number of scientists believed that they were the result of an enhanced 'greenhouse effect', and hence the first signs of human impact on the global climate system. According to these scientists' projections, a globally averaged warming of between 1.5 °C and 5 °C would occur over the next 30 to 50 years, with most accepting an increase of at least 2.5 C. Even if action was immediately taken on an international basis to reduce the emission of CO_2 and other 'greenhouse' gases, it would be several decades before the concentration of these gases stabilised. If emissions were not reduced but continued to grow at predicted levels, they would increase 'greenhouse' gases in the atmosphere by around 50 per cent. The chances of decisive action being taken within the next 10 years were remote for three reasons. First, continuing scientific controversy encouraged a 'wait and see' approach; secondly, within the industrialised nations, there were powerful interest groups, such as the Global Climate Coalition (GCC) in the US, which represented industry and utility sectors, and which was strongly opposed to greater controls; and thirdly, developing nations, such as India and China, showed little enthusiasm for a course of action which would effectively inhibit their industrialisation programmes. Neither country, for example, sent representatives to the 'Rio plus five' Earth Summit, held in New York in June 1997.

What, then, would be the results of global warming on the scale that many scientists were predicting? First, the quality and quantity of water would decline in many regions, leading to drought in some areas. This would exacerbate an already serious situation, where 20 per cent of the world's population did not have access to safe drinking water and 50 per cent lacked water for proper sanitation. According to some estimates, the enhanced 'greenhouse' effect might already have caused millions of deaths through drought. Secondly, sea levels would rise due to melting icecaps and the thermal expansion of oceans, flooding many of the low-lying regions of the world. Estimates of this rise ranged from 20 cm by the year 2030, to 1m by the year 2050, to a worst case scenario of 5 to 8m by the year 2100. A 1-metre rise would have the effect of displacing 70m people in China and 15m in Bangladesh. Thirdly, agriculture would be affected, with crop yields reduced both by water shortages and increased pest destruction. This would be devastating in some developing countries, leading to major famines. Fourthly, forests would also be affected, with increased susceptibility to fire, disease and insect damage. Finally, global warming presented new health hazards, in the form of heat-related illness due to higher temperatures over longer periods, new breeding sites for pests, and a shift in the range of infectious diseases.[25]

All of the above, however, paled into insignificance if one considered the possibility of a 'runaway' greenhouse disaster. According to a survey of 400 climatologists, conducted by Greenpeace, almost half had thought that this terrifying scenario was a possibility, with 10 per cent believing it to be probable.[26] In brief, the 'runaway greenhouse' disaster would arise from a positive feedback loop, through which global warming increased the production of 'greenhouse' gases at an accelerating rate, which in turn would cause a further escalation in the rate of global warming. This process would continue at an exponentially increasing rate, until the planet heated up to a temperature close to boiling point. The conditions on earth, where life of course would no longer be possible, would thus approximate those of Venus, where a dense atmosphere made up mainly of CO_2 is responsible for temperatures of around 450 C.

The 'runaway' process would be triggered once the concentration of 'greenhouse' gases in the air approached a certain level. In the case of CO_2 it would be around 1 per cent; in the case of a cocktail of 'greenhouse' gases, it could be rather less, given that CH_4, for example, has a thirty times more powerful 'greenhouse' effect than CO_2. A number of scenarios for a 'runaway' disaster had been constructed, which showed the build-up of 'greenhouse' gases to the critical level through a combination of some or all of the following factors, all themselves a product of global warming in the first place: (1) rapid decomposure of the vast amount of carbon (C) held in the soil as dead organic matter, and its release into the air as CO_2 and CH_4; (2) release of CH_4, locked up in the continental-shelf sediments and below arctic permafrost; (3) ocean waters becoming less able to take CO_2 from the air as they warm up; (4) loss of marine phytoplankton, also caused by ozone depletion, and a reduction of its capacity to extract CO_2 from the air (a loss of 10 per cent would reduce the annual oceanic uptake of CO_2 by an amount approximating the total annual CO_2 emissions from fossil fuel consumption); (5) increasing net CO_2 production in plants and trees; (6) loss of vegetation through drought, and resulting return of carbon to the atmosphere; (7) release of more water vapour into the atmosphere; (8) warmed oceans giving out much of their dissolved organic carbon as CO_2 due to increased activity by bacteria.[27]

All of the above was, of course, speculative, but nevertheless disturbing when one recalled that a rise of average global temperatures by 2 C, which was the minimum that most scientists expected by 2050, could make the planet warmer than it had been for the past 100m years, and perhaps warmer than it had ever been since life had moved to land 400m years ago. It could be argued – as indeed it seriously was – that just as humanity had the technology to warm the globe, albeit accidentally, it also had the technology to cool it down; that it could, as a last resort, detonate a large number of nuclear bombs, in the hope that the vast clouds of dust thrown up into the atmosphere would put an end to any 'runaway greenhouse' disaster. But it was difficult not to see in such a proposal a prospect as alarming as the disaster it was supposed to be able to avert.

Loss of biodiversity

The word 'biodiversity' is a contraction of the word biological diversity, and thus refers to the notion of variety within the living world. The word came into common usage in the mid-1980s, this in itself a reflection of the growing concern about threats to different forms of life. It could be understood to refer to three separate elements: genetic diversity, species diversity, and ecosystem diversity. Genetic diversity referred to the heritable variation within species; species diversity to the number of different species; and ecosystem diversity to life-supporting habitats, such as coral reefs and rainforests. These three elements were obviously closely interconnected: loss of genetic diversity might threaten the evolutionary potential of a particular species; destruction of ecosystems could lead to species loss; and so on.

The precise measurement of biodiversity is impossible. Nobody has ever known how many species exist on the planet. By the mid-1990s, around 1.7m species had been identified, with estimates of further species ranging from 5m to 100m. The World Conservation Monitoring Centre suggested a conservative working estimate of 12.5m species, the majority of which, of course, were insects and microorganisms.[28] It was suggested that the number of new species to be discovered was limited only by the number of active taxonomists and the rate at which they were able to work. While the measurement of ecosystem diversity was complicated by how an ecosystem was actually defined, the measurement of genetic diversity was impossible under anything other than very specific conditions, given the sheer magnitude of potential genetic variation. It had been estimated, for example, that in both humans and fruit flies the number of possible combinations of different forms of each gene sequence exceeded the numbers of atoms in the universe.[29] The measurement of biodiversity also had to take into account the extent to which a particular species differed from other species: the greater its evolutionary uniqueness, the greater its importance.

Despite these difficulties in measuring global biodiversity, which some biologists reckoned to be at an all time high, there was clear evidence of a reduction in the biodiversity of specific species and habitats. The greatest threat was posed by the destruction of wilderness areas, in particular rainforests and coastal mangroves, which probably contained between 80 per cent and 90 per cent of all species. The Harvard biologist, Edward O. Wilson, calculated in 1997 that at least 50,000 species a year were disappearing as these ecosystems were ripped up. Globally, three-quarters of the world's bird species were declining, and nearly one-quarter of the 4600 species of mammals were threatened with extinction.[30] The extinction rate was increasing, and, according to some estimates, 20 per cent of species in existence in 1985 could have been wiped out by 2000, and well over half of all those that remained by the year 2100.[31] If the large-scale changes in global climate and weather patterns took place as predicted, there was a high probability that these extinction rates would escalate further. There were also threats to genetic diversity within both crops and livestock, as genetic erosion resulted from the continued, exclusive cultivation of a limited number of varieties.

Over geological time, stretching over the 4.5b years of the earth's history (human beings have been around for only 7m or 8m of them) all species have had a finite span of existence. Those which existed at the end of the twentieth century represented about 1 per cent of all that have ever lived.[32] Paleontologists reckoned that there had been five episodes of mass extinction, such as that at the end of the Permian period (250m years ago), which probably eliminated between 77 per cent and 96 per cent of all species. Leaving aside mass extinctions of this kind, background or 'natural' rates of extinction have varied enormously, with periods of high extinction having occurred over the past 250m years at intervals of roughly 26m to 28m years.[33] What was novel about our own time was an escalation of extinction rates due to the activities of one species – mankind. 'It is beyond question', the World Conservation Monitoring Centre concluded, 'that extinctions caused directly or indirectly by man are occurring at a rate which far exceeds any reasonable estimates of background extinction rates, and which, to the extent that it is correlated with habitat perturbation, must be increasing'.[34] It was possible, therefore, that we were witnessing the beginnings of a new period of mass extinction brought about by human agency.

Moving back from a geological to a human timescale, one had to ask the question of whether it mattered. Nature, after all, was not the source of all good, and, as Raymond Tallis had observed, 'pus pouring from one's leg is as natural as a song pouring from a bird's throat'.[35] Nevertheless, there were compelling arguments for the preservation of biodiversity. First, it was important to maintain genetic diversity in crops and livestock, as genetic erosion and uniformity decreased resistance to pests and disease. In this respect, genetic diversity could be seen as a kind of insurance policy for the agriculture of the future. Secondly, medicinal drugs derived from natural sources made an important global contribution to health care. It was true that these sources represented only a small percentage of biodiversity, but natural diversity might be increasingly valued for the 'blueprints' it provided for new synthetic drugs. Thirdly, there was the principle of inter-generational responsibility, which imposed duties of 'stewardship' and prohibited us from destroying what future generations might value. Fourthly, for many people there was an aesthetic and spiritual dimension to biological diversity, which manifested itself as a deep respect for variety in nature for its own sake. While each of these arguments, taken alone, might not present an adequate case for biodiversity conservation, taken together they helped to explain why the increasing threats to the living world provoked such alarm.

Food scarcity

From the 1950s onwards, up until the late 1980s, world food supplies grew at an unprecedented rate. The amount of fish caught in the world's oceans grew from 19m tons in 1950 to 88m tons in 1988, a rise of over 360 per cent. During this period, the global catch per person more than doubled, climbing from just under 8kg to 17kg. From 1950 to 1990, the world's grain harvest almost tripled, increasing from 631m tons to 1780m tons. This worked out as a rise in the grain harvest per person of around 37 per cent, climbing from around 248 to 336kg per person.[36] These per capita increases were all the more impressive when one took into account the fact that, during the same period, the world's population more than doubled, rising from 2.5b in 1950 to 5.3b in 1990. They were made possible by advances in farm and fishing technologies, and driven by a record growth in incomes. Of course, not all regions of the world were equal beneficiaries, and it was a sobering thought that, despite these phenomenal increases in the global food supply, millions of people still died as a result of famines in parts of sub-Saharan Africa, Latin America and Southeast Asia.

By the late 1990s, all the basic indicators suggested that food supplies could not continue to grow at the rates to which the world had become accustomed. In the case of fish stocks, which were supplying one quarter of all the proteins on which humans fed, the absolute limits had already been reached. Fishing technology was so sophisticated that ocean fish stocks were declining due to the sheer volume of fish taken out. Trawlers, able to locate the exact position of shoals, and using vast nets to sweep them up, could work in even the most remote corners of the planet. Historically, the size of the fish catch had been limited only by fishing capacity. But, since the late 1980s, the determining factor had been the sustainable yield of fisheries. As we have seen, fish catches had continued to grow up until 1988, at which point they had peaked at around 88m tons. Between 1988 and 1997, the global fish catch per person had declined by about 9 per cent as the population had continued to grow. To have taken even more fish out of the oceans would have only resulted in decreasing yields in following years. Given the finite nature of fish resources and a continuing growth in population, it was clear that the next generation of children was going to consume far less fish during its lifetime than the previous generation.

Grain was a vitally important component of food supplies, in that it directly supplied human beings with half their calorific intake, and indirectly supplied a substantial proportion of the other half in the form of livestock feed, on which the production of meat, milk and eggs depended. The global grain harvest had continued to rise in the 1980s and 1990s, but at a much slower rate than during the preceding decades and, relative to population growth, it had started to decline. Reaching its peak of 346 km in 1984, world grain production per person had declined by over 9 per cent to 313 km by 1996. This slowdown had been due to five main reasons. First, croplands had suffered from either soil exhaustion or erosion, to the extent that large areas had become unusable. For instance, the grain area of the former Soviet Union had reached an all-time high of 123m hectares in 1979, but had shrunk to 91m hectares in 1995 as heavily eroded land had had to be abandoned. Secondly, croplands had been lost to industrialisation, particularly in densely populated, developing countries. Japan, South Korea and Taiwan had lost nearly half their grainland area since production peaked in 1960; China and India had been rapidly losing cropland due to massive road-building programmes; Indonesia, Vietnam, Thailand and Malaysia were going the same way. Thirdly, the old strategy of boosting crop yields with increasing amounts of fertiliser had become limited by the finite capacity of crops to absorb more and more nutrients. Fourthly, higher temperatures and more extreme weather events which, as we have seen, were increasingly associated with the build-up of 'greenhouse' gases, had had devastating effects on crop yields in both 1988 and 1995. The experience of 1988 had shown that the combination of intense heat and drought could totally eliminate the exportable surplus of grain in the United States, the world's breadbasket. The eleven warmest years since records had begun in 1866 had all taken place since 1979, with the three hottest in the 1990s: if the earth's average temperature continued to rise, it would have a devastating impact on future grain harvests.

The fifth threat to grain production was, of course, water scarcity. One of the main reasons for the near tripling of the world grain harvest between 1950 and 1990 had been a huge expansion of irrigation, which had extended agriculture into arid regions with little rainfall. Most of the world's rice and much of its wheat were now produced on irrigated land. Between 1950 and 1993, the total area of the world's irrigated land had increased by over 160 per cent, rising from 154m hectares to 248m hectares. However, by 1979 the growth in irrigation had fallen behind the growth in population, and by the

1990s there was evidence to suggest that the total area of irrigated land was actually shrinking.[37] If this was the case, then the irrigation water supply per person, which had been declining since 1979, would fall even faster.

The explanation for this decline lay in the depletion of water both from underground aquifers and from rivers. Water tables were now falling in the major food-producing regions of the world, such as the United States and China. Irrigated cropland in Texas, for example, had shrunk by 11 per cent between 1982 and 1992, due to depletion of the Ogallala aquifer. Increasing industrial and residential needs for water were intensifying the competition for supplies between the city and the country. The water table under Beijing had dropped from 5m below ground in 1950 to more than 50m in 1996, raising the question of whether Beijing's water needs in the future could be met without diverting supplies from irrigation. Rivers, too, were under increasing pressure. The great Huang He (Yellow River) in China first failed to reach the sea in 1972, and by the 1990s was running dry for progressively longer periods. The Colorado, the major river in the south-western United States, frequently disappeared into the Arizona desert, rarely reaching the Gulf of California.

Some doubted the gravity of all this. According to projections from the UN Food and Agriculture Organisation, we would continue to see grain surpluses and declining real grain prices through to the year 2010. However, this view was vigorously challenged by some experts, on the grounds that the growth of grain supplies simply could not keep pace with a population growing by an additional 80m people a year, when the scope for increasing harvests was limited by the factors outlined above.[38] Lester Brown, President of the Worldwatch Institute, argued that pressures on food supplies were being further exacerbated by the demands of Asia's rising affluence. When Western Europe and North America had modernised after World War II, creating a consumer economy and boosting consumption for grain-fed livestock products, they had done so with a total population of 440m. Now, Asia was going through a comparable process, but at a much faster rate with the involvement of 3.1b people – more than half the world's population. 'There is no historical precedent', said Brown, 'for so many people moving up the food chain so fast'.[39]

In Brown's view, the politics of surpluses that had dominated the world food economy since the end of World War II were now being replaced by the politics of scarcity. World wheat and corn prices had reached their highest ever in 1996, with carryover stocks (the amount left in the world's grain bins at the start of each new harvest) diminished to the lowest levels on record. Countries which already had grain deficits, such as China, Brazil, Mexico and many states in both the Middle East and North Africa, were expected to have even larger deficits by the year 2030. There appeared to be an assumption that the United States would be able to meet these deficits, but with the diminishing opportunities to expand the growth of the grain supply, which we have noted, this assumption might not have been realistic.

The supply and demand of grain would, of course, balance in the market-place, but in a period of scarcity at the cost of much higher prices. This could lead to growing unrest in developing countries, and in those where the majority of people live on a minimal, subsistence-level diet the consequences could be explosive. Brown foresaw an unprecedented degree of political instability in these countries, with knock-on effects to the affluent world, affecting the profits of multinational companies, the performance of stock markets and the earnings of pension funds.[40] Leslie envisaged desperate governments contemplating biological warfare as a preferable alternative to starvation, and as 'an act of revenge on the disgustingly overfed'.[41] In *Beyond the Limits*, Donella H. Meadows, Dennis L. Meadows and Jørgen Randers raised the spectre of global collapse, arising from the inability or unwillingness of governments to take action until long after the limits of sustainable exploitation of the environment had been exceeded.[42] In this scenario, we would not exactly have reached the point of no return, but the return would be long and hard, and to a very different place.

Population growth

Behind all the manifestations of environmental decline, described above, lay the sudden and unprecedented expansion of the world's population over the course of the twentieth century. Attempting to meet the needs of vastly-increased numbers of people had placed intense strain on the environment, both through the effects of pollution and through the exploitation of the earth's natural resources.

It had taken several million years of human history for the population of the world to grow to 2.5b. Since that figure had been reached in 1950, it had taken just 37 years for it to double. To put it another way, the first billion had been reached in 1804, and while it took 123 years to increase from 1b to 2b, succeeding billions had taken 33, 14, 13 and 11 years respectively. At the close of the twentieth century, with a global population of over 6b, around 80m babies (equivalent to the entire population of Germany) were being born each year at the rate of around 220,000 a day or 9000 an hour. With the possible exception of some species of rodents, humans were now by far the most numerous mammals on earth. Taking into account reptiles, amphibians and birds as well, only the domestic chicken outnumbered humans. As the biologist Edward O. Wilson had observed, we were 'the first species in the history of life to go out of control on a global scale'.[43]

The rates of population growth did, of course, vary enormously from region to region, as can be seen from Table 1.1, which divides the world into six regions and shows differential growth rates from 1950 to 1994.

Figure 1.1   World population growth from year 1 to 2050

Population (in billions)

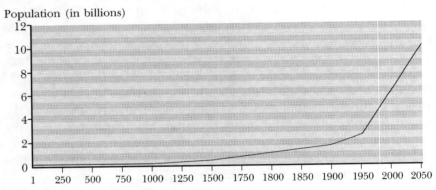

Source: United Nations Population Division, Department of Economic and Social Information and Policy Analysis, 1994,
gopher://gopher.undp.org:70/00/ungophers/popin/wdtrends/histor

Table 1.1   Population increase (millions), 1950–1994,
in the major regions of the world

Region	1950	1994	% Increase
Africa	224.0	708.0	216.07
Asia	1403.0	3403.0	142.55
Europe	549.0	726.0	32.24
Latin America	166.0	474.0	185.54
North America	166.0	290.0	74.69
Oceania	12.6	28.1	123.01
World Total	2520.0	5630.0	123.41

Source: *1994 Demographic Yearbook*, United Nations

In the period from 1950 to 1994, taken as a whole, the developing countries accounted for 89 per cent of global population growth. At the end of this period, they were accounting for 97 per cent of it. However, it is important to remember that it was the more developed countries which had put the greatest strain on the environment. Using 1990 as an example, Paul Ehrlich had argued that the average rich-nation citizen had used 7.4 kW of energy in the course of the year – a continuous flow of energy equivalent to the amount required to illuminate seventy-four 100–watt lightbulbs. The average citizen of a poor nation, by contrast, had used only 1 kW. If energy use was taken as a measure of environmental destruction, it could be shown from these figures that the 1.2b people living in the rich nations had had a far greater destructive impact than the 4.1b living in poor nations.[44] In effect, it could be seen that the relatively small population of the advanced industrialised world, through pollution and the exploitation of non-renewable resources, had accounted for roughly two-thirds of global environmental destruction. On top of this, the sheer number of people trying to feed themselves in the poor countries had had, and was continuing to have, a devastating impact in these regions in the form of deforestation, overgrazing, diminished water supplies, soil erosion and so on.

When the population of the world had risen to 3.5b in 1968, Paul Ehrlich published *The Population Bomb*, in which he examined the implications of a continuing, massive growth in population levels, warning that we were playing 'environmental roulette' and that we faced the prospect of breeding ourselves into oblivion.[45] Although some of his predictions proved to be excessive, he found in his follow-up book *The Population Explosion* (1991), which he co-wrote with Anne Ehrlich, that 'a largely prospective disaster has turned into the real thing'.[46] In the period between the publication of the two books, world population had risen to 5.3b, threats (some unforeseen) to the environment had materialised, and at least 200m people, mostly children, had died of hunger and hunger-related diseases. The consequences of overpopulation, argued the Ehrlichs, were clear for all to see: 'more frequent droughts, more damaged crops and famines, more dying forests, more smog, more international conflicts, more epidemics, more gridlock, more drugs, more crime, more sewage swimming and other extreme unpleasantness'.[47] In 1968, the Ehrlichs suggested, the fuse had been burning. Now the population bomb had detonated.

It could be argued that the worst, in fact, was now over, given that

41

world population growth had slowed from a peak of around 2.1 per cent a year in the early 1960s to 1.6 per cent in the period 1990–5. There was every sign that the so-called 'demographic transition', whereby family sizes decreased as a result of industrialisation, urbanisation and the fall of the death rate, was working its way through most parts of the world. However, when one realised that a decrease in annual population growth from 2.1 per cent to 1.6 per cent merely extended the time it took for a population to double from thirty-four years to forty-four, it became clear why the Ehrlichs had suggested that the population bomb had already exploded.

First, global population was still growing on an exponential curve, in that its increase was proportional to what was already there. Meadows, Meadows and Randers invited us to conceive of this as a water lily that choked out all other life in its pond after thirty days of doubling in size. For a long time, the lily plant would have been so small in size that it would not have seemed worth worrying about. Only when it covered half of the pond might one think about cutting it back. But that would be on the twenty-ninth day, 'when there would be just one day left to save the pond'.[48]

Secondly, even when total fertility rates (the number of lifetime births per woman) had fallen to the 'replacement level' of two babies per woman, population growth had an in-built momentum which kept it on an upward curve for some time afterwards. This was because most developing countries had a very young age structure which ensured that large numbers of young people would enter the parenting ages for the next several generations. Births would thus continue to outnumber deaths long after the 'replacement level' had been reached. The Ehrlichs cited India as an example. In 1990, it had had a population of 850m people with a total fertility rate of 4.3. If over the subsequent thirty to thirty-five years the fertility rate dropped to replacement level and stayed there with no increase in the death rate, then India's population would continue to grow for almost a century, stabilising at around 2b people. This would be as many people living in one nation as populated the entire planet in 1930.[49]

The fact remained, however, that in the 1990s the world was still a long way from stabilising its population. The United States, with its 267m people (mid-1997 figures), was still adding around 1.7m people to itself each year (excluding immigration), but it was in the poorer nations that the really massive population increases were taking place. The fertility rate for sub-Saharan Africa as a whole was still around six. Nigeria, just by itself, with a doubling time of a little over twenty years, could move from its hundred or so million to around half a billion. Pakistan and Bangladesh were expected to double their numbers. The fertility rate in Egypt was still over four, in India and Peru just under four.

Future population trends were notoriously difficult to predict. It was interesting to recall that, in 1951, the United Nations predicted that global population in 1980 would be anywhere between 3b and 3.6b, although it considered the higher figure unlikely. As we now know, the actual figure proved to be around 4.4b, a significant margin of error (34 per cent above the higher limit) in a 30 year projection. Long-range projections varied enormously, but at the end of the 1990s, most were forecasting a world population of between 9b and 10b in 2050 (five times the population of 1950), but with higher estimates going up to 12.5b. If fertility were to stabilise at 2.5 children per couple, global population could reach 28b by 2150.[50] Given these forecasts, it was clear that the worst, far from being over, was still to come.

This was not a view held by the bishops assembling in 1988 to celebrate the twentieth anniversary of Pope Paul's anti-birth-control encyclical *Humanae Vitae*, who declared that 'the world's food resources theoretically could feed 40 billion people'.[51] In a similar vein, Julian Simon had argued in *The Ultimate Resource* (1981) and subsequent articles that resources were infinite, that more people were better than fewer people and that population could and should grow indefinitely.[52] However, these views were considered irresponsible by most population analysts and were not widely shared, not even in Catholic Italy, which, at 1.25, had the second lowest fertility rate in the world (Hong Kong had the lowest at 1.23).

There were, in fact, very real doubts as to whether the planet could sustain a human population of the levels predicted. Even if food and water supplies could in some way keep pace with population growth, increasing industrialisation, which was likely to accompany any 'demographic transition' from higher to lower fertility rates, would place degrees of stress on the environment beyond anything that had so far been experienced. The scale of likely future impacts could be grasped when one recalled that, in the ten years from 1980 to 1990, global industrial production had already exceeded that for all history up to 1950.

'At least in the near future', argued John Leslie, 'a population of as little as ten billion could be expected to cause desertifications and famines, intolerable local water scarcities and levels of pollution, which virtually guaranteed wars'.[53] For the Ehrlichs, what was difficult to reconcile was the contrast between their apprehension of the catastrophes ahead and the apparent complacency of the public and elected officials. In their view, there was no doubt that the population explosion would soon come to an end one way or another. The only question was whether it would happen through humane means or 'by nature wiping out the surplus'.[54]

Environmental pessimism

Behind the narratives of environmental decline outlined in this chapter lay an undercurrent of pessimism. This was not because those who had contributed to the narratives had become fatalistic. On the contrary, the identification of problems was invariably followed by prescriptions for corrective action. Thus, for example, Rachel Carson called for a halt to the chemical barrage of insecticidal poison, and put forward alternatives based on biological methods of insect control.[55] As we have seen, DDT was eventually banned in the West, largely as a result of her work. Colborn *et al* argued for a wholesale review of both the culture and the institutional arrangements which had been built up around the use of synthetic chemicals.[56] The Worldwatch Institute recorded the success of intergovernmental action to reduce the rate of ozone depletion, and continued its efforts to promote 'ecological literacy'. The Ehrlichs campaigned for population control at both a political and personal level ('we don't give baby presents for any child past number two').[57] Environmental pressure groups and Green political parties became established in the West over the last thirty years, achieving some spectacular successes in their own right and affecting the climate of opinion in both industry and mainstream politics. Environmental pessimism arose not from the extinction of hope amongst those who told the story of decline, but from what their story actually revealed.

It was clear, to begin with, that the human species had never before been subjected to such a scale and pace of environmental change. Transforming as the Industrial Revolution of the late eighteenth and nineteenth centuries had been within a few Western nations, it bore no resemblance to the scale of environmental transformation which had taken place over the second half of the twentieth century. As we have seen, there were four key elements: first, levels of pollution, and, in particular, the introduction into the environment of vast amounts of synthetic chemicals, had created conditions for human and animal life which were outside the previous limits of biological experience and which had unknown and unpredictable effects. Secondly, never before had the activities of human beings impacted on the global climate and on conditions in the stratosphere. Thirdly, global population had reached unprecedented levels, exacerbating pollution and exhausting non-renewable resources, water supplies and food-producing land. Fourthly, the activities of just one species – mankind – had escalated the extinction rate of other species, raising the possibility of a new period of mass extinction brought about by human agency. In short, an environment which had taken millions of years to evolve was being radically altered within the space of a generation. Human beings, which had evolved in relation to and as part of this environment, were being forced to adjust from what Carson had called 'the deliberate pace of nature' to make biological adaptations to new environmental conditions at a speed which was unprecedented in the history of the species. Colborn *et al* saw all this as 'a great global experiment – with humanity and all life on earth as the unwitting subjects'.[58]

What would be the result of this experiment? The evidence suggested that there were likely to be unpleasant surprises in store. We had learned from our experiences that what at first could appear beneficial could later have malign consequences which were wholly unforeseen at the time. DDT, for example, had first been used as a pesticide in the 1940s, when it had been widely acclaimed as the answer to pest control, with its developer, Paul Müller, being awarded the Nobel Prize for his efforts in 1948. It was not until the 1960s that fears about its safety had begun to emerge, and it was not until 1972 that its use was legally restricted in the United States. CFCs, first synthesised in 1928 by Thomas Midgeley, who received the Priestley Prize, chemistry's highest award, for his work, were on the market for over forty years before suspicions were voiced about their effect on the ozone layer. It was not until 1987 that international agreement was reached on the phasing-out of their use. As we have seen, both DDT and CFCs continued to be used in developing countries. Who in the 1950s was prepared to predict that the activities of humans could impact on the global climate system?

Given these experiences, it was not unreasonable to suppose that we had already introduced other pollutants into our environment, the effects of which were as yet both unknown and still to present themselves. A pattern could be discerned: we tested chemicals for the most recently recognised hazard, only to discover after the chemical had been declared 'safe' and had been widely used that it had other dangerous properties which had never been anticipated and for which it had never been tested. This had been true of DDT, PCBs, chlordane, lindane, toxaphene, malathion, methoxychlor and many others. The unpredictability of the effects of chemical pollutants was increased by the fact that they could combine both with themselves and other substances in the environment, producing unexpected reactions. For example, when malathion was still being used, it was found that, if it came into contact with certain other organic phosphates, the toxic effect was magnified by fifty times.[59] Similarly, laboratory experiments on breast cancer cells had shown that, while some hormone-disrupting chemicals had no effect when introduced individually, when introduced in combination with other so-called estrogen mimics they could produce a pronounced proliferation of these cells.[60]

Other incidents arose from the unexpected links between what at first appeared to be disconnected phenomena. Taylor gave the example of how fish farms had been developed in Scotland, by feeding large numbers of fish on the larvae of brine shrimps imported from San Francisco Bay. These larvae could be transported in a dormant condition but could still be fed to the fish as live food. However, as the Bay area had become polluted, the supply of larvae had dried up and new supplies had to be brought into Scotland from the Great Salt Lake in Utah. However, when these were put into the fish farms, the fish all died. On investigation, it was discovered that Utah farmers had been using heavy loads of pesticide, which had drained into the lake and had been absorbed by the shrimps. The quantity had not been enough to kill the shrimps, but as the fish fed on the shrimps, the poison accumulated in the fish, eventually killing them. In this way, the attempts of Utah farmers to grow more cereal had had a knock-on effect on Scottish attempts to produce more protein.[61]

We can see, then, that the key elements of environmental pessimism arose, firstly, from the sheer scale and pace of decline and, secondly, from the sense of foreboding this produced in relation to the prospect of unpredictable and unforeseen effects. Colborn *et al* likened this to 'flying blind'. 'Our dilemma', they suggested, 'is like that of a plane hurtling through the fog without a map or instruments'.[62] But there was a third element to this pessimism – what Robert Heilbroner has called 'our collective capacity for response'.[63] This will be discussed in more detail in Chapter 4, but at this point we can look briefly at how it was represented in these narratives in relation to environmental questions.

First, there was the problem of establishing beyond reasonable doubt that a set of practices, or a particular substance, was actually responsible for the damage to the environment that had been identified. Cause and effect was often difficult to prove conclusively, particularly, as we have seen, because of the time lag between the two. This could set up a false sense of security, which was difficult to dislodge. Furthermore, the issues themselves were scientifically complex, and usually subject to a great deal of disagreement amongst the very small number of people who were qualified to form a judgement, and on whom the rest of us had to rely. There were also powerful interests which stood to lose financially from restraints on their activities, and which could be quick to exploit scientific uncertainty. We saw how industry and utility sectors had come together in the United States to form the Global Climate Coalition (GCC), an alliance which sounded 'green' but which in fact campaigned against greater controls. Similarly, a chemical industry which, according to one estimate, accounted for 45 per cent of the world's GNP through the manufacture of chlorinated synthetic chemicals and the products made from them was not going to agree readily that the build-up of these chemicals in the environment was ecologically destructive. Colborn *et al* argued that scientific uncertainty should have made us proceed with far more caution. Given the costs of tackling environmental threats, the sacrifices involved and the interests at stake, however, uncertainty instead became a justification for 'business as usual'.

Secondly, even when it was established beyond doubt that a particular practice or combination of practices would have a destructive impact on the environment, it might take years before this impact was widely felt. Thus, the destruction of the ozone layer remained for most people at the conceptual level only, its effects to be experienced by others at some point in the future. Similarly, the build-up of greenhouse gases was a gradual process, causing the effects of global warming to materialise not in the immediate future but well into the twenty-first century. Problems which lay years ahead, rather than those anticipated in the immediate future, and which might in any case be subject to scientific controversy, could become discounted both in public opinion and in political processes. The long run might never happen; and, if it did, the next generation could adjust to it, with the help of even more advanced technologies which by then would have been developed. But this ran the risk of 'overshooting', like the tanker whose engines are put into reverse when rocks are seen ahead, but whose momentum is such that it is unable to stop before hitting them.

Thirdly, a sense of impotence could arise from the sheer scale of environmental decline and the intractability of the difficulties encountered in attempts to arrest it. Implicit in the narratives which have been discussed in this chapter was a fundamental critique of a global civilisation and economy built on the foundation of fossil fuels and synthetic chemicals. If this critique was accepted, then the magnitude of change required to move towards another kind of civilisation slipped out of the realms of the possible and into those of the fantastic. Not only was this true of the advanced industrialised countries, where it was inconceivable that levels of consumption now widely enjoyed would be easily relinquished, it was even more true of the developing countries, which had seen the West grow rich without undue concern for the environmental consequences, and which were now not about to give up their opportunity of material advancement, on account of environmental problems which had been created by the West in the first place.

Fourthly, the sheer numbers of people expected to inhabit the earth by the year 2050 presented problems of political organisation which had no historical precedent. It could not be assumed that political systems which had evolved in a world containing 1b or 2b people would cope with the strains of 10b people within a deteriorating environment. Heilbroner foresaw a period of 'convulsive change', whereby change was forced upon us by catastrophe rather than calculation.[64]

None of this was to suggest that narratives of environmental decline were 'invented' by the postmodern world. The association of Nature with innocence and goodness, which was a powerful component of 'green' sensibility, had had a long-standing place in European and American literature.[65] It could be found in writers as diverse as Shakespeare, Rousseau and Thoreau and could be traced right back to the classical world, to the work of Virgil, Theocritus and Hesiod. But it was with the development of industrialism, particularly in the England of the late eighteenth and nineteenth centuries, that recognisably modern notions of environmental decline emerged. The old veneration of the 'natural' combined powerfully with critiques of the new industrialism to produce a 'structure of feeling' that proved remarkably enduring. Central to these critiques, early versions of which were associated with Romantic poets such as William Blake, was a deep distrust of science. Not only was science seen to produce, in the technologies of the 'dark satanic mills', the most appalling environmental conditions but also its piecemeal analytical procedures, by failing to see the whole as distinct from the sum of its parts, was seen as a betrayal of the organic view of nature. Science itself thus became an agent of decline – a charge that returned with even greater intensity in our own period and which is discussed as a narrative in its own right in Chapter 3. However, whilst the Romantics can be seen as early 'greens', celebrating and defending the 'natural' as the industrial-scientific world began to take shape, they were not in a position to articulate or fully understand the economic energies which drove this world. For this, it was necessary to wait for the theorising of 'capitalism' which came later in the nineteenth century; and although Marx himself was not blind to the attractions of the bucolic life, famously claiming that communist society would enable him 'to hunt in the morning, fish in the afternoon, rear cattle in the evening [and] criticise after dinner',[66] it was actually William Morris who made the clearest connections at the time between the dynamics of capitalism and environmental degradation. 'Waste' was a central motif of Morris's political writings, and it applied as much to environmental resources as it did to the lives of those he saw destroyed by the pressures of 'competitive Commerce'.[67]

The values of these earlier narratives could still be discerned in the postmodern world. The attachment to the 'natural' was a powerful component of the growing environmental movement and was also reflected in the explosion of interest in 'natural' health products, organic foods and so on. The hold that the 'natural' exercised on the public imagination was well understood by the advertising industry, which used images of pastoral wholesomeness to sell a huge variety of 'unnatural' consumer goods. There was some irony in this, in that it was the industry that produced those goods that was still held responsible, as it had been in the nineteenth century, for the destruction of the 'natural' in the first place. However, the science and technology on which modern industry was built occupied an increasingly ambiguous position: on the one hand, it was their products which were bringing us closer to environmental collapse; on the other, the material and intellectual benefits which they had given us were immeasurable. Furthermore, it was only through science that we understood what was happening to our environment and it was only through the application of science that we had any chance of averting the catastrophes ahead. But this required collective action and, as we saw earlier, the postmodern world seemed incapable of providing it. Although there were many reasons for this, the destructive and uncontrollable energies of global capitalism, which had been foreseen so clearly in the nineteenth century, continued to feature strongly in the explanations of both the extent of environmental decline and of our inability to arrest it.[68] These energies are discussed further in Chapter 4.

Narratives of environmental decline, then, were not new in themselves: an attachment to the 'natural' featured powerfully in the literary history of the West; and recognisably modern concerns for the environment could be identified in the early critiques of industrialism. The values of all these traditions had persisted and could be discerned in the narratives which had emerged in our own times. However, what *was* new was the pessimism that these narratives exhibited, and this arose ineluctably from the material conditions that they described. It was a pessimism which was global in its scope, although its articulation was confined largely to the advanced industrialised world, where environmental issues attracted a great deal more attention than anywhere else. As we saw, developing countries were reluctant to allow environmental concerns to get in the way of the pace of their own industrialisation; and it was in the advanced industrialised world, in any case, where the greatest strains on the environment were being placed.

In the narratives discussed in this chapter, the environmental resources of the planet could be seen as a form of 'capital', which required stewardship on behalf of future generations. But the responsibilities of stewardship had not been properly discharged. Too high a price had been paid for the material benefits now enjoyed in the rich countries of the world, and environmental 'capital' had become dangerously depleted. This 'capital' would become further depleted, yielding diminishing returns in the years ahead, as developing countries continued to claim their share. 'Rationalize as we will', Robert Heilbroner had written in 1974,

> stretch the figures as honesty will permit, we cannot reconcile the requirements for a lengthy continuation of the present rate of industrialisation of the globe with the capacity of existing resources or the fragile biosphere to permit or to tolerate the effects of that industrialisation. Nor is it easy to foresee a willing acquiescence of humankind, individually or through its existing social organisations, in the alterations of lifeways that foresight would dictate.[69]

For Eric Hobsbawm, writing twenty years later, 'stewardship' was simply not possible in a world 'captured, uprooted and transformed by the titanic economic and techno-scientific process of the development of capitalism'. The forces thus generated were now 'great enough to destroy the environment, that is to say, the material foundations of human life'.[70] In the closing weeks of the twentieth century, the independent scientist, James Lovelock, author of the influential Gaia thesis and inventor of the electron capture detector (ECD),[71] delivered an equally pessimistic verdict. Asked whether further environmental controls could still avert the crises ahead, Lovelock replied that it was already too late. 'It's like you're on a steep hill in a car and your brakes fail', he told his interviewer. 'You've got to do something and at least you can take your foot off the accelerator. But you're going to crash anyway'.[72] On a more up-beat note, John Leslie concluded that the probability of the human race avoiding extinction over the next five centuries was 'encouragingly high, perhaps as high as 70 per cent'.[73] But if the avoidance of extinction was the best that could be hoped for, if this really was the 'bottom line' of the environmental debate, then the sense of pessimism lying behind the narratives of decline discussed in this chapter could be readily appreciated. As Colborn *et al* observed, 'there may be fates worse than extinction'.[74]

Notes

1. Carson, *Silent Spring*, p. 167.
2. Ibid. p. 32.
3. Ibid. pp. 229–39.
4. Taylor, *The Doomsday Book*, p. 127.
5. Colborn, Dumanoski and Myers, *Our Stolen Future*, p. 138.
6. Leslie, *The End of the World*, p. 45.
7. Colborn, Dumanoski and Myers *Our Stolen Future*, p. 240.
8. Ibid. pp. 26–46.
9. Ibid. pp. 167–97.
10. Ibid. pp. 196–7, 208.
11. Leslie, *The End of the World*, p. 44.
12. Ibid. pp. 43–4.
13. Ibid. p. 43.
14. Ibid. p. 51.
15. Electrical Association, *Environmental Briefing*.
16. See Worldwatch Institute, *State of the World 1997* and Electrical Association, *Environmental Briefing*.

17. Leslie, *The End of the World*, p. 51.
18. Brown, 'Illegal trade in banned CFC gases exposed'.
19. Leslie, *The End of the World*, p. 51.
20. Ibid. p. 52.
21. Ibid. p. 54.
22. Lovelock, *Gaia*, p. 39.
23. Leslie, *The End of the World*, p. 54.
24. Ibid. pp. 55–8.
25. See Justus and Morrissey, *Congressional Research Service Issue Brief 89005*, pp. 2–4. See also Leslie, *The End of the World*, pp. 56–7.
26. Leggett, 'Running down to Rio'.
27. Ibid. p. 41; Leslie, *The End of the World*, p. 61.
28. World Conservation Monitoring Centre, *Biodiversity*, p. 3.
29. Ibid. p. 2.
30. Worldwatch Institute, *State of the World 1997*, p. 13.
31. Leslie, *The End of the World*, p. 69.
32. Dawkins, *River out of Eden*, p. 8.
33. World Resources Institute, 'Biodiversity', p. 1.
34. World Conservation Monitoring Centre, *Biodiversity*, p. 6.
35. Tallis, *Newton's Sleep*, pp. 53–4.
36. Worldwatch Institute, *State of the World 1997*, pp. 23–5.
37. Ibid. pp. 29–31.
38. Ibid. p. 38.
39. Ibid. p. 35.
40. Ibid. p. 39.
41. Leslie, *The End of the World*, p. 66.
42. Meadows, Meadows and Randers, *Beyond the Limits*, pp. 136–7.
43. 'Global Population and Resource Use', *The Guide to Florida Environmental Issues and Information*, Chapter 1, Florida Conservation Foundation.
44. Ehrlich, 'Too many rich people'.
45. Ehrlich, *The Population Bomb*.
46. Ehrlich and Ehrlich, *The Population Explosion*.
47. Ibid. p. 23.
48. Quoted in Leslie, *The End of the World*, p. 73.
49. Ehrlich and Ehrlich, *The Population Explosion*, p. 60.
50. United Nations Population Division (UNPD), *Long-Range World Population Projections*.
51. Ehrlich and Ehrlich, *The Population Explosion*, p. 19.
52. Simon, *The Ultimate Resource*.
53. Leslie, *The End of the World*, p. 72.
54. Ehrlich and Ehrlich, *The Population Explosion*, p. 17.
55. Carson, *Silent Spring*, pp. 240–57.
56. Colborn, Dumanoski and Myers, *Our Stolen Future*, pp. 246–9.

57. Ehrlich and Ehrlich, *The Population Explosion*, p. 229.
58. Colborn, Dumanoski and Myters, *Our Stolen Future*, p. 250.
59. Carson, *Silent Spring*, pp. 44–5.
60. Colborn, Dumanoski and Myters, *Our Stolen Future*, p. 140.
61. Taylor, *The Doomsday Book*, pp. 18–19.
62. Colborn, Dumanoski and Myers, *Our Stolen Future*, p. 246.
63. Heilbroner, *An Inquiry into the Human Prospect*, p. 62.
64. Ibid. p. 132.
65. See Williams, *The Country and the City*, for an account of this association in English literature.
66. Marx and Engels, *The German Ideology*, p. 54.
67. See, in particular, Morris, 'Art and socialism'.
68. This is not to imply that the communist regimes were any the less destructive of their environment.
69. Heilbroner, *An Inquiry into the Human Prospect*, p. 136.
70. Hobsbawm, *Age of Extremes*, p. 584.
71. The ECD is an extremely sensitive measuring instrument, capable of identifying minute quantities of certain chemical substances. It was the ECD which 'first made possible the discovery that pesticide residues were present in all creatures of the Earth, from penguins in Antarctica to the milk of nursing mothers in the USA' (Lovelock, *Gaia*, p. x). Lovelock also reckoned that the discovery of the ozone hole would have been delayed for ten years had it not been for the ECD (see note 72).
72. Interview with James Lovelock, *Newsnight*, BBC 2, December 1999.
73. Leslie, *The End of the World*, p. 146.
74. Colborn, Dumanoski and Myers, *Our Stolen Future*, p. 238.

2

Moral Decline: Warfare, Human Rights and the Crime Explosion

And the price of failure, that is to say, the alternative to a changed society, is darkness.

Eric Hobsbawm, *Age of Extremes*(:)
The Short Twentieth Century 1914–1991

Introduction

A S NOTED IN THE INTRODUCTION, it was within the sphere of the moral that the idea of decline had appeared in its most rhetorical, relative and narrowly ideological forms. Narratives of moral decline were regularly used as a polemical device to serve quite specific political interests. It is not suggested that the narratives discussed in this chapter have not served political interests of their own; nor, indeed, that the moral and the ideological can ever be separated. But an attempt has been made to withstand the centrifugal pressures of moral relativism and focus on narratives which, if not aspiring to a universal status, have at least been pitched on some widely shared moral ground. These relate: to the morality of nuclear and post-nuclear warfare; to the incidence of torture, genocide and political murder; and to the crime explosion which has manifested itself more or less throughout the Western world since the 1960s.

The accounts of warfare in the postmodern world presented a moral paradox. On the one hand, the nuclear terror of the Cold War could be seen as the result of a morally degenerative logic, which had profoundly damaging effects on 'the structure of feeling' of the period; on the other, its ending unleashed new forms of 'internal', 'informal' and 'tribal' warfare, facilitated by the 'democratisation of the means of destruction'. At the same time, torture, genocide and political murder persisted, despite the fact that documentary evidence of these atrocities, in both words and images, was more widely disseminated than at any other time in history. In the West, a crime explosion of unprecedented proportions symbolised a breakdown of social order and the ascendancy of an anti-social individualism. This was attributed to the increasingly Darwinian qualities of late capitalism (discussed further in Chapter 4) and the disintegration of family life. It was possible to see how these various narratives, reflecting apparently irreversible trends, might have intertwined to form a global 'metanarrative' of moral pessimism.

Warfare

From the mid-1960s on, the world witnessed the biggest arms build-up in all history. Both the United States and the Soviet Union had tested thermonuclear devices (H-bombs) during the previous decade, demonstrating their capacity to produce weapons of a destructive power which was theoretically unlimited. By 1954, the Americans had already tested a fifteen-megaton H-bomb, known as 'Mike', producing an explosion well over one thousand times as large as that which destroyed Hiroshima, and in 1962 the Soviet Union had tested a bomb with a staggering yield of fifty-eight megatons. (The scale of this can be grasped if one remembers that a one-megaton bomb produces the explosive power of 1m tons of TNT, and that the amount of high explosive used during the entire course of World War II was equivalent to around three megatons.) In the escalating arms race that followed, driven forward by ideological imperatives, by fears (both real and imagined) of the other side's capabilities, and by the interests of what Eisenhower identified as early as 1961 as the 'Military-Industrial Complex', the volume of warheads and their systems of delivery multiplied. At one level were developed the so-called strategic weapons, inter-continental ballistic missiles (ICBMs), launched from submarines or from silos deep under the ground, and capable of delivering multiple warheads (MIRVs) over distances of many thousands of miles. At another, were the 'battlefield' nuclear devices, closely integrated with conventional weapons, and deliverable as artillery, air bombs, landmines and even mortars. In case these sound anodyne, it should be remembered that the Hiroshima bomb, which killed at least 130,000 people, was by present-day standards a small one and would today fall into the 'battlefield' class. In the course of the Cold War, the destructive technologies became ever more formidable, as new generations of weapons succeeded the old, each side increasing its capacity to inflict ever greater devastation on the other. Titan I gave way to Titan II; the SS5 to the SS20; Minuteman I to Minutemen II and III; Polaris to Poseidon and then to Trident; Cruise and Pershing in Europe; and so on. With around one third of the world's scientists engaged in defence research, the nuclear arsenal reached astronomical proportions. By 1984, an estimated 54,000 nuclear warheads were in existence, with an explosive power equivalent to 1m Hiroshimas. Just 1 per cent of this would have been enough to annihilate every large and medium-sized city in the world.

The effects of a nuclear strike have been well documented, and it will be sufficient here to give just a brief outline of what happens when a thermonuclear device explodes and of what the predicted consequences of a more extensive nuclear exchange are likely to be.[1] At the moment of explosion, there is first of all a surge of radiation which, in a one-megaton air burst, will deliver a lethal dose of radiation to unprotected human beings within an area of around six square miles. Secondly, and almost simultaneously, an electromagnetic pulse is generated which, in a high altitude detonation, can knock out electrical equipment over a wide area. A report from the US Defence Department's Civil Preparedness Agency, for example, stated in 1977 that a multi-kiloton bomb exploded 125 miles above Omaha, Nebraska, would damage solid-state electrical circuits throughout the entire continental United States, and in parts of Canada and Mexico as well.[2] Thirdly, once the fusion and fission reactions have blown themselves out, a fireball materialises, incinerating everything within it or close to it, and sending out a thermal pulse as a wave of blinding light and intense heat. In a one-megaton explosion, this pulse lasts for about ten seconds and will cause second degree burns on exposed skin and set fire to easily ignitable materials, such as fabrics or dry leaves, up to a distance of nine and a half miles. Fourthly, as the fireball expands, it sends out a blast wave in all directions, which is experienced as a sudden and shattering blow, followed by a hurricane-force wind. The blast from a one-megaton explosion will demolish buildings, uproot trees, blow down pylons, and overturn vehicles within a radius of four and half miles. Human beings standing in the open will be swept up by the wind and carried along by it, hitting other objects and being hit by other flying debris. Those inside buildings are likely to be crushed as the buildings collapse. In built-up areas, huge firestorms may arise, engulfing the entire target area and killing even more people than the original heat and blast. Finally, as the fireball burns, it rises, condensing water from the surrounding atmosphere and forming the characteristic mushroom cloud. If the explosion has taken place at ground or near-ground level, thousands of tons of dirt and debris will be sucked up into the mushroom cloud and returned to earth as 'early' fallout, exposing humans to potentially lethal radiation disease. Air-bursts, such as those used at both Hiroshima and Nagasaki, will also produce fall-out, but in much smaller quantities than that produced in ground-bursts. (In contrast, air-bursts produce much greater blast effects.) The extent of 'early' fallout will depend upon weather and other conditions, but, according to one official assessment, under average conditions a one-megaton ground-burst will lethally contaminate over one thousand square miles.[3] 'Lethal contamination' is considered to be the amount of radiation which, if delivered over a short period of time, will kill half the able-bodied young adult population.

These, then, are what may be considered the five primary and local effects of a single nuclear explosion. However, despite military doctrines of 'flexible response', 'graduated response', 'counterforce', and so on, all of which were at one time or another promulgated by NATO and premised on the belief that a nuclear exchange could be containable or 'limited', the overwhelming balance of opinion amongst experts was that the use of nuclear weapons at any level would quickly escalate into a major strategic conflict.[4] The effects described above would thus be multiplied hundreds or thousands of times, killing millions and causing social disintegration on a worldwide scale. The infrastructure of our highly complex and inter-dependent societies would be rapidly destroyed, leaving a world without food supplies, water, electricity, fuel or manufactured products. Those not killed by the immediate impacts would face an extremely hostile environment. Many scientists believe that a nuclear exchange of anything over 100 megatons would throw so much debris into the atmosphere that the world would be shrouded in darkness for up to six months. This would produce a 'nuclear winter' during which temperatures could drop by anything from 15° to 50°C, depending upon weather conditions. When the sun returned, its rays would shine through a severely depleted ozone layer, exposing surviving human beings to potentially lethal doses of ultraviolet radiation. On top of this, the entire surface of the planet would be contaminated as nuclear fallout, driven into the stratosphere at the time of the explosions, would circulate around the globe, falling to earth over a period of months and years. Millions would die of famine and disease, and millions more would experience the most appalling psychological damage. This was the world imagined in *Threads*, a drama-documentary shown on BBC television in 1984, which attempted to represent the effects of a nuclear strike on the city of Sheffield, following an East-West exchange of 3000 megatons. The film ends with a few survivors, ten years after the war, scratching out a living on the land, existing in brutalised social relationships and incapable of using language in anything but its most basic and functional form. Even this vision assumed too much for the British Medical Association, which argued that the UK no longer possessed the skills or primitive technologies which would enable its people to return to the rural civilisations of the past.[5] John Leslie envisaged a return to Stone Age conditions, with the planet able to support only around five million hunter-gatherers, who would be as liable to extinction as more or less any other large mammal.[6] Jonathan Schell postulated that only the 'hardy species', such as moss, grass and insects (which have very high tolerances of radiation), would thrive after a nuclear holocaust and that the United States could thus become a 'Republic of Insects and Grass'.[7] In the final analysis, however, Schell suggested, there was not much point trying to understand what such a world would be like, because for most people it wouldn't be like anything, because they would be dead. The right vantage point from which to view a nuclear holocaust was that of a corpse, but from that vantage point, of course, there was nothing to report.[8]

Whether or not these terrifying scenarios would actually materialise during the Cold War ultimately depended upon the effectiveness of a policy of pure deterrence which came to be known as 'mutually assured destruction' (MAD). This was an extremely dangerous doctrine, which operated on the principle that a nuclear strike from one side would be met automatically by massive retaliation from the other. Neither the Soviet Union nor the United States would therefore use nuclear weapons, because for either side to do so would bring about its own immediate destruction. This policy probably came closest to breaking down during the Cuban Missile Crisis of 1962, when President Kennedy reckoned at one point that the chances of war with the Soviet Union had risen to 'somewhere between one out of three and even'[9]. But the risks were always there, with threats coming from three different directions. First, both sides engaged in 'games of chicken', in which each tried to convince the other that it was prepared to risk destruction rather than abandon its aims. The games were at times hair-raising, as when Henry Kissinger advocated rapid and brutal escalation 'to a point where the opponent can no longer afford to experiment'.[10] President Nixon was attracted to the 'Madman Theory' of the Presidency, which involved convincing his enemies that he was irrational and unstable, and thus capable of risking a holocaust rather than concede even a minor advantage.[11] Such games raised political and military tensions to potentially catastrophic levels. Secondly, there is evidence to suggest that there were military strategists on both sides who were not convinced that 'mutual destruction' was always 'assured'. Soviet enthusiasm for antiballistic missile systems (ABMs) in the 1960s, for example, was seen by the Americans as an attempt to gain a decisive technological advantage which might make a nuclear war 'winnable'. President Reagan's Strategic Defense Initiative (SDI), which raised the prospect of an antiballistic missile umbrella covering the whole of the United States, provoked precisely the same reaction in the Soviet Union in 1983. Even a precautionary civil defence initiative, such as the widespread building of underground shelters, could be interpreted by the other side as a preparation for war. In such a climate of paranoia, the side that feared a pre-emptive first strike might well launch its own pre-emptive attack; meanwhile, the other side, assuming that the enemy would reason in the same way, would have even more reason to strike first; and so on. 'The Russians', Robert McNamara wrote in 1985, 'knew that a first strike was not always excluded from US strategic thinking';[12] and the Americans, records the military historian, Martin van Creveld, began to fear a Soviet first strike from the mid-1970s on, following the deployment of MIRVed SS-18 and SS-20 missiles which seemed to some military experts to have been specifically designed for a first strike against the US and its allies.[13]

The third main threat to a peace based upon the balance of terror came not from intentional but accidental nuclear war. With the flight times of missiles reduced to just a few minutes, command authorities lived in a use-'em-or-lose-'em world, in which they would have to respond almost instantly to the warning of an enemy attack, deciding either to launch their own missiles or risk seeing them destroyed in their silos. There is even speculation that launch systems might have been computerised to the extent that a combination of warning systems would have automatically triggered the launch.[14] Under 'launch-on-warning' conditions, the reliability of attack-detection systems was critical. It is thus sobering to recall quite how frequently false alarms were recorded. A US Senate investigation found, for example, that between January 1979 and June 1980 there were 147 'serious' false alarms, such as the one generated by a defective computer chip at NORAD (North American Air Defense Command) which gave notice of an imminent Soviet attack. Other experts estimated that on average there were one or two occasions each year when a false alarm persisted long enough to trigger a nuclear alert.[15] Under these circumstances, no one could rule out with complete certainty the possibility of a catastrophic combination of technological and human error – just as no one could ever rule out, for example, the possibility of another air disaster, however good the safety precautions. Despite widespread views to the contrary, the US and Soviet military establishment did not physically require essential codes from their respective presidents to launch an all-out strategic attack. The commander and officers of a US ballistic missile sub-marine, for example, had between them all the necessary information to launch a nuclear strike. Furthermore, the notion of psychologically unstable personnel in charge of nuclear weapons did not exist only within the realm of TV dramas and Hollywood movies. In an article in *Scientific American*, B. G. Blair and H. W. Kendall reported that

> of the roughly 75,000 members of the US Military with access to nuclear weapons and related components, nearly 2,400 had to be removed from duty. Seven hundred and thirty abused alcohol or drugs, and the rest had psychological or emotional problems, were insubordinate or engaged in criminal behaviour.[16]

During the Cold War, then, for the first time in history, the human species acquired the military technology to extinguish itself on a global scale and, according to many accounts, came very close to doing so. The science writer, Nigel Calder, found that many distinguished scientists had by the end of the 1970s become deeply pessimistic about whether the planet would survive. Compelled to investigate – 'to lift the stone again and see what was now crawling underneath' – Calder found that the outlook was 'quite surprisingly grim'. The risk of a nuclear holocaust, he concluded, was 'growing with every year that passes'.[17] Schell argued that deterrence, having rationalised the construction of a 'doomsday machine', at best offered a slightly extended term of residence on earth 'before the inevitable human or mechanical mistake occurs and we are annihilated'.[18] According to Bailey, we were simply 'a society preparing for war'.[19] The historian E. P. Thompson argued that we were drifting ineluctably towards nuclear warfare, independently of the intentions of political leaders.

> I do not argue, [he said] from this local episode or that: what happened yesterday in Afghanistan and what is happening now in Pakistan or North Yemen. I argue from a general and sustained historical process, an accumulative logic, of a kind made familiar to me by the study of history.[20]

These profound anxieties were reflected in one of the best known symbols of the period, the 'Doomsday Clock', which appeared in each issue of the *Bulletin of Atomic Scientists* and whose hands moved back and forth towards midnight as the world lurched from crisis to crisis.

To many, the nuclear terror appeared as both a symptom and cause of moral decline. In Jeff Nuttall's *Bomb Culture*, first published in 1968, Nuttall had suggested that the repressed violence implicit in nuclear deterrence had produced morally sick societies, in which disassociation from feeling had become necessary to exist in a world constantly threatened by annihilation.[21] This, Nuttall argued, was reflected in the violence, sick humour and celebration of insanity to be found in much contemporary culture, from the work of William Burroughs and the Beat writers of the 1950s through to the dark undercurrents which ran through the explosive pop music scene of the mid- to late 1960s. Nuttall saw a widespread numbing of moral sense, as people experienced a 'vacuum where the future used to be'.[22] For growing numbers of young people, a Dionysian immersion in sensation, for which drugs were an indispensable accessory, provided an effective means of distraction as they passed the time until extinction. Such was the madness of 'sane' society that notions of insanity had to be re-evaluated. In this, Nuttall was following the psychiatrist R. D. Laing who had argued that schizophrenics were no more mad than the supposedly sane were truly sane. 'We can no longer assume', Laing had written,

> that such a voyage (schizophrenia) is an illness that has to be treated . . . Can we not see that this voyage is not what we need to be cured of, but that it is itself a natural way of healing our own appalling state of alienation called normality?[23]

From a different perspective, Harry T. Nash also examined the disassociation of feeling, but in a very specific context. In an essay entitled 'The bureaucratization of Homicide', Nash turned his attention to the behavioural characteristics of those officers in the US Department of Defense whose job it was to select sites in the Soviet Union which would be hit by nuclear warheads in the event of a war.[24] Nash was particularly well qualified to undertake this examination, having himself served as an intelligence analyst within the Air Targets Division of the Air Force. Having left the Department of Defense to take up an academic post, Nash found himself many years later haunted by memories of his work with Air Targets, wondering how he and his colleagues had calmly planned 'to incinerate vast numbers of unknown human beings without any sense of moral revulsion'.[25] Nash realised that a complex bureaucracy had evolved, in which various forms of abstraction were deployed to divert those within it from thinking about the homicidal implications of what they were actually doing. Thus, language took on an anaesthetic quality, as 'tactical' nuclear weapons came to be called 'baby nukes' and the latest versions of intercontinental ballistic missiles were referred to as 'the newest members of the ICBM family'. The neutron bomb, a small 'device' producing twice the radiation of an 'ordinary' nuclear bomb and designed to destroy people rather than buildings, was referred to as a 'radiation enhancement weapon' or, more colloquially, a 'cookie cutter'. The relationship of weaponry to human life became almost incidental, as defence analysts absorbed themselves in the numbers game of the arms race, assembling lists and tables, matching missile for missile, warhead for warhead. A preoccupation with the mechanics of administration was encouraged, and work in the Department took on the qualities of office life in a large bank or insurance company. Nash was struck by the extraordinary 'ordinariness' of it all, recalling the phrase 'the banality of evil', which Hannah Arendt had used to characterise the bureaucratic mechanisms established by the Nazis to distance the individual from the reality of genocide.

While Nash focused on the moral degeneration of military bureaucracies, E. P. Thompson saw the moral decline of entire cultures (both East and West). In his essay 'Protest and survive' (1980), Thompson argued that the necessary condition of nuclear warfare was a deformation of culture and that this deformation began with language. Just as Nash had seen language take on an anaesthetic quality within military discourse, Thompson saw it as anaesthetising a wider public by reducing the most monstrous realities to 'a flat level of normality'. On both sides, our minds were being prepared as 'launching platforms for exterminating thoughts', as we demonised the enemy and learnt to see them as non-people. 'Wars commence in our culture', wrote Thompson, 'and we kill each other in euphemisms and abstractions long before the first missiles have been launched.'[26]

For Thompson, the nuclear terror was thus both a symbol of a 'hideous cultural abnormality' and the cause of widespread moral contamination. Like Nuttall, Thompson saw the insidious effect of a repressed violence which had 'backed up' into the economy, the ideology and the culture of the opposing powers. This, he argued was 'the deep structure of the Cold War'. Thompson even detected a tremor of excitement within our culture at the prospect of the violence to come, as if the experience of living for so long in expectation of it had produced a kind of ennui which would only be dispelled when it was finally unleashed. Everything moved, he argued, on its degenerative course, 'as if the outcome of civilisation was as determined as the outcome of this sentence: in a full stop'.[27]

Well, as we all know, the inevitable proved not to be inevitable. The collapse of the Soviet Union in 1991 produced such profound changes in superpower relations that by 1993 the military historian, Martin van Creveld, was able to say that we had reached the point where nuclear war between the superpowers – or what was left of them – seemed 'out of the question'.[28] Under the START II treaty, signed by Presidents Bush and Yeltsin in 1993, both Russia and the United States agreed to eliminate almost three-quarters of their deployed 'strategic' nuclear weapons by the year 2003, agreeing a limit of 3500 on each side, and eliminating all MIRVs. In 1997, Clinton and Yeltsin signalled their intentions to make further reductions under START III, aiming for a new limit of 2500 by 2007, and agreeing to look again at the questions of 'tactical' nuclear weapons and of 'transparency'. Belarus, Ukraine and Kazakhstan voluntarily returned to Russia nuclear weapons which had been inherited from the Soviet Union. The arms industry contracted, so much so that a study published by the Stockholm International Peace Research Institute (SIPRI) in 1993 concluded that the era of ever-increasing military expenditures was now over.[29] The democratic world, for the first time in fifty years, could no longer be threatened on a global scale.

Did this abrupt and extraordinary conclusion to the Cold War bring to an end those narratives of moral decline which the prospect of warfare in the postmodern world had engendered? There were certainly those who thought it should. George Bush spoke of the coming of 'a New World Order', in which partnership, peacekeeping and peacemaking would become the ruling ethos of international relations. Francis Fukuyama, in *The End of History and the Last Man* (1992), declared that the era of global conflict was over and that our historical pessimism, a legacy of the first half of the twentieth century, should now be left behind.[30] But there were others who, far from celebrating the end of superpower confrontation, saw only the unfolding of a terrible new world marked by savagery, instability and disorder. Prominent amongst these was Martin van Creveld, who argued in *The Transformation of War* and *On Future War* (both 1991) that we would actually look back on the Cold War as the last golden age, when the superpowers imposed a system of international discipline which, in most parts of the world, preserved stability and prevented local and regional tensions from breaking out into bloody and murderous conflicts.[31] There had, of course, been exceptions, such as on the Indian sub-continent and in sub-Saharan Africa, but these had almost always been in parts of the world where superpower affiliations had been at their loosest. With the restraints of the Cold War removed, van Creveld saw an explosion of what he termed 'Low Intensity Conflict'. This encompassed many different forms, from guerrilla war to revolution to terrorism, but they all shared the common characteristic of involving at least one party which was not a state. Van Creveld believed that we were witnessing the end of 'traditional' wars, by which he meant those that were declared by governments and fought by 'legitimate' armies. Such wars had been rendered largely 'unfightable' due to the threat posed by nuclear weapons, but in their place had come a widespread return to 'tribalism', where violent conflicts involved whole societies and in which the traditional distinctions between Government, Army and the People were no longer preserved. This had been facilitated by the increasing number of weak states, a process which had been gathering pace since 1945, but which had rapidly accelerated with decolonisation and the collapse of the Soviet Union. There were fewer than sixty states when the United Nations was founded in 1945, but by the end of the 1990s there were almost two hundred. According to another military historian, John Keegan, only two dozen of these could be regarded as well governed.[32] 'Tribalism' had also been exacerbated by conditions of poverty and extreme deprivation which, in many parts of the world, made the prospect of warfare appear as a step up rather than a step down. Van Creveld noted that in some circumstances war ceased to be a means to an end (Clausewitz's 'continuation of policy by other means') and became, for the participants at least, a liberating end in itself. Furthermore, if 'tribal' conflicts broke out in weak states, then the legal monopoly of armed force could be wrested out of the hands of government, with the result that existing distinctions between war and crime would break down. This had already happened in many countries, such as in Bosnia, the Caucasus, Cambodia, Angola, Somalia and Rawanda. Keegan noted that these were some of the poorest places on their respective continents and that war, once a struggle over riches, was now 'the calling of the wretched of the earth'.[33]

Van Creveld believed that this pattern of conflict would spread. It was already common in much of the Third World, had spread to the Second and could now even be found in the First. For him, the continuing stability of states, and even their very existence, was now threatened by the new forms of 'internal' and 'informal' war, which were replacing the 'strategic' wars, legitimised by governments, that had dominated the nature of warfare in the West for the three hundred years before Hiroshima.[34] Support for this thesis could be found in the work of other analysts of international relations. In *The Clash of Civilizations and the Remaking of the World Order* (1996), Samuel Huntington argued that there was much evidence for the relevance of the 'sheer chaos' paradigm of world affairs, which stressed the breakdown of governmental authority, the break-up of states, the intensification of ethnic and religious conflict, and vast new refugee flows.[35] In 'The coming anarchy' (1994), Robert Kaplan invited us to imagine the cartography of the future in three dimensions: above the two-dimensional map of city states and remaining nations would hover a shifting pattern of cross-national or sub-national 'power centres', reflecting a fluid network of sectarian groupings, criminal organisations and private security agencies. In direct contrast to the peace and tranquillity awaiting Fukuyama's 'Last Man', Kaplan gave us the 'Last Map . . . an ever-mutating representation of chaos'.[36]

In *Age of Extremes*, Eric Hobsbawm cautioned the strong and stable states, such as those in the European Union, against thinking themselves immune from the insecurity and carnage observable in the unhappier parts of the Third World and the ex-socialist countries. The gap between rich and poor countries, he argued, was steadily increasing, with a large section of the Third World dropping out of the world economy altogether. In his view, this was now the source of a growing resentment which would perhaps prove to be the greatest cause of international tension in the years to come. What made this resentment so dangerous was the ease with which arms and explosives could be acquired as a result of what Hobsbawm termed 'the democratisation of the means of destruction'.[37] With an arms industry squeezed by cutbacks in the military expenditure of governments, it was likely that weapons would become even more easily available as arms manufacturers sought new markets.[38] However, what was most alarming was the prospect of nuclear or biological weapons falling into the hands of terrorist groups or 'rogue' states. There continued to be a great deal of concern both about the security of weapons-grade nuclear material in the former Soviet Union and about the number of highly-qualified, badly-paid and potentially disaffected nuclear technicians who might be tempted to sell their expertise to the 'wrong' people.[39] Chemical and biological weapons presented an even greater threat. Despite the growing number of countries signing international agreements prohibiting the development of these weapons, more and more countries were in fact suspected of secretly accumulating them, with seventeen countries being named in 1995.[40] In 1975, Robert Heilbroner had warned that the prospect of desperate people using nuclear terrorism to fight wars of redistribution should not be dismissed as a paranoid fantasy;[41] in the 1990s, John Leslie envisaged 'desperate governments contemplating biological warfare as a preferable alternative to starvation, and as an act of revenge on the disgustingly overfed'.[42]

The ease with which chemical and biological (CB) agents could be manufactured also placed them within reach of terrorist organisations. A former assistant director of the US Arms Control and Disarmament Agency calculated that a major biological arsenal could be built with $10,000 worth of equipment in a room 15 by 15 feet, with equipment no more sophisticated than 'a beer fermenter and protein-based culture, a gas mask and a plastic overgarment'.[43] Unlike any other weapon, biological agents can become more dangerous over time, rapidly multiplying, and firmly establishing themselves within the environment. In March 1995, we witnessed the first major chemical weapons attack by a non-state group, when, in one of the most secure countries in the world, the Aum Shinryko ('Supreme Truth') religious sect released sarin nerve gas into the Tokyo subway system, killing 12 and injuring 5500. Further attacks were almost certainly planned. The sect included a number of experienced scientists, some of whom were reported to have been experimenting with other substances, such as anthrax.[44] It was also reported that the leader of the group had visited Zaire in 1992, ostensibly to help Ebola victims, but with the real objective of getting hold of samples of the Ebola virus – a virus which causes a horrifying, haemorrhaging disease, second only to Rabies in lethality, killing 90 per cent of those it infects within one week. Other examples of planned CB attacks included those of the member of a white supremacist organisation in Ohio, who succeeded in buying through mail order three vials of bubonic plague culture from a Maryland biomedical supply company.

These accounts of warfare in the postmodern world present us with a depressing moral paradox. On the one hand, as E. P. Thompson and others argued, the nuclear terror could be seen as the result of a morally degenerative logic, which had profoundly damaging effects upon what Raymond Williams called 'the structure of feeling' and which, sooner or later, would end in the most appalling catastrophe. On the other hand, we find in van Creveld, Hobsbawm and Huntington the emergence of what amounts to a nostalgia for the Cold War, brought on by what they see as the violent chaos unleashed by the end of it. It is a return of the repressed on a grand scale which, if the thrust of the argument is accepted, is set to continue on its course of proliferating conflict. John Leslie concluded that under these conditions security could only be achieved 'by very intrusive policing' and that most people would probably come to accept that there was no alternative to the loss of privacy that this would involve.[45] Keegan went further. The growing chaos predicted by van Creveld, far from undermining states with a tradition of stability, would quickly turn them totalitarian. People could not tolerate chronic insecurity, Keegan argued, and eventually they would sanction whatever mechanisms of social control were necessary to restore order.[46] With authoritarianism, comes the greatest danger of extreme human rights abuse. Such abuses have engendered their own narratives of moral decline, and it is these which will be considered in the next section.

Torture, genocide, and political murder

When Amnesty, the human rights campaigning organisation, was founded by Peter Benenson in 1961, it declared unequivocally that state persecution of the individual had become 'the gravest social problem of the 1960s'.[47] Benenson had been spurred into action after reading in a newspaper that two Portugese friends had been overheard criticising the Salazar regime whilst having a meal in a Lisbon restaurant, and had subsequently been reported, arrested and imprisoned for treason. By the end of its second year of operation, Amnesty had recorded human rights abuses in sixty-nine countries, had 'adopted' 2180 'prisoners of conscience', and had announced that in two thirds of the world people did not have the freedom to express their political or religious views.[48]

The tone of Amnesty's reports darkened perceptibly as the sixties progressed, and by 1966 Amnesty (now renamed Amnesty International) had found itself compelled to extend its investigations into the allegations of torture in prisons, which were being voiced around the world. The 1966/7 report, for example, contained accounts of the torturing by British interrogators of political detainees in Aden, of the confinement of Somalis in Kenya in concentration camps, and of the use of 'punishment cells' to extract confessions from political prisoners in Uganda.[49] This proved to be just the tip of the iceberg, and by 1970, the Chairman of Amnesty International's Executive, Sean MacBride, was referring to 'the brutality and arbitrariness which disgraces the era'[50], echoing a theme which had been elaborated upon the previous year when the Council of Christian Churches had met at Baden. 'No one', the Council had proclaimed,

> can fail to be alarmed by the mounting violence and brutality of our times. Massacres, tortures, summary executions and arbitrary imprisonments have become such common currency that the natural reaction of horror tends to be blunted. Thus a degradation of human values is taking place.[51]

MacBride retained his position at Amnesty until 1974 (when he was awarded the Nobel Peace Prize), his introductions to the annual reports becoming increasingly bleak. In his penultimate Amnesty statement, clearly shocked by the evidence of the systematic development of torture, involving both formalised training and the application of more sophisticated technologies and methods, MacBride spoke of a 'massive breakdown of public morality and of civilization itself'.[52]

The evidence of torture and other atrocities which Amnesty was routinely accumulating led to the launch in 1972 of a worldwide campaign and to the publication in 1973 of Amnesty's *Report on Torture*. Defining torture as the systematic and deliberate infliction of acute pain by one person on another, for the purposes of obtaining information, administering punishment or general intimidation, the report presented a horrifying account of the deployment of torture in sixty-one countries in all the continents of the world (except Antarctica and Australia). Table 2.1 gives a summary, which is by no means exhaustive, of the methods of torture used.

Table 2.1 Methods of torture

Application of electric shocks, particularly to the head and genitals
Beating, flogging or whipping
Burning with cigarettes
Castration
Combination of beating soles of feet, multiple electric shocks and insertion of a truncheon in the anus or vagina (known as *Falanga*)
Combination of hanging, near-drowning in filthy water, and multiple electric shocks (known as *pau de arara* or parrot perch)
Detention in inhuman conditions
Drug torture (eg. administration of animazin, sulfazine, haloperidal, triftazin, etc.)
Food and sleep deprivation
Forcing victim to stand up with legs apart for hours or days (known as *el planton*)
Forcing victim to watch others being tortured
Inserting red hot iron into anus
Mutilation of body with knife or other sharp instruments
Placing victim on red-hot grill
Pouring acid over victim's head
Rape
Release of CS gas into windowless cells
Simulated execution
Solitary confinement in complete darkness
Strapping victim to bed without sanitation for days
Tearing out of finger-nails
Tightening iron bands around victim's skull
Water torture, such as repeatedly plunging head into dirty water, wrapping victim in wet canvas (known as 'roll-up')

Source: Amnesty International, *Report on Torture, 1973*, pp. 109–217

The *Report on Torture*, re-iterating a point which is constantly made in Amnesty surveys of human rights abuses, made it clear that the report did not claim to present a comprehensive account of torture throughout the contemporary world, and that because a specific country was not cited, this did not mean that no abuses were taking place there. Indeed, given that official co-operation was often necessary in order to establish whether or not torture had actually been practised, it was against precisely those regimes which were most suspect that proof was most difficult to obtain. As Amnesty's policy was to publish only those allegations which it had been able to substantiate, the extent and scale of torture was almost certainly much greater than that actually described in the report.[53] The authors were not able to make comparisons with the more distant past, but felt able to state with some assurance that 'the practice is both more widespread and more intense today than it was fifteen years ago'.[54] A distinctive feature had been its technological development, involving the use of both electrical appliances and drugs. Given that it had become illegal, the practice had also gone 'underground' and was therefore far more difficult to detect and record. The debate in the past had often been between those who advocated the use of torture and those who argued for its regulation. Now, the debate was said to be between 'abolitionists and liars'.[55]

Is it possible to say that Amnesty's high-profile campaign marked a turning point, and that after the publication of the 1973 report the incidence of torture worldwide began to recede? Unfortunately not. In 1978, MacBride's successor, Thomas Hammarberg, was drawing attention not only to the emergence of new trends in torture, such as the incarceration of political prisoners in mental asylums in eastern Europe, but also to the appearance of 'death squads' in Argentina, Chile and Guatemala. In this 'depressing' picture, Hammarberg complained, 'the leaders of too many nations continue to condone or instigate terrorist methods against their own citizens'.[56] Looking back over this period, Hobsbawm concluded in the 1990s that it had represented 'the darkest era or torture and counter-terrorism in the history of the West'.[57]

With explicit references to Orwell's dystopia, Amnesty named 1984 'Year of the Torturer', publishing its second report on the subject, *Torture in the Eighties*. Announcing that one-third of the world's governments had either used or tolerated torture in the 1980s, the report was as shocking as its 1973 predecessor. What was so strongly evoked in the personal testimonies which the report relentlessly presented was the sense of the victim's helpless isolation as the torturers began their work. Here for example, is the account given by Asyse Eker, a twenty-three year old woman, of how she was tortured by the Turkish Secret Service in April 1972. Having described how she was attacked in the street, taken to the basement of an isolated building and administered violent electric shocks, she goes on to recount what happened next:

> My whole body and head shook in a terrible way. My front teeth started breaking. At the same time my torturers would hold a mirror to my face and say: 'Look what is happening to your lovely green eyes. Soon you will not be able to see at all. You will lose your mind. You see, you have already started bleeding in your mouth.' When they finished with electric shocks,

they lifted me up to my feet and several of those I mentioned above started beating me with truncheons. After a while I felt dizzy and could not see very well. Then I fainted. When I came to myself, I found I was lying half naked in a pool of dirty water. They tried to force me to stand up and run. At the same time, they kept beating me with truncheons, kicking me and pushing me against the walls . . . As if all this was not enough, Umit Erdal [one of the torturers] attacked me and forced me to the ground. I fell on my face. He stood on my back and with the assistence of someone else forced a truncheon into my anus . . . They next made me lie on my back and tied my arms and legs to pegs. They attached an electric wire to the small toe of my right foot and another to the end of a truncheon. They tried to penetrate my feminine organ with the truncheon. As I resisted they hit my body and legs with a large axe handle. They soon succeeded in penetrating my sexual organ with the truncheon with the electric wire on, and passed current. I fainted. A little later, the soldiers outside brought in a machine used for pumping air into people and they said they would kill me. With a leather strap, they hanged me from my wrists on to a pipe in a corridor. As I hung half-naked, several people beat me with truncheons. I fainted again. When I awoke, I found myself in the same room on a bed . . . I was bleeding a dark, thick blood.[58]

As well as these harrowing personal stories, the report accumulated further details of the techniques of torture then in use, such as the practice in Guatemala of using quicklime inside a hood made of the inner tube of a tyre, which was placed over the victim's head; or the forcing of children to watch their mothers being tortured in the women's block of Tehran's Evin jail. Trained doctors were reported to be in attendance at some sessions, their role being to ensure that the victim did not escape into unconsciousness or death, and that he or she survived until the next session. There was even a kind of torturers' sub-culture, with its own terminology. Thus, in Chile, the victim was taken to *el quirófano* – the operating theatre in which he was made to lie on a table for a long period of time with the upper half of the body unsupported; or he was placed on *la parrilla* (the grill), which was the metal bed to which he was strapped while electric shocks were administered. In Zaire, the prisoner was forced to drink his own urine, known as *le petit déjeuner*, after which came *le déjeuner*, when he was systematically beaten on the shoulders.

Torture in the Eighties acknowledged that there were many more news stories on the subject than there were a decade ago, and there is some evidence that this trend has continued. The Committee for Human Rights, for example, which is a New York-based international human rights organisation, launched its 'Witness Program' in 1992, distributing video cameras to hundreds of human rights observers throughout the world. The aim of this programme was to record violations as they occurred, including evidence of torture, supplementing the traditional written reports of organisations such as Amnesty, and at the same time providing the visual images which were so necessary to ensure maximum media coverage. The assumption behind this programme, an assumption shared by all those organisations engaged in recording and publicising human rights abuses, was that the broadcasting of such abuses would promote international outrage, and that such outrage, in turn, would bring those abuses to an end. This did not happen.

Despite the end of the Cold War, and the opening up of former totalitarian states to international scrutiny, the evidence suggests, according to the *Final Report of the International Conference on Torture*, held in Stockholm in 1996, that 'torture is as prevalent today as when the United Nations Convention against Torture and Cruel, Inhuman and Degrading Treatment or Punishment ("Convention against Torture") was adopted in 1984'.[59] This was borne out by Amnesty International's most recent (at the time of writing) annual report, which claimed that, during 1996, tens of thousands of detainees were subjected to torture or ill-treatment, including rape, in at least 124 countries, including Cuba, Egypt, Myanmar, the Russian Federation and Nigeria, and that several hundred people actually died as a result of torture in custody or in inhuman conditions in at least 46 countries, including Cameroon, India, Libya, Venezuela and the Federal Republic of Yugoslavia. The report also carried evidence of hundreds of thousands of "disappearances" in at least 39 countries and of thousands of extrajudicial executions in at least 69 countries. As with previous reports, Amnesty cautioned that these figures were based only on known violations and should be regarded as a conservative estimate.[60] In any attempt to comprehend the nature and scale of torture in the contemporary world, we should also take into account those companies which form part of the torture industry, such as the UK company which supplied and exported a complete torture chamber to Dubai in 1990; and the numerous companies, based in Europe, North America, Russia and elsewhere, which make and supply instruments of torture, such as batons capable of administering electric shocks of up to 150,000 volts.[61]

I now turn to the issue of genocide, which has been more prevalent in the contemporary world than many of us would care to recall. Strictly speaking, the term 'genocide', coined by Raphael Lemkin in

1944 to conceptualise the horrors of the Jewish Holocaust,[62] refers to the destruction of a group of people on account of their membership of a national, ethnic, racial or religious group. In this conception, which was enshrined by the United Nations General Assembly in its 1946 Convention, 'genocide' can refer not only to the killing of such groups, but also to other methods of destruction, such as enforced sterilisation or the removal of children from one group to another. At the same time, it specifically excludes the destruction of people who are victimised on account of their politics or social class. For these reasons, analysts of genocide have come up with the term 'politicide' to describe the intentional killing of people by governments for political reasons, and the even broader term 'democide' to encompass all forms of government murder, including those which are neither genocidal nor political, such as the working of POWs to death by the Japanese army in World War II.[63] The significance of these distinctions can be seen in Rudolph Rummel's 1994 attempt to quantify democide in the twentieth century, in which he concluded that while around 39m people had been killed through genocides, when all forms of government murder were put together the total rose to 170m people. This, it should be noted, excluded war deaths, which Rummel was careful to distinguish from 'democide in time of war'. While war deaths result from the 'legitimate' casualties of war, such as soldiers and civilians killed in battle or battle-related disease, 'democide in time of war' refers to the forms of killing which would now be prohibited by the Geneva Convention and classified as war crimes or crimes against humanity. Into this latter category fall, for example, the reprisal killings of Czechs and Yugoslavs by the Nazis, and those who died in Soviet Labour camps during the Second World War.[64] The scale of state killing in the course of the twentieth century has been so colossal that the reality of it is almost beyond our capacity to imagine. Even the estimated 39m genocide deaths – around 23 per cent of Rummel's total – exceed all the war dead of all this century's international and civil wars, including both World Wars, the Korean and Vietnam Wars, the Russian and Mexican Revolutions, and the Spanish and Chinese Civil Wars.[65]

These statistics alone were enough to lend credence to the view that the twentieth century had been the most violent in human history. But was it possible to suggest that after the end of the Second World War, when the full horror of the Holocaust had been revealed, that the tendency of governments to murder groups of their own citizens did at least diminish? And furthermore, did not the collapse of totalitarian governments throughout the Communist world in the early 1990s reduce the risks of democide? Barbara Harff, a leading genocide scholar, thought not. 'Fifty years after World War II', she argued in 1996, 'We do not heed the lessons of the Holocaust . . . Never again, we the "civilised world" promised the few survivors . . . That promise has been broken some forty-eight times.'[66] Harff's statement came after conducting research into victimisation by the state of ethnic, religious, national and political groups in the period 1948 to 1995. In this research, she found that over seventy communal and political groups had been victimised in forty-eight episodes of genocide and politicide, with a death toll of anything between 9m and 20m people. In episodes of this kind, it was rarely possible to ascertain the number of deaths with any degree of precision, but Harff found that even the lower figure of 9m exceeded the total number of battle-related fatalities in international and civil wars over the same period.[67] In this respect, what Rummel had shown to be true for the twentieth century as a whole, Harff had shown also to be true for the period since 1945. Furthermore, the majority of genocides and politicides identified by Harff had taken place in more recent years, with thirty-two of the forty-eight having occurred since 1965 (see Table 2.2).

What conclusions could be drawn from this appalling record of state violence? Could it be shown that there were certain conditions which were conducive to democide? Most analysts agreed that the common denominator was power, and that the more autocratic the regime the more likely it was to use violence against its own citizens. Conversely, democratic governments by and large did not engage in genocide or political mass murder. However, when autocratic regimes collapsed, they were as likely to be replaced by a different form of autocracy as they were by democratic government. The collapse of the Soviet Union, for example, did not lead, as so many had hoped, to the triumph of democracy, but to the re-emergence of dictatorships, xenophobia and new forms of repressive government. Jan Pronk reminded us that, historically, state violence had often been an essential part of state formation.[68]

Barbara Harff and Ted Robert Gurr suggested that potentially democidal situations could be identified by examining the circumstances in which dominant groups systematically discriminated, as a matter of public or social policy, against ethnic, religious, national or regional minorities.[69] Such discrimination might take the form of denying economic or political opportunities, the prohibition of

Table 2.2 Genocides and politicides, 1945–95

Country	Dates	Number of Victims
USSR	1943–1947	500,000–1,100,000
USSR	11/1943–1/1957	230,000
USSR	5/1944–1968	57,000–175,000
China	2/12/1947	10,000–40,000
USSR	10/1947–1950	200,000–300,000
Madagascar	4/1947–12/1948	10,000–80,000
PR China	1950–1951	800,000–3,000,000
North Vietnam	1953–1954	15,000
Sudan	1956–1972	100,000–500,000
PR China	1959	65,000
Iraq	1960–1975	10,000–100,000
Angola	5/1961–1962	40,000
Algeria	7/12/1962	12,000–60,000
Paraguay	1962–1972	900
Rwanda	1963–1964	5,000–14,000
Zaire	2/1964–1/1965	1,000–10,000
Burundi	1965–1973	103,000–205,000
Indonesia	10/1965–1966	500,000–1,000,000
South Vietnam	1965–1972	475,000
China	5/1966–1975	400,000–850,000
Guatemala	1966–1984	30,000–60,000
Nigeria	5–10/1966	9,000–30,000
India	1968–1982	1,000–3,000
Equatorial Guinea	3/1969–1979	1,000–50,000
Pakistan	3–12/1971	1,250,000–3,000,000
Uganda	2/1971–1979	100,000–500,000
Chile	9/1973–1976	2,000–30,000
Pakistan	1973–1977	5,000–10,000
Ethiopia	1974–1979	30,000
Angola	1975–1995	250,000–500,000
Cambodia (Kampuchea)	1975–1979	800,000–3,000,000
Indonesia	12/1975–continuing	60,000–200,000
Argentina	1976–1980	9,000–30,000
Zaire	1977–1983	3,000–4,000
Afghanistan	1978–1989	1,000,000
Burma	1978	under 10,000
Uganda	1979–1/1986	50,000–100,000
El Salvador	1980–1992	20,000–70,000
Mozambique	1980–1992	500,000(?)
Iran	1981–1989	10,000–20,000
Syria	4/1981–2/1982	25,000–45,000
Sudan	1983–continuing	500,000–1,500,000
Ethiopia	1984–late 1980s	?
Burundi (possible)	1988	50,000–100,000(?)
Iraq	1988–1994	?
Somalia	5/1988–1989	?
Bosnia	5/1992–1994	200,000
Rwanda	1994	500,000

Source: Harff, Barbara and Ted Robert Gurr (1996), 'Victims of the State: Genocides, Politicides and Group Repression from 1945 to 1995', in Albert J. Jongman

(ed.), *Contemporary Genocides: Causes, Cases, Consequences,* Leiden: PIOOM, pp. 49–51.
    Geno/politicide is defined as the promotion, execution and/or implied consent of sustained policies by governing elites or their agents – or in the case of civil war either of the contending authorities – that result in the deaths of a substantial proportion of a communal and/or politicised communal group.

valued cultural practices, or the restriction of autonomies enjoyed by other groups. Whether or not discrimination of this kind would escalate into violence and killing would depend upon the character-istics of the ruling regime, the extent to which there had been a history of violence and the response to discrimination by the victi-mised groups. If these groups attempted to defend their interests by mobilising politically, they increased further the risks of repressive and retaliatory measures.

    Taking all these factors into account, Harff and Gurr tried to identify, throughout the world, all those groups subject to extensive discrimination, and to assess which of them faced the greatest threats. In 1995, they concluded that there were fifty-two of such groups in thirty-six different countries, facing a 'high risk' of further victimisa-tion under conditions which could conceivably degenerate into genocide or politicide.[70] This amounted to over 190m people.

    Torture, genocide and political murder represent the most ex-treme forms of human rights abuse. To some readers, it may come as something of a shock to be reminded of both the scale and frequency of their incidence over the past few decades, and of the vast numbers of people still at risk in the foreseeable future. The moral degradation of those directly responsible can hardly be questioned. But Barbara Harff goes further, and suggests that, when those in a position to intervene fail to do so, they too became morally culpable by implicitly accepting the moral standards of those who perpetrate the atroci-ties.[71] She sees this as a form of moral relativism, often disguised under the rhetoric of sovereignty, in which it is maintained that the political sovereignty and territorial integrity of states are sacrosanct and cannot be violated.[72] These arguments can suit both parties, particularly when there is a mutual interest in securing commercial deals and maintaining trade arrangements. The notion of cultural difference can also be invoked, and then deployed to question the very idea of universally applicable human rights, as it was in 1996 by Ohn Gyaw, the Burmese Minister of Foreign Affairs.

    We are seriously concerned, [he said] by the growing tendency of certain Western countries to politicise the question of human rights. We firmly believe that the international community should take a more holistic approach to the question of human rights and not be pre-occupied with individual rights and freedoms.[73]

According to Harff's and Gurr's 1996 research, 16m people in Burma were then under threat.[74] In the literature of torture and death described above, there were two persistent responses: first, the un-diminished horror and outrage at the unspeakable cruelties which governments were still able to inflict upon their own citizens in the late twentieth century; secondly, frustration at the international community's inability or unwillingness to take preventative action, and at its toleration of a 'culture of impunity' which allowed govern-ments to believe that they could, literally, get away with murder. But in what sense was this a narrative of decline? Could it really be said that the atrocities of the last thirty years represented a deterioration of international moral standards? The statistics which we have ex-amined here suggest, after all, that, although governments continued to torture and kill their own citizens, the death toll over this period, staggering as it was, represented a relatively small proportion of the 170m democide deaths estimated by Rummel for the whole of the twentieth century. There is, furthermore, something obscene, on account of its abstraction, in the attempt to measure either moral decline or moral progress on the basis of a statistical comparison, when the statistics being compared refer to the systematic extermina-tion of millions of human beings. Would it not be more appropriate to suggest that, as far as atrocities of this kind were concerned, the postmodern world became neither more nor less morally degraded, but merely added to the depressingly familiar evidence of the un-changing human capacity for brutality?

This was not a view shared by Stanley Cohen. In his article, 'Witnessing the truth', Cohen pointed out that in these matters the last thirty years could be distinguished from any other period in history in one key respect, namely, by an unprecedented capacity to accumulate information on human atrocities and to disseminate that information around the world.[75] This was facilitated both by the growth of international organisations, such as Amnesty, dedicated to the exposure of human rights violations wherever and whenever they occurred, and by the development of a global media industry capable of the instant transmission of images, sounds and words from virtually anywhere on the planet. Cohen argued that the human rights move-ment was one of the very few survivors of the Enlightenment project, in that it not only upheld the ideal of universal values and standards, but also assumed that accounts of their transgression would produce universal moral and emotional responses.[76] However, these responses did not materialise and, as noted above in connection with the 'Witness Program', the publicising of violations, no matter how shocking, did not bring them to an end. Whether this was explained through fashionable concepts such as 'compassion-fatigue' or whether it was attributed to an overwhelming sense of helplessness, the fact remained that the speaking of truth to power had had little effect. As Cohen concluded, 'we do not need to accept the vanities and silliness of post-modernist theory to understand that the issue is not the abstract right to know, but what does it mean anymore "to know" '.[77] On one level, the relationship between knowledge and action in the moral sphere was an old Enlightenment problem,[78] but although the problem might conceptually be the same, the context had changed beyond recognition. It was in this sense that we could speak of a narrative of decline: we knew so much more, and yet it made so little difference.

Crime, the family and social disintegration

A revulsion towards killing, torture and the deployment of weapons of mass destruction will not be readily dismissed as 'moral panic'. The same cannot be said about the conviction, held by many in the West, that their societies have been disintegrating under the pressures of increasing crime, the collapse of any kind of moral consensus and an experiment in 'family diversity' which has gone seriously wrong. Stanley Cohen, for example, who, as we have seen, was deeply concerned with the moral implications of human rights abuse, was dismissive of the moral concerns about social life in Britain expressed by 'editors, bishops, politicians and other right-thinking people'.[79] In *Folk Devils & Moral Panics*, Cohen argued that from time to time societies were subject to periods of 'moral panic', during which people or events were identified as a threat to societal values, demonised by the media and then subjected to a moral crusade. Such crusades, according to Cohen, were ideological in nature and ostensibly conducted in the name of society. However, in reality, they were driven by the interests of particular social groups and directed towards those whom they had labelled 'deviant'. The deviant 'folk devils' providing the focus of Cohen's book were the armies of Mods and Rockers which fought each other on the beaches of Britain's south coast during the 1960s, but the process which Cohen described could be applied to the many other groups which have fulfilled and which will continue to fulfil a demonic role in the public imagination. 'More moral panics will be generated', said Cohen, 'and other as yet nameless, folk devils will be created. This is . . . because our society as present structured will continue to generate problems for some of its members – like working-class adolescents – and then condemn whatever solution these groups find'.[80]

In *Hooligan: A History of Respectable Fears* (1983), Geoffrey Pearson went further, arguing that widespread fears in Britain of worsening street crime, growing hooliganism and declining moral standards, far from being a defining characteristic of our own period, formed part of a long historical tradition, the evidence for which could be found in virtually every generation.[81] In support of his thesis, Pearson presented a genealogy of these fears, from the 'muggers' of the 1970s inner-cities, back through the 'garotters' and 'Hooligan' gangs of Victorian London, to the 'Unruly Apprentices' of the seventeenth and eighteenth centuries. Although the specific focus of these fears (Cohen's 'folk devils') altered with changing social circumstances, for Pearson the underlying logic remained broadly the same. The fears emanated from the 'respectable' elements in society and they were always directed towards groups of (usually young) people from the materially disadvantaged underclass. Another constant factor was a powerful sense of nostalgia, through which the present was always compared unfavourably with the past. Here, Pearson was re-visiting territory explored by Raymond Williams in *The Country and the City*, where Williams had observed and analysed a preoccupation in English literature with the mourning of an idyllic, but elusive, rural past. In trying to track this idyll down, Williams found himself on a 'moving escalator' which took him forever backwards until he arrived, inevitably, at the Garden of Eden.[82] Pearson found himself in a similar predicament, although he suggested that the closer he came to his own time, the more recent the decisive period of decline had appeared to be. Thus, by the 1970s, it was 'twenty years ago' that was most often cited as, if not a golden age, then at least a time of moral stability before the descent into lawlessness had begun. But when Pearson looked at the 1950s, he found precisely the same kind of fears and the same conviction that social order was breaking down. 'Nostalgia', he concluded, was

> one of the raw materials of the human condition out of which the
> immovable preoccupation with declining standards and mounting dis-

order is fashioned . . . Each succeeding generation [was] remembering
the illusive harmony of the past while foreseeing imminent social ruin in
the future.[83]

In this account, the discourse of rising crime and deteriorating moral
standards became just one more example of the 'ageless mythologies
of historical decline'.[84] Postmodern Britain (which in this respect
might have stood for any other contemporary Western democracy)
exhibited no more violence or disorder than at any other time, and
the forebodings which this violence generated, far from representing
a break with the past, expressed only a continuity with it. If the long
history of 'respectable' fears told us anything, said Pearson, 'then it is
surely that street violence and disorder are a solidly entrenched
feature of the social landscape'.[85] Like Cohen, Pearson argued that
these fears served the interests of particular groups and classes. But,
for Pearson, they were also part of a long historical tradition in which
fears of social disintegration were actively promoted in order to
mobilise support for authoritarian social policies. Pearson saw this
as a sub-conscious return to the pre-democratic past, where ruling
interests were preserved by force.[86]

Although Pearson was careful to acknowledge both the realities of
criminal violence in contemporary Britain and the strength of feeling
aroused by it, his central argument was that the problem was
exaggerated for political purposes and that our understanding of
it was constrained by 'the blinding certainties of myth'. Even though
criminal statistics might show what Pearson himself referred to as a
'galloping crime rate' from the end of World War II onwards,[87] such
statistics, he went on to say, told us 'nothing worth knowing about the
historical realities of crime and violence'.[88]

Anyone who has attempted to discover what the real incidence of
crime has been over a specified period of time, or who has tried to make
comparisons between one period and another, will certainly concede
that crime statistics need to be approached with a great deal of caution.
Although they are often used by politicians and the media as a kind of
'barometer of crime', it is important to bear in mind that they are a
measure not of the actual incidence of crime but only of the number of
crimes which the police have recorded. Between the two lies the so-
called 'dark figure', the number of crimes which, for various reasons
are either not reported or are reported but not recorded.

In Britain, it is estimated that of all recorded crimes around 80 per
cent are those reported to the police by the public, with the re-

mainder being 'discovered' by the police themselves.[89] The total volume of recorded crime is thus heavily dependent on the public's willingness to report crimes. Whether or not a crime is reported can depend upon many factors, including the degree to which the crime is experienced by the victim as being 'serious', expectations of how the police will respond and fears of involving the police (in cases of domestic violence, for example). Increases in reporting rates have been attributed to greater police sensitivity (in rape cases, for example), to reductions in the public tolerance of petty crime, to the conditions of insurance policies and even to the increase in the ownership of telephones. It has also been suggested that the break-up of traditional communities has resulted in more people looking to the police to help deal with crime, whereas formerly many forms of criminal behaviour would have been dealt with in the community itself.[90] The numbers of crimes which the police will 'discover' themselves will depend upon police resources, strategies and priorities, particularly in relation to 'victimless' crimes. Police interest in a pop festival, for example, will almost certainly boost the number of recorded drug offences; conversely, when police interest in a particular form of illegal activity declines, as it did with homosexuality from the late 1950s onwards when decriminalisation was anticipated, then the number of recorded offences will rapidly decline.

The volume of recorded crime is determined not only by patterns of reporting but also by counting procedures. Malcolm Young suggested that in Britain the police only started to keep accurate records of reported crimes from the mid-1960s onwards, when politicians demanded it and when the police themselves realised that statistics could be used to win additional resources.[91] However, even then, there were inconsistencies in how specific crimes were counted. If a thief, for example, used a stolen credit card on several occasions, did this count for one offence or several? How many offences should be attributed to a man who assaults his partner over a period of months or even years? Should 'trivial' offences be excluded and, if so, where should the line be drawn between the 'trivial' and the 'serious'? The answers to these questions could produce widely varying statistics. Different police forces would give different answers and, although 'counting rules' were established in 1971, there was still some ambiguity. Maguire cited the case of Nottinghamshire, which for several years in the late 1970s had an unusually high crime rate, and one ostensibly far higher than that of its neighbouring counties. This proved to be largely due to the Nottinghamshire police practice of recording a very high proportion of the offences reported by the public, regardless of how trivial they were.[92] The records of some other police forces were skewed in the opposite direction, reflecting a tendency on the part of the police either not to believe the reports of some members of the public or not to take the reported offences seriously. There was also evidence of 'cuffing', the practice of omitting some reported offences, either to avoid work or to improve clear-up rates. According to Pat Mayhew and Natalie Aye Maung, for both good and bad reasons around 40 per cent of 'crimes' reported to the police did not end up in the official statistics.[93]

Changes in either the law or in administrative procedures will also have a dramatic effect upon official crime statistics. Pearson pointed out that the 'crime wave' of the mid-1930s was the result not of a crime explosion amongst juveniles but of the 1933 Children and Young Persons Act, which had the effect of bringing many more young people before the juvenile courts. Similarly, the increasing use of formal cautions in the 1970s, as opposed to the more informal system of unregistered cautioning, also added substantially to the crime figures.[94] Maguire noted that the 1977 decision of the Home Office to include in the official statistics the previously excluded offences of criminal damage of £20 or less increased at a stroke the 'total volume of crime' by 7 per cent.[95] This exemplified how arbitrary the classification of 'notifiable offences' (that is, those included in the official statistics) could be. Furthermore, there were contradictions within this classification. It embraced 'indictable' offences (those subject to trial in a Crown Court) but excluded 'summary' offences (those tried in the 'lesser' magistrates court). Yet, some of the most common 'indictable' offences, involving relatively small amounts of loss or damage, such as shoplifting or theft from vehicles, were arguably far less serious than some of the uncounted 'summary offences', such as common assault, cruelty to children and indecent exposure.[96]

Given this catalogue of contradictions, changing definitions and inconsistencies of both reporting and counting, what are we to make of the picture presented to us by the official crime statistics?

Figure 2.1 charts the increases in crimes in Britain recorded by the police since records began in 1876 up until 1994. Despite the Home Office ruling mentioned above, criminal damage offences, involving losses of less than £20 have been excluded for the sake of consistency, although no adjustments have been made for inflation. On the face of it, it appears that the crime rate remained broadly the same until around 1930, rose gradually until around 1950 and then rocketed over the next thirty-five years. Five hundred thousand crimes were recorded in 1950, 1.6m in 1970, 2.5m in 1980 and 5m in 1994. In terms of crimes recorded per 100 population, this represented 1 in the 1950s, 5 in the 1970s and 10 in 1994. Over the same period, equally spectacular rises were recorded in most other Western democracies.[97]

Figure 2.1 Crimes recorded by the police, 1876–1994

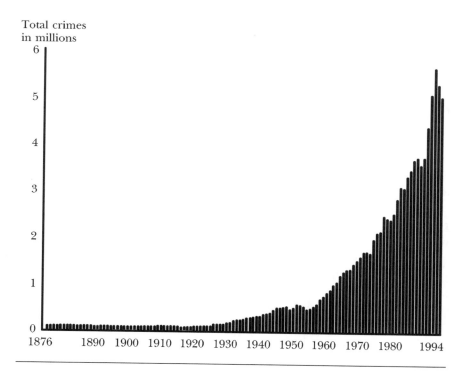

Total crimes in millions

Source: Home Office (1995), *Information on the Criminal Justice System in England and Wales, Digest 3*, London: p. 2
Crime is defined here as 'notifiable offences', excluding criminal damage of less than £20

Do we ignore these figures and agree with Pearson that they tell us 'nothing worth knowing about the historical realities of crime and violence'? Should we follow criminologists from the 'institutionalist' school and conclude that crime statistics, far from representing any kind of 'objective reality', are no more than the products of system-

atically biased social and organisational processes? From this perspective, crime statistics themselves should be the object of sociological enquiry, yielding insights not about crime but about the
agencies which produce the statistics. Or should we go further than
this, adopting the 'radical perspective', which questions not only the
methods of representing crime, but also the definitions of crime
itself, the structures of law and the operation of the criminal justice
system? This brings us back to Cohen's formulation that it is 'society
as present structured' which generates the problems and which then
criminalises many of those who suffer most from the problems which
society creates.

In retrospect, it seems that Pearson's judgement of *plus ça change
c'est la même chose* was both hasty and a little complacent. The
interpretation of official crime statistics was, and continues to be,
highly problematic, but evidence started to come in which supported
the view that crime *was* rapidly rising, even if the rate of increase was
not quite as rapid as the official statistics suggested. This evidence
came in the form of victimisation surveys, which had been introduced
into the United States and much of Europe in the 1970s and which
were developed in Britain in the 1980s. These surveys involved asking
a large sample of people (around 10,000 in Britain) whether they had
been victims of any of a specified series of crimes. On the basis of their
responses, national totals could then be estimated for a number of
different offences.

As the organisers of the British Crime Survey (BCS) were quick to
point out, a victimisation survey could not provide a figure which
purported to represent the 'total volume of crime'. Crimes against
commercial or corporate victims, for example, such as shoplifting
and vandalism, were not included in the surveys, nor were fraud,
motoring offences and the so-called 'victimless' crimes, such as the
possession of drugs. Sexual offences, though asked about, were very
rarely reported to BCS interviewers, so these also remained outside
the scope of the findings. Nevertheless, the BCS and the official
statistics shared enough common ground for conclusions to be drawn
about both the volume of crime (the 'dark figure') and rates of
increase in a number of key areas. These included burglary, most
forms of theft, vandalism against household property and vehicles,
robbery and wounding.

What were these conclusions? As far as the volume of crime was
concerned, between 1982, when the BCS was first conducted, and
1996, the BCS consistently revealed, within the categories of offence

that were comparable, a far higher number of crimes than those recorded by the police. On average, for every one incident recorded by the police around four were revealed by the BCS. The precise ratios changed from survey to survey, the highest being 1:4.5 in 1982, the lowest being 1:3.4 in 1991. In 1995, the latest year for which figures were available at the time of writing, the ratio was 1:4.3, with 2.8m offences recorded by the police against 12 million estimated by the BCS. There was some variation within these average ratios, depending upon the category of offence, but the overall message was the same: the official statistics represented only a small proportion of the total number of crimes committed. For the first time in Britain, the 'dark figure' had begun to emerge, as it had across Europe and the United States. The amount of 'new' crime revealed was so great that the Home Office had to consider how the figures might be presented in such a way as to deflect a wave of 'moral panic'.[98]

Perhaps even more significantly, the BCS also corroborated the picture of rising crime which the official statistics had presented and about which so many criminologists had been sceptical. Over the period 1981 to 1995, for those crimes which could be compared, the police statistics showed an increase of 91 per cent while the BCS showed an increase of 83 per cent. The 'authors' of the BCS pointed out that although there were some discrepancies in the two sets of figures, the overall direction was consistent.[99] Data from surveys was not, of course, available in Britain before 1981, but if the years following 1981 showed that BCS figures broadly confirmed the trends revealed in the police statistics then it was reasonable to assume that they would have done so in the years preceding 1982.

By the early 1990s, the scepticism towards the notion of rising crime, exemplified by sociologists such as Pearson, had become much less common. Maguire noted that it had become 'broadly accepted throughout the discipline [of criminology] that the incidence of certain forms of crime, at least, had substantially increased'.[100] Coleman and Moynihan acknowledged the existence of 'the modern crime problem', whose true beginnings could be traced back to around 1955.[101] Sally Field, in her study of crime trends in post-war England and Wales, found 'a striking picture of consistent long-run growth in crimes whose origins are diverse'.[102] This pattern was repeated in virtually every Western democracy, although in the 1990s there was evidence to suggest that in some countries (including Britain) the rates of increase had slowed down or even gone into reverse.[103] However, in relation to the massive increases of the previous three decades, a slowing-down or even decline in the crime rate had only a marginal impact on the overall position.

What were the nature of the crimes? Figure 2.2 breaks down into different categories the total of 19.1m crimes estimated by the BCS to have taken place in 1995.

Figure 2.2 Proportion of BCS crimes in different categories

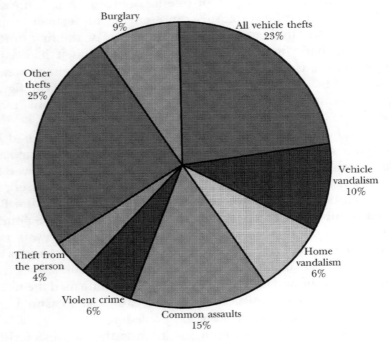

Source: Home Office (1996), *The 1996 British Crime Survey,* London: HMSO

The volume of one type of crime relative to another has remained fairly constant throughout all of the 'sweeps' conducted by the BCS. It will be seen that most crimes are against property, and that nearly six incidents in every ten are thefts or attempted thefts. Motor vehicles emerge as the most common target, with a third of all incidents involving theft of, theft from, or damage to vehicles. This has led some commentators to conclude that, although the evidence of rising rates of crime may be irrefutable, at least most of the crime is fairly petty. If one then works out the statistical averages of falling victim to particular kinds of offence, then the idea that Britain and the rest of the industrialised world are experiencing a crime crisis can once again seem wildly exaggerated. As Hough and Mayhew pointed out in their first report on the British Crime Survey, the average person could expect a robbery once in every five centuries, an assault resulting in injury once every century, the family car to be stolen once every 60 years, and a burglary in the home once every 40 years.[104]

This reassuring picture of a world in which only the very unlucky become victims of crime has been subject to vigorous challenge from Jock Young and others adhering to the so-called 'left realist' school of criminology. From their perspective, such a picture ignored both the burgeoning area of 'white-collar' crime (such as corporate fraud, tax evasion and so on) and the disproportionate impact of 'conventional' crime on the disadvantaged communities which were least able to cope with it. In what the authors considered to be the founding text of 'left realism', Lea and Young distanced themselves from 'left idealists', who rightly acknowledged the extent of 'white-collar' crime but who consistently failed to recognise the devastating impact of 'conventional' crime on precisely those people whose interests the 'left idealists' purported to serve.[105] Pearson, as we have seen, argued that fear of crime was exaggerated by the 'respectable' classes; but in focusing on 'respectable' fears, he had ignored the much more well-grounded fears of the disadvantaged and the vulnerable who were actually on the receiving end of most criminal activity. It was the interest of the 'left realists' in how the impact of crime was unevenly distributed amongst the population which led to a more nuanced appreciation of how crimes affected some more than others.

Lea and Young emphasised the point that crime was concentrated both in certain areas and also within certain groups.[106] This was well brought out in local crime surveys, such as those conducted in Merseyside (1984), Islington (1986 and 1990) and Edinburgh (1990), which showed that in some areas, predominantly those blighted by poverty, crime rates bore little relation to the reassuring picture suggested by statistical averages. The first Islington survey, for example, found that a third of all households in this inner-city area had been the focus of burglary, robbery or sexual assault within the previous twelve months. Age was another important factor: young, white females were twenty-nine times more likely to be subjected to assault than white females over 45.[107] Special surveys of women, most conducted by feminist researchers, revealed far higher rates of actual or threatened sexual violence than those suggested by the national crime surveys.[108] Research in both Britain and the United States showed how levels of risk for many types of crime were also related to membership of racial groups. In the United States, for example, although on average males faced a greater risk of homicide than females, black females in fact had a higher homicide rate than white males.[109] If crime statistics were 'averaged out', Lea and Young argued, they concealed massive differences in both the experience of and anxieties about crime which were intricately related to gender, class, race, age and location. In short, it was simply not possible to lump together the view from the middle-class suburbs, protected by burglar alarms and neighbourhood watch schemes, with that of deprived urban areas, subject to militarised policing, where 'multiple victimisation' was routinely experienced. When the *Guardian* newspaper did just this in January 1998, running the headline 'Crime "crisis" based on myth', it was powerfully refuted by Young:

> The traditional conservative myth [he wrote] has been replaced by the traditional liberal myth that crime is not really a problem. From the point of view of the public on embattled estates, the battered women suffering at the hands of her partner, the policeman on the beat and indeed the majority of criminological research there has over the last 30 years been a crime crisis.[110]

Young was, of course, careful to distance himself as much from the 'crime myths' of conservatives as he was from those whom he regarded as left-wing apologists for crime. In accepting that crime was a major social problem, he saw himself as engaging not in 'moral panic' but in 'moral realism'. From this perspective, it was morally irresponsible not to recognise that crime had a profound effect upon the lives of many people, particularly those least able to cope with it. But while conservatives saw crime as a question of individual (a)morality, 'left realists' such as Young placed criminal behaviour firmly within a social and political context. According to Lea and Young, many forms of crime were symptomatic of a general breakdown of social order into a kind of Hobbesian war of all against all. It was the symbol of 'a world falling apart . . . a lack of respect for humanity and fundamental decency'.[111] This was caused, not, as right-wing criminologists or politicians would have it, by wilful wickedness or a biological disposition to crime, but by 'the fundamental structural problems of capitalism'.[112] These were not poverty and unemployment in themselves, but a widespread sense of unjustified inequality, 'of being excluded from the "glittering prizes" of capitalist society'.

Lea and Young termed this 'relative deprivation', a concept which in their view could be used to explain why crime rates continued to rise throughout the post-war boom when income and employment levels were generally rising.[113] 'Relative deprivation' was endemic in modern capitalist societies, whose culture was characterised by 'rampant individualism' and 'pure egoism'. Such values were part of the core dynamic of capitalism, which relentlessly broke down collective and community traditions. This dynamic is analysed further in Chapter 4. Crime itself was a reflection of these values, a selfish and individualistic response to the problems of economic decay, social fragmentation and growing inequalities thrown up by advanced capitalism. With the gradual collapse of political alternatives, into which the energies of discontent might be channelled, more and more of the marginalised turned to crime. But, according to Lea and Young, while 'left idealists' took a romanticised view of such crime as a form of heroic rebellion, 'left realists', although accepting that it had its roots in the inequitable nature of society, recognised that its victims tended to be those who were themselves poor and disadvantaged. As Jeremy Seabrook had observed, 'the dispossessed turn on each other . . . The rich, meanwhile, can sleep safely in their beds.'[114]

Needless to say, this construction of crime, and, in particular, the moral exoneration of the individual criminal on account of the iniquities of capitalism, was not universally accepted; nor was it always conceded that the rich 'could sleep safely in their beds'. The perception of crime as a symptom of social disintegration was widely shared, but the disintegration was seen by many (on the left as well as on the right) not primarily as a consequence of capitalist economic relations but of an unprecedented collapse in the stability of the traditional family. Lea and Young dismissed this as the conservative 'fallacy of autonomy', but further work on the subject subsequently emerged which was neither exclusively conservative nor obviously fallacious.

In his book *Rising Crime and the Dismembered Family* (1993), Norman Dennis, who describes himself as an ethical socialist, argued that during the period associated with postmodernity two features of everyday life in England had experienced an extraordinary transformation. The first was the massive growth in crime; the second was the disintegration of family life as it 'had been understood for at least the preceding one hundred years'.[115] As Lea and Young had done, Dennis sought to explain why crime had first rocketed during the decades of low unemployment and rapidly rising living standards, when, according to criminological theories which were fashionable at the time, crime should have decreased as unemployment came down. However, whereas Lea and Young, as we have seen, characterised crime as a function of 'relative deprivation' within a capitalist culture which promoted unjustifiable inequalities, Dennis saw the determining factor as the collapse of the traditional family and, in particular, the decline of fatherhood. Furthermore, just as conformist intellectuals had resolutely maintained 'the growth of crime as an illusion' consensus before 'stampeding' out of it in the face of irrefutable evidence, they were now displaying a comparable blindness towards the growing seriousness of the problems of citizenship and child-rearing.

Given that crime was overwhelmingly the activity of young males, Dennis argued that we should start with this fact in any explanation of why crime had risen so dramatically over the last thirty years. What was it that had changed so profoundly within this group of people during this period to cause so many of them to go 'on the rampage'? For Dennis, the 'relative deprivation' experienced in advanced capitalist societies was inadequate as an explanation for two reasons. First, 'relative deprivation' was a constant element of human experience, and one which could always be cited as a cause of crime. Given this, it was difficult to argue convincingly that the capitalism of postmodernity produced more 'relative deprivation' than that of, say, the first half of the twentieth century, let alone the nineteenth century. Secondly, it was a totalising theory which could not explain why some took the anti-social, individualistic path of crime, while others, under the same material circumstances, handled their resentments in a more constructive manner. Dennis's explanation for the crime crisis was the disintegration of family life, resulting in the collapse of a socialising network which had both curbed the excesses of young males and at the same time prepared them for responsible citizenship through the traditional route of marriage and fatherhood. This was a complex process of cultural transmission, derived from the experience of generations, and one which was now being abandoned wholescale. Moreover, the question of a man's obligations towards his children and the mother of his children was no longer part of the public sphere and had become a matter of purely individual concern. In short, it had been privatised.

In support of his thesis, Dennis pointed to the massive increase in both the divorce rate and the number of single-parent families. In Britain, only 1 in 80 marriages taking place in 1951 had ended in divorce before the sixth anniversary; but by 1981, this had risen to 1 in 9, an increase of almost 900 per cent. Another way of measuring the increase was to look at the number of divorce petitions being filed. Thirty-two thousand were filed in 1961, rising to 111,000 by 1971 and 192,000 by 1990. Divorce rates then began to level off, but, according to Dennis, this was only because fewer people were bothering to get married.[116] In the early 1990s, there was 1 divorce for every 2 marriages.[117] Marriage was either being preceded by long periods of cohabitation or being replaced by it. However, there was strong evidence that 'trial marriages', as unmarried cohabitation was once called, far from improving the long-term prospects of a partnership, had actually made them worse. Furthermore, children were being born with ever-increasing frequency outside marriage, accounting by 1991 for 30 per cent of all births. A growing proportion of these births were to never-married lone mothers, the number of which had shown a staggering rise from 1.2 per cent of all families with dependent children in 1971 to 6.4 per cent in 1991.[118] All of these changes had had a profound effect upon the conditions under which children were being raised. Many were now routinely experiencing a bewildering range of family mutations, which might include separation, divorce, single-parent family, parent and live-in lover, remarriage of one or both parents, life in one step-parent family with visits to another step-parent family, the break-up of one or both step-parent families, and so on.

The trends which Dennis identified were broadly replicated in all Western democracies, although there were some variations between them. Divorce, for example, was at its highest in the United States, where by the early 1990s half of all marriages were ending in dissolution. The rate of out-of-wedlock childbirth had, as in Britain, also escalated, jumping from around 5 per cent in 1960 to 27 per cent in 1990. The impact of all this, both on children and on the fabric of social life in general, was examined by Barbara Dafoe Whitehead in her provocatively entitled article, 'Dan Quayle was right' (1993).[119]

It must be said, first of all, that Whitehead approached this highly contentious subject with a great deal of caution. She was well aware that when a parent took the decision to end a marriage, it was often an extremely painful decision and only taken as a last resort. Furthermore, most parents were only too conscious of the pain that separation and divorce would inflict upon their children, and Whitehead knew that to remind them of it could thus seem particularly cruel and unfeeling. Indeed, such were the depths of feeling aroused by these issues that attempts to discuss them dispassionately had very often been construed as veiled attacks on already vulnerable single mothers and their children. Those who persisted in their attempts were frequently dismissed as 'declinists, pessimists, or nostalgists, unwilling to accept the new facts of life'.[120] Nevertheless, Whitehead argued, the evidence from the accumulated research which was now coming in had such serious implications that it could no longer be reasonably ignored. Two clear conclusions could be drawn from it. The first concerned the impact on children themselves; the second, the broader social consequences of this impact.

During the 1970s there was, according to Whitehead, a widespread assumption that family disruption would not cause lasting harm to children and could actually enrich their lives. Instead of living within the often claustrophobic, repressive nuclear family, the child of a broken marriage could have access to a wider network of parents, step-families, new friends and so on. Moreover, if children were brought up within single-parent families, either for all of for part of their childhood, they would be no more likely to experience emotional or economic problems than children from two-parent families. Whitehead argued that these assumptions were simply no longer tenable in view of the mounting evidence from longitudinal research studies, such as those conducted by Sarah McLanahan, Judith Wallerstein and Nicholas Zill.[121] These studies revealed that, as far as divorce was concerned, there was a very real division between the interests of the parent and those of the child. While for many parents divorce could be a liberating experience, heralding new beginnings (one study showed that half of all divorced adults reported greater happiness), children experienced only loss and grief. Furthermore, children did not easily 'get over' divorce, as had been commonly assumed, but often experienced difficulties well into adult life. In her study, Wallerstein had found that five years after divorce, more than a third of the children were experiencing moderate or severe depression. At fifteen years, many of the adults, by then into their thirties, were still struggling to form strong loving relationships of their own. Zill had found that 'the effects of marital discord and family disruption [were] visible twelve to twenty-two years later in poor relationships with parents, high levels of problem behaviour, and an increased likelihood of dropping out of high school and receiving psychological help'.[122] Children in single-parent families were also more likely to suffer greater problems than those in two-parent families which had stayed together. According to Whitehead, they were six times as likely to be poor and to stay poor longer, two to three times more likely to have emotional and behavioural problems, and significantly more inclined to drop out of school, get pregnant as teenagers, abuse drugs or be in trouble with the law.[123]

Whitehead argued that this, in itself, was a serious enough problem, but that it was, additionally, compounded by its collective impact on social life in general. Just as in the 1970s there had been a widespread belief that the experience of different forms of family life could be enriching for the individual child, there had been a comparable belief that 'family diversity' could add to and enhance the traditions of social pluralism on which the American nation had been constructed. However, this too had proved to be a romantic illusion. According to Whitehead, the evidence suggested that the break-up of the traditional family, far from enriching the quality of social life, was actually a central cause of some of America's most intractable social problems, one of the most serious of which had been the crime explosion. Whitehead pointed to the volume of studies which showed, for example, that, even after income had been taken into account, boys from single-mother homes were significantly more likely to commit crimes and to end up in the juvenile justice, court and penitentiary systems. The conclusions of academic research were reinforced by the personal testimony of the many city mayors, police officers, social workers, probation officers and court officials who consistently pointed to family break-up as the most important source of rising rates of crime.[124] This did not mean, of course, that all children from dissolved marriages or single-parent families were automatically more likely to experience difficulties than those from intact two-parent families. Some children in the former category would always 'do better' than some in the latter. But this did not invalidate the general trend, as some researchers had tried to claim.[125] It merely proved that, inevitably, there was an overlap between the two distributions, with the better end of the worse distribution doing better than the worse end of the better distribution.

For Whitehead, it was very clear that the disintegration of the traditional family was instrumental in the development of a wider social disintegration. Recalling de Tocqueville's observation that an individualistic society depended upon a communitarian institution like the family for its continued existence, Whitehead argued that the maintenance of the family as an effective moral force was essential to a free, democratic society. The family had a key role in the transmission of citizenship, teaching lessons of 'independence, self-restraint, responsibility and right conduct'. If the family failed in this task, then the entire experiment in democratic self-rule was jeopardised.[126] On the evidence of the latest research, Whitehead concluded, it *was* failing. This failure was due to a seismic structural change in its nature – a change which, far from representing social progress, represented 'a stunning example of social regress'.[127]

In an even more politically-charged book, *Farewell to the Family?*, written with the intention of influencing government policy towards the family in Britain, Patricia Morgan went further. The breakdown of the family could not even be seen as social 'regress', because this implied a return to a social condition that had already existed. Morgan argued that such a condition had never existed. All societies which had survived had been built upon marriage, and children had always been raised in 'traditional' families, even if in some societies these traditions had encompassed polygamy and (to a lesser extent) polyandry. What was entirely novel about our own time, Morgan maintained, was the diminution of fatherhood and a human society built increasingly on the mother/child unit. In anthropological literature, a widespread failure to marry was a sign of impending disaster, an inability to maintain 'society's infrastructure' and 'bridges of social connectedness'. In Morgan's view, we were now engaged upon a historically unprecedented social experiment, in which the human costs were likely to be 'socially, politically and morally un-acceptable'.[128]

In this discussion of crime, family breakdown and social disintegration, I have drawn on literature relating primarily to Britain and the United States. However, as I have mentioned, the trends which have been described have been replicated to a greater or lesser extent throughout the West. A sense of social disintegration, of which rising crime is the most potent symbol, has given rise to narratives of moral decline which are derived, on the one hand, from a critique of the moral deficiencies of late capitalism and, on the other, from a perception of diminishing moral responsibility within the family towards the interests of children. In the former, moral injustices, such as high unemployment and grossly unequal distributions of wealth, are systematically perpetuated by ruling interests in the name of competition and free markets; in the latter, the basic building-block of society, the family, is undermined through the moral failure to provide secure and stable environments for the bringing up of children. Although these narratives reflect very different value systems, they are not incompatible in every respect. First, they both seek to provide structural explanations for the growth of crime. The individual offender, certainly, makes his own choices; but these choices are strongly influenced by broader circumstances which are not of his own making. Secondly, the break-up of the family can itself be seen as a function of the rampant individualism which is so closely associated with the culture of advanced capitalism. This is the classic dilemma faced by conservatives who on the one hand promote neo-liberal economic policies but on the other deplore the social fragmentation which comes with them. In these narratives, moral decline is thus part of a general societal decline, with the individual subject to forces over which he or she has little control and which appear to be both enduring and very difficult to reverse.

Moral pessimism

It is easy to see how the narratives of moral decline which have been examined in this chapter can be read as a 'metanarrative' of moral pessimism. As I noted in the discussion of environmental pessimism (Chapter 1), this is not because those who tell the stories of decline have themselves withdrawn into submissive fatalism. On the contrary, many were or are actively engaged in 'resistance' as well as analysis. Both E. P. Thompson and Harry Nash, for example, were deeply involved in campaigns for nuclear disarmament; Amnesty International continues to exert whatever pressures it can on governments engaged in human rights abuses; Barbara Harff urges genocide scholars to engage as much in the practical questions of intervention as in the theoretical analysis of why such atrocities take place; John Lea and Jack Young outline practical measures both for deterring crime and dealing more effectively with offenders; Patricia Morgan suggests changes to government family policy; and so on. The moral concerns which have been the focus of these different narratives have been clearly articulated, supported by evidence, often amplified by the media and addressed in practical ways. However, the manifestations of moral decline which the narratives reveal appear deeply embedded in the postmodern world and show no signs of receding. It is this which gives rise to a sense of moral pessimism, as can be seen if we remind ourselves briefly of how each of the narratives considered in this chapter were concluded.

In looking at the evolution of warfare over the past thirty years or so, we noted that the human species, for the first time in history, had acquired the military capacity to extinguish itself on a global scale. During the Cold War, it came close to doing so. The end of the Cold War, with its global network of alliances, brought to an end the immediate threat of superpower confrontation and a nuclear armageddon. However, the collapse of the superpower system, and the balance of terror on which it rested, released 'tribal' tensions which had been long repressed and which were now bursting out into brutal conflicts in many parts of the world. Instead of the much heralded 'New World Order', based on partnership, peacekeeping and peacemaking, many saw only the unfolding of a terrible new world of savagery, instability and disorder. The growing gap between rich and poor, both within and between nations, was a powerful and continuing source of resentment. 'We are entering a bifurcated world', Robert Kaplan had written. 'Part of the globe is inhabited by Hegel's and Fukuyama's Last Man, healthy, well fed and pampered by technology. The other, larger part is inhabited by Hobbes's First Man, condemned to a life that is "poor, nasty, brutish and short"'.[129] Such conditions were morally repugnant and dangerously volatile. With the 'democratisation' of weapons of mass destruction, the nuclear threat had not disappeared: it had merely been transformed. Nuclear weapons could not be 'dis-invented' and it was only a matter of time before they proliferated. India and Pakistan had already forced themselves into the 'nuclear club', conducting a series of underground tests in May 1998, to the general jubilation of their respective citizens who danced in the streets when they heard the news. However, it was not the nuclear arsenals of 'legitimate' governments which were most feared (though the expectation of a regional cold war on the sub-continent was hardly reassuring), but the prospect of weapons of mass destruction (including biological and chemical agents) being acquired by terrorist organisations or 'rogue' states. The growing instability of the postmodern world, with the proliferation of new kinds of 'internal' and 'informal' warfare, was expected by many to presage a widespread growth in repressive and authoritarian forms of government.

Evidence of torture continued to accumulate. The authors of the first Amnesty International *Report on Torture* had concluded in 1973 that the practice of torture had become both more widespread and more intense than it had been fifteen years before. The second report, *Torture in the Eighties* (1984), had come to the conclusion that one third of the world's governments had either used or tolerated torture in the 1980s. The 1996 *International Conference on Torture* had declared that torture was still as prevalent as it had been in 1984. Genocide and politicide continued to take place with appalling frequency. There had been forty-eight such episodes since 1945, the majority taking place after 1965. Between 9m and 20m people had died in these episodes – more than all of those killed in battle, or as a result of battles, in international and civil wars over the same period. Millions more people continued to be in danger. In 1995, fifty-two groups of people in thirty-six countries faced serious risks of victimisation under conditions which could conceivably degenerate into genocide or politicide. This amounted to 190m people. However, despite the enormity of these atrocities, it was still possible to say that the second half of the twentieth century saw fewer genocides and less political murder than the first. But what caused some analysts to see in this a process of decline was the persistence of these atrocities when documentary evidence of their incidence, both in words and images, was more widely disseminated than at any other time in history.[130]

The perception of a more brutal, violent and indifferent world was strengthened, within the West at least, by reports of a crime explosion from the 1960s onwards. Initially, these reports were dismissed by some sociologists as no more than 'moral panic'. However, 'moral panic' gave way to 'moral realism', as most criminologists came to accept that there were historically unprecedented levels of at least some forms of crime and that they had a disproportionate impact on those who were already economically and socially disadvantaged. Crime symbolised the breakdown of social order, an untrammelled, anti-social individualism, without respect for humanity or fundamental decency. Recent aetiological explanations for the crime explosion had, on the one hand, focused on the increasingly Darwinian qualities of late capitalism and, on the other, on the disintegration of the family and with it a secure environment for the bringing-up of children. While neither explanation denied the possibility of moral choice, both placed an emphasis on structural conditions. At the end of the 1990s, these conditions appeared well-entrenched: there was no alternative to capitalism on offer (even using the word 'capitalism', implying that it was possible to look at it from the 'outside', could seem old-fashioned) and the trends in family life were widely seen to be irreversible.

When these narratives are all put together, it is not difficult to imagine how a sense of moral pessimism might arise. It is a pessimism that is sometimes associated exclusively with the West as it struggles to come to terms with its diminishing power and influence in the post-colonial world. As Keith Tester reminds us, the decline of one civilisation can be the emancipation of another.[131] This is a proposition which also exercised Samuel Huntington, who wondered whether the West was capable of reversing its 'internal processes of decay' or whether its 'sustained internal rot' would accelerate its eclipse by other more dynamic civilisations.[132] For Huntington, the moral decline of the West, which he believed was in the process of committing cultural suicide, was a major preoccupation. Nevertheless, this was subsumed into the even greater preoccupation with moral decline in all civilisations,[133] or, to put it another way, the decline of 'Civilisation' in the singular. Here, Huntington was careful to avoid making claims for the universality of Western cultural values, on the grounds that universalism was no more than imperialism by another name. But this did not mean that he was acceding to the kind of moral relativism that was criticised earlier in this chapter. On the contrary, Huntington argued that there were basic moral commonalities, derived from the shared human condition, which could be found in all civilisations. These included, on the one hand, moral concepts of truth and justice and, on the other, negative injunctions against moral transgressions such as murder, deceit, torture and tyranny. There was no incompatibility, Huntington argued, between the renunciation of universalism, the acceptance of cultural diversity and the search for shared moral ground. Indeed, in the final analysis, the clash between civilisations, which Huntington saw as inevitable in the post-Cold War world, would be overshadowed by the greater clash within civilisations – the clash, which all were experiencing, 'between Civilization and barbarism'. For Huntington, as he surveyed the growing violence, crime and chaos unfolding in many parts of the world, there appeared the possibility of 'an unprecedented phenomenon, a global Dark Ages . . . descending on humanity'.[134] In this perspective, moral pessimism, along with much else, had become globalised.

Notes

1. For this account, I have drawn largely on the following sources: British Medical Association, Board of Science and Education, *The Medical Effects of Nuclear War*; Calder, *Nuclear Nightmares*; Schell, *The Fate of the Earth*; Wilson, *The Disarmer's Handbook*; Thompson and Smith (eds), *Protest and Survive*.

2. Schell, *The Fate of the Earth*, p. 18.
3. Ibid. p. 19.
4. See British Medical Association, Board of Science and Education, *The Medical Effects of Nuclear War*, pp. 26–30.
5. Ibid. pp. 123–4.
6. Leslie, *The End of the World*, p. 27.
7. Schell, *The Fate of the Earth*, pp. 62–5.
8. Ibid. p. 26.
9. Quoted in Leslie, *The End of the World*, p. 28.
10. Quoted ibid. p. 29.
11. Schell, *The Fate of the Earth*, p. 205.
12. Quoted in Leslie, *The End of the World*, p. 30.
13. van Creveld, *Nuclear Proliferation and the Future of Conflict*, p. 40.
14. Leslie, *The End of the World*, pp. 34–5.
15. Ibid. p. 33.
16. Blair and Kendall, 'Accidental nuclear war'.
17. Calder, *Nuclear Nightmares*, p. 10.
18. Schell, *The Fate of the Earth*, p. 217.
19. Bailey, *Pessimism*, p. 109.
20. E. P. Thompson, 'Protest and survive', p. 56.
21. Nuttall, *Bomb Culture*, pp. 105–36.
22. Ibid. p. 48.
23. Quoted ibid. p. 112.
24. Nash, 'The bureaucratization of homicide', pp. 62–74.
25. Ibid. p. 63.
26. E. P. Thompson, 'Protest and survive', p. 51.
27. Ibid. p. 57.
28. van Creveld, *Nuclear Proliferation and the Future of Conflict*, p. 63.
29. See Wulf, *Arms Industry Limited*.
30. Fukuyama, *The End of History and the Last Man*, p. 12.
31. van Creveld, *The Transformation of War* and *On Future War*.
32. Keegan, 'Who says a Hitler could never happen again?'.
33. Keegan, *A Brief History of Warfare*, p. 14.
34. van Creveld, *Nuclear Proliferation and the Future of Conflict*, p. 126.
35. Huntington, *The Clash of Civilizations*, p. 35.
36. Kaplan, 'The coming anarchy', p. 75.
37. Hobsbawm, *Age of Extremes*, pp. 560–1.
38. Wulf, *Arms Industry Limited*, p. 26.
39. Philips, 'West moves warily to counter the threat of nuclear anarchy'.
40. Cole, 'The specter of biological weapons', p. 32.
41. Heilbroner, *An Inquiry into the Human Prospect*, p. 43.
42. Leslie, *The End of the World*, p. 66.
43. Cole, 'The specter of biological weapons', p. 31.
44. Fairhall, Norton–Taylor and Radford 'Saddam's deadly armoury', p. 15.

45. Leslie, *The End of the World,* p. 42.
46. Keegan, 'Who says a Hitler could never happen again?'.
47. Amnesty, *Annual Report 1961/2,* p. 1.
48. Amnesty International, *Annual Report,* p. 2, and *Annual Report 1962/3,* p. 8.
49. Amnesty International, *Annual Report 1966/7,* pp. 7–11.
50. Amnesty International, *Annual Report 1969/70.*
51. Quoted Ibid.
52. Amnesty International, *Annual Report 1972/3,* p. 4.
53. Amnesty International, *Report on Torture,* p. 109.
54. Ibid. p. 29.
55. Ibid. p. 29.
56. Amnesty International, *Annual Report 1978,* p. 4.
57. Hobsbawm, *Age of Extremes,* p. 446.
58. Quoted in Amnesty International, *Torture in the Eighties,* p. 10.
59. Amnesty International, *International Conference on Torture,* p. 1.
60. Amnesty International, *Annual Report 1997.*
61. Amnesty International, *Annual Report 1996,* pp. 9–17.
62. See Rummel, 'The Holocaust in comparative and historical perspective', p. 18.
63. Ibid. pp. 19–20.
64. Ibid. p. 23.
65. Ibid. p. 23.
66. Harff, 'Rescuing endangered peoples', pp. 119–20.
67. Harff and Gurr, 'Victims of the state,' p. 37.
68. Pronk, 'The UN after 50 years', p. vii.
69. Harff and Gurr, 'Victims of the state', p. 38.
70. Ibid. pp. 54–8.
71. Harff, 'Rescuing endangered peoples', p. 117.
72. Ibid. pp. 121–2. Harff wrote this before the NATO intervention in Kosovo. It has been argued that NATO's actions marked a significant departure from the kind of moral relativism which Harff describes. However, the decision to conduct the campaign from the air and not risk NATO ground troops was seen by some analysts as symptomatic of moral cowardice. Moreover, in other parts of the world, such as Chechnya, the principle of the inviolability of sovereignty remained unchallenged.
73. 'Human Rights, Human Wrongs', Channel 4, 7 December 1997.
74. Harff and Gurr, 'Victims of the state', p. 55.
75. Cohen, 'Witnessing the truth', pp. 41–2.
76. Ibid. p. 36.
77. Ibid. p. 45.
78. See, for example, Schiller, *On the Aesthetic Education of Man,* pp. 25–9, for an extensive investigation of this dilemma.

79. Cohen, *Folk Devils & Moral Panics*, p. 9.
80. Ibid. p. 204.
81. Pearson, *Hooligan*.
82. Williams, *The Country and the City*, pp. 18–22.
83. Pearson, *Hooligan*, pp. 221 and 229.
84. Ibid. p. 223.
85. Ibid. p. 242.
86. Ibid. p. 231.
87. Ibid. p. 20.
88. Ibid. p. 219.
89. See Maguire, 'Crime statistics, patterns, and trends', p. 250.
90. Ibid. p. 259.
91. See Coleman and Moynihan, *Understanding Crime Data*, p. 35.
92. Maguire, 'Crime statistics, patterns, and trends', pp. 255–6.
93. Mayhew and Maung, *Surveying Crime: Findings from the 1992 British Crime Survey*, p. 2.
94. Pearson, *Hooligan*, pp. 216–17.
95. Maguire, 'Crime statistics, patterns, and trends', p. 248.
96. Ibid. p. 248.
97. Ibid. p. 257.
98. Ibid. p. 264.
99. Home Office, *The 1996 British Crime Survey*, p. 4.
100. Maguire, 'Crime statistics, patterns, and trends', p. 260.
101. Coleman and Moynihan, *Understanding Crime Data*, p. 117.
102. Field, *Trends in Crime and Their Interpretation*, p. 4.
103. Mayhew and van Dijk, *Criminal Victimisation in Eleven Industrialised Countries*, pp. 34–70.
104. Hough and Mayhew, *The British Crime Survey*.
105. Lea and Young, *What Is to be Done about Law & Order?*, p. 11.
106. Ibid. p. 26.
107. Quoted in Maguire, 'Crime Statistics, Patterns, and Trends', p. 267.
108. Ibid. p. 267.
109. Lea and Young, *What Is to Be Done about Law & Order?*, pp. 32–3.
110. Young, Letter to the *Guardian*, 8 January 1998. Young's letter had been provoked by a page 1 story on 6 January, written by the Home Affairs Editor, Alan Travis, under the headline 'Crime "crisis" is a myth', in which Travis claimed that the 1996 British Crime Survey had shown that the public was wrong to believe that crime was rising dramatically.
111. Lea and Young, *What Is to Be Done about Law & Order?*, p. 55.
112. Ibid. p. 59
113. Ibid. p. ix
114. Ibid. p. 271
115. Dennis, *Rising Crime and the Dismembered Family*, p. 1.

116. Dennis, *Rising Crime and the Dismembered Family*, p. 5.
117. *International Statistical Year Book*, CDROM, 1999.
118. Dennis, *Rising Crime and the Dismembered Family*, pp. 5–6.
119. Whitehead, 'Dan Quayle was right'.
120. Ibid. p. 50.
121. See: McLanahan, 'The consequences of single parenthood for sub-sequent generations'; Wallerstein and Blakeslee, *Second Chances*; and Zill, Peterson, Moore and Furstenberg, *1976–1987 National Survey of Children: Waves 1, 2 and 3*.
122. Quoted in Whitehead, 'Dan Quayle was right', p. 66.
123. Ibid. p. 47.
124. Ibid. p. 77.
125. See Dennis, *Rising Crime and the Dismembered Family*, pp. 46–8.
126. Whitehead, 'Dan Quayle was right', p. 84.
127. Ibid. p. 80.
128. Morgan, *Farewell to the Family?*, pp. 152–3.
129. Kaplan, 'The coming anarchy', p. 60.
130. For a further exploration of the moral implications of this, see Tester, *Moral Culture*. Tester asked whether those who were 'consumers' of relatively distant violence and horror were in some way 'guilty'. He concluded that they were 'metaphysically guilty' (pp. 146–52).
131. Ibid. p. 150.
132. Huntington, *The Clash of Civilizations*, p. 303.
133. Huntington classifies the major contemporary civilisations as follows: Chinese; Japanese; Indian; Islamic; Western; Orthodox Russian; Latin American; and African. Huntingdon, *The Clash of Civilizations*, p. 45.
134. Huntington, *The Clash of Civilizations*, p. 321.

3

Intellectual Decline: Science and Art

Few seem haunted by an insufficiency of meaning
(Raymond Tallis, *Newton's Sleep: Two Cultures and Two Kingdoms*)

Introduction

NARRATIVES OF INTELLECTUAL DECLINE, constructed around the practice of science, have proliferated and intensified since the 1960s. These narratives acknowledged the material and intellectual benefits which science had unquestionably brought but maintained that the price paid had been too high. Such a view formed part of an older counter-Enlightenment tradition and could be seen, in particular, as a stronger version of the Romantic critique of science which had emerged in England in the late eighteenth and early nineteenth centuries. The reasons why such a critique should have returned with greater intensity in our own period are examined. Despite the robust defence of science put forward during the 'science wars' of the 1990s, the misgivings around science, both as a mode of cognition and as a transforming power, could not be allayed.

Underpinning this narrative was a theological preoccupation with the vision of humanity that science had bequeathed: that of accidental man alone in a meaningless, valueless universe. Despite the theological aspirations of science (as, for example, in the search for a Theory of Everything), science was not actually capable of confronting the questions of meaning and purpose which religion addressed. Religion, however, had been comprehensively undermined by science and could no longer fulfil its old function. But, according

103

to some (neo-Kantian) critics, art had taken its place and was capable of providing at least some experience of the transcendental meanings which religion used to supply.

This claim was difficult to reconcile with the narratives of decline which had also built up around art. On the one hand, there was a conviction that the 'modernist impulse', which lay behind the greatest artistic achievements of the twentieth century, had finally exhausted itself, culminating in the cul-de-sac of a weary and cynical postmodernism. On the other, a corrosive relativism was seen to be at work within the general culture, which denied judgements of value, degraded the conditions for the reception of art and led to a 'dumbing down' of both cultural institutions and intellectual life. In this view, the 'consoling vision' of art, like that of religion, had gone for good.

Science

The construction of a narrative of intellectual decline around the practice of science can seem strangely perverse given the scale of twentieth-century scientific achievement. In field after field, from medicine to agriculture, from energy to communications, spectacular advances had been brought about by scientific discovery and application. Science had transformed virtually every aspect of human life, becoming the indisputably dominant form of epistemological inquiry, and producing what Theodore Roszak had called a progressive 'scientization of culture'.[1] It was the irresistible effectiveness of science, the fact that science worked, which explained these transformations, leading to what Brian Appleyard had identified as 'the modern conviction that for every problem there is a scientific solution'.[2] Francis Fukuyama had gone further, suggesting that it was science which had given directionality to history and, moreover, that this directionality was irreversible.[3] From a rather longer historical perspective, Robert Sinsheimer had reminded us of the extraordinary point to which science has brought us in the history of evolution. Having taken billions of years to evolve, *Homo sapiens* had now developed the means to intervene in the evolutionary process itself, acquiring the capacity through the manipulation of genes to alter forever the evolutionary future both of human beings and of other forms of life.[4]

For natural philosophers such as Paul Davies, it was not so much the practical applications of science which had been astounding, but the extraordinary insights into the hidden order of the universe which science had begun to yield. Sub-atomic physics had given us entry to the strange world of the quantum, where matter and the observer of matter became entangled in profound ways; astrophysics had revealed extraordinary coincidences without which life could not have arisen in the universe; mathematics, having lain dormant in the human brain for many thousands of years, had emerged to find a quite beautiful mathematical unity reflected in the laws of the cosmos. Many scientists even believed that they were within sight of a completely unified physics, a so-called Theory of Everything, in which all the forces of nature, all the particles of matter, space and time, would be amalgamated into a single descriptive scheme. In Davies' account, scientists were inspirational breakers of the 'cosmic code', now offering scientific answers to questions which were essentially theological.[5] Such was the imaginative pull of science that, according to George Steiner, the most gifted and creative minds were no longer attracted to the arts but sought expression instead in the sciences.[6] Isaiah Berlin had claimed that the development of the natural sciences and technology was, quite simply, 'the greatest success story of our time'.[7]

Nevertheless, this 'heroic' vision of science came under intense attack from the mid-1960s on. There was, of course, nothing new in this, and challenges both to the validity of scientific truth and to the value of scientific achievement had persisted since Bacon, Galileo and Descartes first deployed their methods to such devastating effect in the sixteenth and seventeenth centuries. Scientific rationalism might have liberated people from superstition and ignorance, at the same time transforming the material conditions under which they lived, but there had always been those who claimed that it had succeeded only in replacing one form of tyranny with another. Such claims could be seen as part of a counter-Enlightenment tradition, which ran from the epistemological relativism of the seventeenth-century Italian philosopher, Giambattista Vico, through the German and English Romanticism of the late eighteenth and early nineteenth centuries, down to various forms of postmodernism from more recent times.[8] However, what was new was both the intensification of these claims and the appearance of new forms of radical scepticism.

For example, in his seminal work on *Scientific Knowledge and Its Social Problems* (1971), Jerome Ravetz argued that the long golden age of science was now definitely over and that the natural sciences, facing problems of an entirely new order, were in danger of decline and dissolution. The vision of science as the pursuit of the Good and the True had become 'seriously clouded' and the traditional idea of the 'noble scientist' had disappeared from view.[9] In a special issue of *Daedalus* (1974), for which scholars from both within science and outside were commissioned to examine the changing relationship between science and its public, Edward Shils noted the 'relatively new' phenomenon of secular antagonism towards science. It had, he suggested, become significantly more vehement since the 1960s, condemning what had been accepted unreservedly only fifteen or twenty years before, and resulting in the 'present radical rancour against science'.[10] Contributing to the same issue, Amitai Etzioni and Clyde Nunn recorded the views of a number of observers that science in the United States was experiencing a 'crisis of legitimation', that the public's reaction to science was one of deepening disillusion and that science and technology had taken a 'severe pounding' from which it would not recover.[11] Writing in Britain, Colin Dollery declared in 1978 that the age of optimism within medical science had ended, a view endorsed in the US twenty years later by Leslie Garrett, who contrasted the modest claims of medical science in the 1990s with the confident predictions of the 1950s and 1960s.[12] However, it was not only the 'external' impacts of science which came under attack. In a 1988 survey of the sociology of scientific knowledge (SSK) and, more broadly, of what had come to be known as the 'social study of science' (SSS), Steve Woolger documented the growing scepticism within several disciplines towards the 'internal' workings of science and towards the claims to truth which arose from them.[13] This was territory explored by Jean-François Lyotard who, in what was later seen as a defining analysis of the 'postmodern condition',[14] had attempted to show how the legitimacy of scientific 'truth' was deeply implicated in relations of wealth, power and efficiency. For philosophers of science such as Rom Harré, scientific discourse was just another form of narrative, a mode of storytelling with no higher claim to truth than that offered by philosophy, literature or literary criticism.[15] The historian Margaret Jacob had written of a 'vast transformation' in our perception of science, starting in the 1960s and taking place at both scholarly and popular levels.[16] As a consequence of this transformation, she went on to say, the heroic model of pure, value-free science lay 'in shambles'.[17]

What accounted for these narratives of scientific decline? How were they constructed? What precisely was the nature of the decline being represented? A good starting point is the influential work of Theodor Roszak, who, in the late 1960s and early 1970s, attempted to formulate a systematic critique of science, technology and scientific rationalism which might bring a sharper focus to the growing unease around science that had emerged out of the 1960s dissident counter culture.[18] Roszak did not deny the extraordinary achievements of science. Indeed, so powerful had science become, so completely had it colonised the culture of the West, that, for Roszak, it was not just another subject for discussion, it was *the* subject. But therein lay the problem. The 'success' of science, both as a mode of cognition and as a transforming power, had been bought at a terrible price. Moreover, the 'mindscape' of scientific rationality had become so pervasive that it was becoming almost impossible to conceive of reality in alternative ways. In Roszak's view, it was this 'mindscape' which had done so much to produce the cynicism, emptiness and despair which he saw lying at the heart of contemporary Western culture. 'We conquer nature', he argued, ' we augment our power and wealth . . . but the despair burrows in deeper and grows fatter; it feeds on our secret sense of having failed the potentialities of human being'.[19]

How was Roszak able to load so much on to the practice of science? What was it that science possessed that could provoke such a vehement denunciation? Central to Rozak's thesis and, as we shall see, to those who have developed it in more recent years, is what he saw as the de-humanising tendency of science. He traced this back to the very beginnings of the scientific revolution, when Bacon and Descartes first instituted 'objectivity' as the fundamental property of scientific enquiry. Even though an epistemology of total objectivity might never be attained, as many scientists would concede, a psychology of objectivity could and would become the standard mental apparatus for all scientific activity. It was this impersonal method, what others have approvingly called the 'view from nowhere', which divorced man from himself, objectified nature and, ultimately, turned the act of scientific knowledge into an act of alienation. As Bacon had predicted with uncanny foresight, the deployment of such methods would prove to be extraordinarily powerful, yielding its 'harvest' – the massive expansion of knowledge and the development of technology – in the generations to come. But, according to Roszak, the acquisition of this 'power-knowledge' and its assumption of cultural supremacy in the modern world was bought at the cost of an increasingly reductionist, reified and instrumental view of human beings and other forms of life. This was the distinctive psychic disease of our age which explained the capacity of human beings to turn on their environment and their fellows with 'the cool and meticulously calculated rapacity of industrial society'.[20]

In Roszak's view, the power and productivity of science, magnified by its industrial application, depended upon an increasing specialisation of knowledge. Indeed, so fragmented had science become that it no longer made sense to speak of it as a 'field' of knowledge, only as an endlessly multiplying array of sub-fields.[21] The 'objectivity' of the scientific method, the exclusion of the human from its epistemology, had already had the effect of separating knowledge from value; the fragmentation of science into higher and higher degrees of specialisation made the separation irreversible. Roszak's vision was of a titanic scientific experiment, spiralling out of control in all directions, while humanity could only stand back and see what the final, tragic destiny of the sum of its parts would turn out to be. It was this vision which prompted Roszak to make the startling assertion that science did not work and that it was only the wilful refusal to look beyond a narrow instrumentalism that gave credence to the claim that it did.[22] By this he meant that, although science provided solutions to specific problems, from a broader perspective it could be seen that those solutions often either gave rise to even greater problems or only solved problems that had been created by science in the first place. Thus, for example, only when value had been separated from knowledge could it be said that thermonuclear weapons 'worked'; and only highly specialised forms of knowledge, which ignored the broader picture, could have produced an industrialism capable of bringing the world so close to environmental collapse.

Roszak was careful to distance himself from those who wished to turn their back on the modern world and return to a kind of 'paleolithic primitivism'.[23] However, he maintained that scientific industrialism always promised more than it delivered, promoting a kind of technological idolatry which was both deeply unsatisfying and ultimately unsustainable. He likened the technological society of his time to a world's fair in its last days, 'indefinably sad and shoddy despite the veneer of orthodox optimism' and exhibiting a 'vile tackiness'.[24] To those who argued that clear distinctions had to be drawn between 'pure' science and its (mis)application to technology, Roszak replied that such distinctions were disingenuous, ignoring the political and sociological contexts in which the practice of science was now located. Corporate investment in science had, of course, always been made in the expectation of financial returns; but, increasingly, governments were also looking for more direct returns from their research funding. They had become much less susceptible to the old argument that pure research could be counted upon to produce practical benefits in unexpected and unpredictable ways. In the background, there were in any case always cohorts of technicians in waiting, whose whole training had been directed towards the monitoring of theoretical research for its potential applications. The separate realms of science and technology were, for Roszak, a fiction; instead, there was only the 'single, on-going, all-embracing process of Research and Development'.[25]

From this account, it is clear that Roszak placed scientific rationalism at the root of both the destructiveness and discontents which he associated with modernity. As a mode of cognition, it had de-personalised the world, driven out other ways of knowing and destroyed meaning. As a transforming power, it had achieved its extraordinary 'success' through the application of a rigorously narrow focus which simply screened out anything beyond its immediate frame of reference. Roszak's account of the reductive, machine-like qualities of the industrial world, and of the alienation produced in human beings, was in many respects similar to Marxist and neo-Marxist critiques. In Marx, and in subsequent revisions of Marx, the de-humanising characteristics of scientific industrialism were a function of exploitative economic relations. In Roszak, it was the ideology of science itself which was determining, and from this all else flowed.

Given Roszak's work, it is surprising that Brian Appleyard should assert twenty years later that his own *Understanding the Present* was the first attempt to provide an alternative, critical history of science.[26] Appleyard covered much of the same ground as Roszak, but his book provides an interesting illustration of how Roszak's narrative of scientific decline, far from being a temporary reflection of 1960s counterculture, persisted and re-emerged in an even more intense form in the 1990s. Like Roszak, Appleyard wrote of the 'terrifying success' of science, but while, for Roszak, the globalisation of 'scientized culture' was still to come, for Appleyard it was now a reality. The effectiveness of science had proved to be an irresistible force and the material benefits it could bestow were universally demanded. But intrinsic to science were qualities of domination which could not permit the co-existence of alternative belief systems. Science was not just a supplier of goods which could simply be 'purchased' without further effects: it was also a corrosive force which destroyed cultures, undermined traditions and denied other ways of knowing.[27]

So what, it might be asked, if science had these effects? Surely it was just completing the job, started by the Enlightenment, of removing the last vestiges of superstition and untested knowledge? This might be so, Appleyard answered, but then it was necessary to consider the limits to the kind of knowledge triumphant science had bequeathed. Science was brilliantly effective at telling us how to do things and how things worked; but, despite the theological aspirations of those such as Jacob Bronowski, Carl Sagan and Stephen Hawking (who aspired to 'know the mind of God'), science could tell us nothing about purpose and meaning. It could, however, tell us a great deal about the absence of meaning.

The vision of accidental man alone in a meaningless, valueless universe runs through Appleyard's book, as it does through a great deal of twentieth century art and literature. Even Paul Davies, whose up-beat account of modern science was referred to above, acknowledged that 'one of the depressing things about the last three hundred years of science is the way that it has tended to marginalise, even trivialise human beings'.[28] Although Davies went on to suggest that developments in quantum physics might eventually show that human beings had some significance in the universe after all, thus restoring some of the human dignity which classical science had taken away, Appleyard maintained (as did Roszak) that the psychological and cultural impact of 'new' science should not be over-stated. Much had been made of the disappearance of mechanical certainty in quantum physics, with those such as Fritjof Capra arguing that close parallels could now be clearly drawn between the most advanced scientific theories of the West and ancient traditions of eastern mysticism.[29] Even if these claims were credible – and to Appleyard they exhibited little more than wishful thinking at a banal level of generality – it showed a fundamental misunderstanding of science to suggest that sub-atomic physics had somehow replaced traditional science. Whatever was discovered at the sub-atomic level (and there had arguably been no further revolutions in physics since 1927), much of the Newtonian universe remained in place. The project of traditional science continued to shape the culture of the world.

For Appleyard, like Roszak, this science had progressively stripped human beings of meaning and purpose. The more we knew, the more insignificant we became. In the biological sciences, for example, the discovery of DNA in 1953 had, according to Richard Dawkins, finally destroyed any lingering belief that life occupied a privileged position within the universe. 'Up until 1953', Dawkins observed, it was still possible to believe that there was something fundamentally and irreducibly mysterious in living protoplasm. No longer. Even those philosophers who had been disposed to a mechanistic view of life would not have dared for such total fulfilment of their wildest dreams.[30]

The undisguised triumphalism of this kind of assertion was not only offensive to Appleyard; he considered it misconceived. The psychology of objectivity, which, as we noted above, was a fundamental property of scientific enquiry, had resulted in a strange distortion: a vision of the world which effectively pretended that the very mechanism which had created that vision, the reflexive self, was not there. The scientific observer maintained the fiction that he had somehow stepped outside the self, observing from a point somewhere outside the universe. But he would, of course, then have to observe the self observing the self, and so on, in an infinite series of regressions which would never finally arrive at the sought-after condition of objectivity. This attempt to exclude the self from the scientific world-view explained the paradox of a science which continued to expand the boundaries of its knowledge and yet at the same time could be experienced as a kind of epistemological prison. It was this, according to Appleyard, that had prompted Wittgenstein to declare that even when all the scientific questions had been answered, the problems of life remained 'completely untouched'.[31]

Although the formal opposition of religious institutions towards science had all but disappeared (in 1992 the Vatican even provided a formal acknowledgement of the injustice of its condemnation of Galileo), it will be clear that the religious impulse was far from absent in the critical discourses around science which have been discussed so far. Roszak's position on this was explicit. The scientific revolution had repressed religious sensibilities, and the result was an intolerable spiritual impoverishment which could only be addressed by some form of religious renewal. The religion to which he referred was not the religion of churches, orthodoxy and doctrine, but 'religion in its perennial sense . . . Vision born of transcendent knowledge'.[32] Appleyard was more guarded, but nevertheless the theological inflection to his examination of science was unmistakable: science had destroyed meaning, leaving a spiritual vacuum. There was no longer any reason for existence and, without this, on what grounds could societies maintain a belief in their own continuation?[33]

The conviction that scientific knowledge was insufficient had, of course, been a central theme of the Romantic reaction against science in the late eighteenth and early nineteenth centuries. William Blake, for example, famously denigrated science for its 'single vision' and prayed that we might be saved from 'Newton's sleep'.[34] Thomas Carlyle, strongly influenced both by German Romanticism and by his own responses to the emergence of industrialism (which he was the first to name), argued that 'Machinery' was now the defining characteristic of the age, 'in every outward and inward sense'. By this he meant that just as machines had begun to dominate production processes, mechanistic modes of thinking had begun to dominate intellectual processes. There had been advances in the material world, as Carlyle was quick to acknowledge, but this could not compensate for the moral and imaginative impoverishment of the inner life. A healthy culture, Carlyle argued, could only arise from the cultivation of both the inward and the outward. While we had excelled in the latter, the former had become dangerously neglected.[35] Shelley, although fascinated by science, had come to a similar conclusion: 'The cultivation of those sciences', he asserted, 'which have enlarged the limits of the empire over the external world, has . . . proportionally circumscribed those of the internal world; and man, having enslaved the elements, remains himself a slave'.[36] For Shelley, as for Carlyle, this disjunction between the internal and the external had been brought about by an excess of the 'calculating principle', the dominating characteristic of scientific rationalism. In Shelley's analysis, such a disjunction could only be healed, both in individuals and in the wider culture, by the development of the imagination – 'the great instrument of moral good' – and by a strengthening of the 'creative faculty'. In this, Shelley was following Wordsworth who, in what effectively became a manifesto for Romanticism, had argued in 1800 that poetry and the arts were uniquely qualified to nurture the imaginative and affective qualities of human beings that seemed to him to be so endangered by the development of scientific industrialism.[37]

In a well-known formulation, Alfred North Whitehead summed up these reactions as 'a protest on behalf of the organic view of nature and also a protest against the exclusion of value from the essence of matter of fact'.[38] The former protest was a response to the perceived limitations of a scientific method which investigated nature through piecemeal, analytical procedures and which could not see the whole as distinct from the sum of its parts. The latter was a response to science's aspiration towards objectivity and the exclusion of the distinctively human from its representation of reality.

This is all very familiar and it is really quite striking how closely key elements of the (post)modern critiques of science which we have reviewed so far in this chapter were based upon the same ground as that staked out 200 years earlier by Blake, Wordsworth, Carlyle and Shelley. However, what is also striking is the increased intensity of the attacks. As Raymond Tallis has pointed out, Romantic hostility to science was by no means unqualified.[39] Wordsworth admired Newton's vision, though remained fearful of the mechanistic world picture that might be derived from it. Carlyle was not antagonistic to science per se, only to the spread of 'mechanical thinking' beyond what he considered its proper sphere. Shelley, as noted above, was fascinated by science, and believed that it could become a liberating force if only it could be accompanied by a commensurate moral development. Even Blake was prepared to concede the enormous, if in his view misguided, nature of Newton's achievements. As Leo Marx has observed, in comparison with contemporary critiques, the English Romantics would have to be considered as 'moderates'.[40]

Why should contemporary attitudes have hardened thus? Why should a neo-Romantic critique of science have emerged in a stronger form and with even greater intensity than that put forward by the Romantics themselves? First, as we have already discussed, there was the extraordinary, global 'success' of science, which had not only transformed the West but had also penetrated every society and culture in the world. Neither the methods nor the impacts of science could be escaped. Even in the humanities, where much of the scholarly hostility to science was to be found, we could at the same time observe the paradoxical attempt to acquire the authority of science through the incorporation of scientific assumptions and procedures, as, for example, in the development of semiotics, structuralism and aspects of post-structuralism. If, in the first half of the nineteenth century, Carlyle had thought that science already represented a kind of epistemological imperialism, it was not difficult to see, at the end of the twentieth century, how those with a historical sympathy for Carlyle's position might wish to update and re-present his case with a far greater urgency. As Appleyard observed, science and technology had not advanced at an even and gradual pace; 'they have suddenly exploded all about us. Their sheer, profligate effectiveness is something utterly novel'.[41]

The second reason for an increasing unease around science was the experience of both a growing dependency upon it and a corresponding sense of incomprehensibility. Advocates of greater scientific literacy, such as C. P. Snow and, more recently, Raymond Tallis, might suggest that this could be overcome by a more determined educational effort, both within schools and within the general population, but this was not realistic. We were surrounded by the products of the most complex technologies, the workings of which the majority of us would never understand. Even if we considered ourselves specialists in one field – competent, for example, to repair a fault in a personal computer – this was of little help when problems presented themselves in another. Furthermore, the omnipresent technologies on which we depended were simply not designed to be understood – they were designed to be used. As Hobsbawm had observed, fax machines did not operate better when used by professors of electronics.[42] Most of the time we were shielded from both our dependency and our ignorance; but on occasion we were reminded sharply of it, as in the run-up to the year 2000 when the consequences of widespread computer failure, arising from the so-called 'millennium bug', were spelt out.

However, it was not only at the level of technology that science mystified. Within physics, for example, the break with sense experience and 'common sense', inaugurated by the discoveries of Planck and Einstein over a hundred years ago, had still not been assimilated into the general culture, and it was difficult to imagine how it might be. Concepts such as four dimensional space-time, wave-particle duality and Heisenberg's uncertainty principle might have acquired a common currency as a result of attempts to popularise science, but it was impossible to grasp the implications of these concepts or to integrate them adequately into one's own understanding of the world unless one was the beneficiary of a highly specialised scientific training. As physicists pursued their investigations into the ultimate constituents of matter (currently superstrings), and as cosmologists speculated upon what existed prior to the creation of the universe (pre-Big Bang scenarios), the rest of us did what little we could to translate these highly complex theoretical models into terms that might make sense to us. In this, we were assisted by science writers of many kinds, but even here we often found the adoption of an ironic tone, as those writers struggled to communicate the incommunicable. Take, for example, a full-page story in an up-market British Sunday newspaper, which attempted to explain to its readership why Europe's leading centre for research into high-energy particle physics was preparing to build an 'antimatter' factory. Under the headline 'Antimatter set to blast scientists to other side of the cosmos', the author explained that twenty kilograms of 'antimatter', which differed from matter in that the electric properties of its atoms were reversed, would be enough to power a spaceship across the galaxy. However, although the existence of 'antimatter' had been first postulated by Paul Dirac in 1928, and although in theory the universe should have produced equal quantities of matter and 'antimatter', no traces of 'antimatter' had ever been found. Furthermore, manufacturing it was extremely difficult: attempts to produce 'antihydrogen' had resulted in only nine atoms of the stuff, and this, 'rather inconveniently', had all disintegrated within 'a few billionths of a second'. The twenty kilograms needed to power the spaceship would take 'billions of years' to make. Nevertheless, the author concluded, the new factory could perhaps shed light on 'why people and not antipeople have prevailed in the cosmos'.[43] The very notion of 'antimatter' was, of course, meaningless in everyday terms and, as Hobsbawm had pointed out, provided just one more example of the theoretical 'turn' in all of the natural sciences (with the possible exception of molecular biology), after which no preconceived notions of reality were allowed to interfere with the progress of theoretical calculation: reality was what the theoreticians told the practitioners to look for, and they would catch up with it as and when they could.[44] As far as the rest of us were concerned, we stood, according to Roszak, in much the same relationship to the language of contemporary science as did the mediaval peasantry to the Latin mass.[45]

The third and perhaps most potent cause of the renewed hostility to science arose from its role in the development of the technologies of death. Nothing illustrated so clearly as this the old anxieties expressed by the Romantics about the separation of knowledge from value. Although, in retrospect, one might have expected the neo-Romantic revolt against science to have been triggered by the industrialised carnage of World War I, most historians of science suggest that it was not until after World War II, and in particular until the terrifying crises of the Cold War, that disillusion towards the supposedly benign qualities of value-free, progressive science really set in at both the scholarly and popular levels. Margaret Jacob, for example, looking back at how younger historians were reframing their understanding of science in the 1960s, recalls how the story of progress, and of the triumph of science over ignorance and superstition which began with Galileo, 'seemed all but hollow'.[46] For her, it was quite clear: faith in the heroic model of science had collapsed 'under the impact of the bomb'.

115

Fourthly, the destructive effects of scientific industrialism, which in nineteenth-century England had so alarmed, amongst others, Wordsworth, Ruskin and Morris, had by the 1960s culminated in the real possibility of a historically unprecedented environmental collapse. Those who adhered to notions of scientific and technological progress argued that this might be so, but that it was science which had alerted us to the problems and that it was science which would find the solutions. This, it was argued, was the dynamic of a techno-scientific economy through which social gains far outweighed the losses. However, although there might have been historical justifications for this point of view, maintaining it, as we saw in Chapter 1, now required an act of faith that many people were increasingly reluctant to make as the narratives of environmental decline unfolded.

Fifthly, and this is connected to the previous two points, there was a growing perception that contemporary science had become unacceptably dangerous. This, of course, was also an old Romantic fear, famously expressed by Rousseau in his 'Discourse on the moral effects of the arts and sciences':

> Let men learn for once that nature would have preserved them from science, as a mother snatches a dangerous weapon from the hands of her child. Let them know that all the secrets she hides are so many evils from which she protects them, and that the very difficulty they find in acquiring knowledge is not the least of her bounty towards them.[47]

If Rousseau feared the consequences of scientific knowledge in 1750, it is not difficult to understand how these fears might have reappeared in a more intense form in an age which had already seen the development of nuclear fission and genetic engineering and which now looked forward to the coming revolution in molecular nano-technology. Indeed, the reader of this passage today cannot be but struck by the modern resonance of its concerns. Robert Sinsheimer, for example, a biophysicist at the California Institute of Technology (Caltech), used much the same argument as Rousseau when he called in 1978 for further constraints to be put upon scientific research. Our scientific endeavour, Sinsheimer suggested, had been underpinned by an unspoken faith in the resilience of nature – 'as we probed it, dissected it, rearranged its components . . . bent its forms and diverted its forces to human purposes'. In short, we pressed ahead, believing that nature did not 'set booby traps for unwary species'. But the time had come to reconsider this belief. As we delved more deeply into matter and into life, acquiring the power to shape not only the physical nature of the planet but also the evolutionary future of living forms, did we not run the risk of pushing the resilience of nature beyond its limits, disrupting biological equilibria and destroying our ecological niche? For the past four hundred years, the West had attributed the highest possible value to the acquisition of knowledge – and particularly the acquisition of scientific knowledge. In the seventeenth, eighteenth and nineteenth centuries, the technological innovations which had arisen from this knowledge, and the social and cultural consequences which had flowed from it, had been largely benign. But, according to Sinsheimer, at some point in the twentieth century, the balance had begun to shift. The unrestricted advance of scientific knowledge no longer represented the highest form of human achievement.[48]

It is worth noting at this point the extent to which 'dangerous science' has already featured as an important sub-theme in each of the previous two chapters. The harmful effects of pollution and, in particular, of the introduction into the environment of vast amounts of synthetic chemicals were discussed at some length in Chapter 1. The proliferation of weapons of mass destruction (nuclear, chemical and biological) was considered in Chapter 2. For a recent account of other forms of dangerous science, the reader might usefully turn to John Leslie's discussion of the risks associated with genetic engineering, computers, nanotechnology and high energy physics.[49] In brief, the threat from genetic engineering came from the possible introduction of new toxins and allergins into foods and from the unpredictable consequences of the interaction of genetically modified material with its environment. Just as some synthetic chemicals had produced devastating – and wholly unexpected – effects many years after they were first manufactured and used, might not the genetic modification of some organisms also have unforeseen and equally dangerous consequences? Indeed, genetic engineering posed the greatest danger of any technology yet introduced, in that genetic 'mistakes', once out of the laboratory, could reproduce themselves without limit and never be recalled. The transfer of genes from one form of life to another, such as the use of 'anti-freeze' genes from fish to create frost-resistant tomatoes, was a particular focus of concern, in that it provoked fears of dangerous diseases spreading across species. There was also widespread concern about the genetic engineering of crops to resist pesticides and herbicides, or even to resist pests themselves: might not their genes escape into wild plants, creating new forms of virtually indestructible 'superweed'? What effect would such crops have on humans once they had become incorporated into the standard diet? No one knew the answers to these questions. Nevertheless, genetic engineers pressed ahead, arguing that the history of life itself was one long genetic experiment, and that they were only contributing to a process in which Nature had been engaged for billions of years. But this was precisely the point: genetic engineers could perform in a day what Nature might have taken a million years to achieve. There was no way of knowing what dangers might arise from this extraordinary compression of time.

Computer-caused disasters ranged from the possibility of nuclear accidents, at either the civil or military level (including accidental nuclear war) to the total paralysis of energy and communication systems, triggered by 'landslides in cyberspace' or by particularly malignant computer viruses which could mutate, self-replicate and 'lie low' for many years. The growth in computer processing power, and our increasing dependence upon it, had been extraordinarily rapid, with some experts predicting the development of systems intricate enough to rival the human brain by 2030. This took us into the realms of artificial intelligence (AI), and while some scientists, such as Roger Penrose, remained sceptical about the 'Hard AI' holy grail of the self-conscious computer, others such as Eric Hofstadter and H. P. Moravec, not only foresaw the disappearance of the distinctively human but actually looked forward to the eventual transition from carbon to silicon-based evolution. For Appleyard, it seemed quite logical that science, having conceptually removed the soul from the body, should now proceed to do so physically as well.

The coming revolution in nanotechnology, as a result of which it would be possible to construct atomic-scale machines to perform tasks in molecular environments, was announced in Richard Feynman's classic 1959 Caltech lecture, 'There's plenty of room at the bottom'. Such machines, which would effectively be able to control the structure of matter, could be put to an enormous range of uses, from cleaning up waste by altering its molecular structure to travelling through the blood stream in order to perform miniature surgery. Although none of these machines had yet been built (their components would be around one millionth of a millimetre in size), theoretical and computational models proved that they did not violate existing physical laws and that there was no fundamental barrier to their development. According to Eric Drexler, the future application of nanotechnology promised to eclipse even the vast transformations brought about by the technology revolutions of the twentieth century.[50] However, at the same time, as with any powerful technology, there were risks. The disaster scenario most commonly imagined, known as 'the gray goo problem', involved the construction and release of a runaway, self-replicating machine, about the size of a bacterium, but tougher and virtually omniverous. Such a runaway might 'blow like pollen and reproduce like bacteria', reducing 'the biosphere to dust in a matter of days'. Although Drexler thought it unlikely that such a disaster could happen by accident (Leslie was not so sure), both were aware of the destructive uses to which nanotechnology could be put. For Drexler, it could 'give nuclear war some company as a potential cause of extinction';[51] for Leslie, we could but 'hope that the temptations of war, terrorism and crime will be removed . . . before any nanotechnological revolution hits us'.[52]

The amount of energy that could be created in laboratory experiments increased roughly tenfold during each decade of the twentieth century. This was largely due to the development of particle accelerators which eventually became capable of producing, over tiny areas, energy releases far greater than those produced by the explosion of thermonuclear bombs; by the beginning of the 1990s, such 'collision energies' could reach around four thousand billion electron volts. The fifty-four mile long Superconducting Supercollider (SSC), which the Americans started to build in Texas in 1993 but subsequently stopped on the grounds of cost, would have increased these energies by a further factor of ten. Although the cancellation of the SSC was a setback, in Leslie's view, it did not represent a permanent obstacle to the continuing pursuit of higher and higher energies; indeed, with the development of the next generation of accelerators, involving radically different technologies, it was quite possible that the pace of growth might be maintained. If this was so, we could – by simple extrapolation – expect to produce energies greater than those released by the collision of cosmic rays well before the end of the twenty-first century and to see 'Planck-scale' energies by the year 2150. The magnitude of these energies was extremely difficult for the layman to grasp. But it was such that, according to some scientists, it could conceivably bring about 'the ultimate ecological catastrophe' which not only destroyed all life, but also the possibility of life. In this scenario, a new generation of particle accelerators triggered, with an enormous release of energy, the formation of a bubble of 'real vacuum' which expanded close to the speed of light, advanced through and beyond the galaxy, causing all protons in its path to decay. Our own 'vacuum state' – that is, the space in which we lived – simply disappeared in a microsecond of gravitational collapse.[53]

These worst-case scenarios were, of course, speculative and highly contentious. At the scholarly level, some scientists doubted the theoretical basis of the calculations and dismissed the conclusions as science fiction; others conceded the theoretical possibility but thought the reality so unlikely as to be barely worth consideration; others thought the potential dangers real enough but believed that the rigours of scientific safety procedure would prevent catastrophe. From all these perspectives, the fears generated by 'dangerous science' at the popular level were simply the latest manifestation of the old, Romantic, Frankenstein syndrome, amplified by often sensational reporting in the media and irresponsible comment from the inadequately informed. However, this could not explain away the fact that, as we have seen, some distinguished scientists had themselves begun to voice concerns at what they saw as the reckless advance of both science and its applications. These could not be dismissed as ill-informed and unscientific. Moreover, the world we inhabited was no longer that of Dr Frankenstein: the 'dangerous science' of postmodernity was of an altogether different magnitude.

The sixth reason for disenchantment arose from the notion of 'dirty science'. One focus of this was the 'military-industrial' complex, which grew up in a symbiotic relationship to the Cold War and whose influence on the development of scientific knowledge had been enormous. For example, according to Margaret Jacob, the imperatives of the defence industry had had a fundamental impact on both teaching and research within the science and technology departments of the major American universities. Physics had increasingly narrowed its concerns to those areas thought to have military applications. Jacob recalled, for instance, how confirmation of Einstein's theory of general relativity came to be seen as 'a critical step toward improving ballistic missile accuracy by accounting for minute gravitational effects'.[54] Hobsbawm identified a new breed of scientific researcher who, unlike his counterpart of previous generations, accepted the policies of his paymaster unquestioningly, preferring not to look too critically at the wider implications of his work. There appeared to be no difficulty in recruiting staff to conduct research into chemical and biological warfare.[55]

The 'military-industrial', however, was not the only 'complex' with which science was seen to have compromising relations. A 'medical-industrial' complex was also identified, signalling (particularly in the

US) a growing convergence between medical science and business. Arnold Relman, a former editor-in-chief of the *New England Journal of Medicine* and one of the first to name this 'complex', argued in 1992 that the decisive transformations had taken place since the 1970s. In his account, there had been an erosion of medical ethics as physicians and researchers increasingly entered into financial arrangements with drug manufacturers and investor-owned health-care facilities. Clinical investigators, for example, were holding equity interest in companies whose products they were testing; others were serving as paid consultants or scientific advisors; respected academics were being hired by drug companies to give lectures or write articles about the manufacturers' new products; and physicians were investing in health-care facilities to which they could then refer their patients. In all of these cases, the belief that these experts were offering rigorously impartial advice was strained by the realisation that the expert had a direct financial interest in the outcome of the advice. In Relman's view, the new market in healthcare that was emerging, in which medical science had become a competitive industry, represented a breach of the medical profession's ethical contract with society.[56]

The 'genetic-industrial' was identified as yet another 'complex' through which scientific research was increasingly driven by the imperatives of profit. One example of this was the development of a crop seed which grew normally and resulted in excellent harvests, but which had been genetically modified to produce biologically sterile grain. This had the advantage of terminating Nature's 'unprofitable' habit of reproducing itself, requiring farmers to buy new seed each year rather than to sow the grain which they had harvested themselves. The biotechnology company, Monsanto, had developed another seed (named Biotech) which had been genetically modified to increase the sales of the company's flagship herbicide, Roundup, through the introduction of a gene which would make it immune to the toxic effects of this – but no other – herbicide. Developments of this kind, which were arguably not in the interests of the wider public, had been made possible by a close alignment of research into the life sciences with the needs of the biotechnology industry. Indeed, according to Richard Lewontin, Professor of Population Genetics at Harvard, there was by 1992 'no prominent molecular biologist . . . without a financial stake in the biotechnology business'. By 1999, Lewontin was suggesting that this was even becoming a threat to democracy, in that it was now more and more difficult for governments to find sources of independent and impartial advice. Under these conditions, questions of scientific alternatives, which were essentially political, were instead paraded as the merely technical; and in this way, what was profitable came to affect, or even determine, what was 'scientifically true'.[57] Such a challenge to the truth claims of science formed only part of a much broader assault on both the institutions and the epistemology of science, through which it was suggested that scientific knowledge, far from being objective and universally true, was no freer from ideological contamination than any other 'discursive practice'.[58] Charges of this kind were of a different order altogether from those levelled by the Romantics and their successors who, as we have seen, were exercised by the limitations of scientific rationalism but who, nevertheless, entertained no serious doubts about the inherent validity of the scientific method itself.

Let us pause at this point to summarise. It has been suggested that, since the 1960s, narratives of intellectual decline around the practice of science have proliferated and intensified. These narratives can be seen as part of a counter-Enlightenment tradition and, in particular, as a stronger version of the Romantic critique of science which emerged in England in the late eighteenth and early nineteenth century. In this strong version, science is represented as a dominating power which, in its separation of knowledge from value, divorces man from himself, de-personalises the world and turns the act of scientific knowledge into an act of alienation. Incapable of permitting the co-existence of alternative belief systems, it becomes a corrosive force which destroys cultures, denies other ways of knowing and progressively strips human beings of meaning or purpose. It has been extraordinarily successful in its application to technology, from which 'pure' science can no longer be separated, but the specialisation which has made this possible has promoted a narrow instrumentalism which ignores the broader consequences of its actions. Scientific rationalism thus stands accused both of producing a 'mindscape' of despair and of bringing the world close to self-destruction. This is an unacceptably high price for the material and intellectual benefits which science has unquestionably also brought. As to why such a critique should have emerged so forcefully in our own period, six reasons were put forward: the global reach of science and its penetration (through technology) of every society and culture in the world; the experience of a growing dependency upon science and a corresponding sense of incomprehensibility; the role of science in the development of weapons of mass destruction; the ecological and environmental impact of scientific industrialism; the potential dangers inherent in further scientific advance; and the prominent role of military and business interests in the direction of scientific research.

These narratives were, of course, subject to robust responses from within the scientific community. In 1994, for example, alarmed by the scale of hostility towards science in the US, Paul Gross and Norman Levitt, respectively Professors of Life Sciences and of Mathematics at Virginia and Rutgers Universities, called upon scientists to go on the offensive, particularly against the 'academic left' whose relativist distortions they believed to have had an increasingly pernicious effect upon the public understanding of science.[59] The following year, in *Newton's Sleep*, Raymond Tallis, Professor of Geriatric Medicine at the University of Manchester, staked out his defence of science, which he subsequently extended into an impassioned defence of Enlightenment values in general.[60] For Tallis, it was not 'Newton's sleep' (Blake's shorthand for all that was wrong with the scientific worldview) that we should distrust and denigrate but, on the contrary, the 'anti-science and organic daydreams' peddled by those who wilfully denied the facts of progress. Central to Tallis's case was the simple conviction that the material benefits bestowed upon humanity by the application of science to technology outweighed all other factors. Taking a middle-aged man (presumably from the West) as an example, Tallis asked us to consider his position:

> Unlike most human beings in history (indeed most organisms) he will not have died before reaching adult life. His surviving to what is now called 'middle' age makes him part of an even more privileged few. His own children will not be the minority survivors of a continuous, natural massacre of the innocents. He will be well fed. He will not be riddled with numerous undiagnosed and untreatable infestations. Any illnesses he has will be cured or, if incurable, significantly palliated. He will not have brought to his middle years the long-term effects of childhood malnutrition or chronic illness. His clothes, if not *haute couture*, will be infinitely superior to the smelly bug-ridden rags that have ineffectively insulated shivering humanity throughout most of history . . . At night he will sleep in a comfortable bed, safe from cold and rain and the depredations of insects and wild animals. Supported above the abyss of pain, hunger, cold and other unalleviated miseries contingent upon material want, he is privileged beyond the wildest dreams of his ancestors.[61]

In the light of these transformations, to speak of the 'de-humanising tendency' of science was, for Tallis, ludicrous. There was nothing more de-humanising than material impoverishment, illness and unrelieved hard labour; and pain was the greatest de-humaniser of all. It was precisely these conditions which science had done so much to ameliorate. The 'single vision' might have produced the atomic bomb, but it had also produced penicillin, electricity and sanitation. The West, of course, had been the greatest beneficiary of science, but the developing world, far from rejecting science, wanted more of it. What, asked Tallis, did those critics of science-based technology propose to put in its place? Although they rarely articulated it as such, they could offer only one alternative: a return to the inefficacies of myth, superstition and magic. These were the 'other ways of knowing' which science 'denied', nothing more than the old discredited forms of knowledge from which enlightened science had struggled so hard to liberate us. To reject science was to embrace irrationalism, and, for Tallis, irrationalism (of the blood and soil variety, for example) presented far greater dangers to humanity than the deployment of reason. Of course, reason could be represented as nothing more than a manifestation of ideology,[62] but, Tallis argued, if we accepted this, we effectively abandoned ourselves to the capricious forces of unreason. As for the loss of humanity's significance in the cosmos, we never had any in the first place. Surely the destruction of such a fundamental illusion could not be an unmitigated loss?

A critique of science, whether as a mode of cognition or as a transforming power, was always going to be vulnerable to responses of this kind. The culture of the West (and increasingly of the entire world) was so infused with both the epistemology of science and the effects of its technology that it was actually no longer possible to speak seriously of alternatives. Even the formulation of an argument against science could end up undermining itself simply by relying on the very conventions (scientific rationalism) which it wished to challenge. Critics of science could thus be easily dismissed as self-contradictory (if not dishonest) purveyors of apocalyptic delusions. For Tallis, such critics also displayed an alarming ignorance of the needs and desires of ordinary people, preferring instead to cast themselves in the role of 'soul doctors' to a civilisation which they considered to be 'irredeemably sick'. Almost exclusively confined to the academy, these critics were represented by Tallis as 'hysterical humanists', reacting to their own sense of marginalisation by decrying modernity. From this perspective, we were left with the distasteful spectacle of comfortably employed intellectuals, pathologising the advanced industrial society which made their employment possible, and denying all hope of progress.

Yet, when the dust of the 'science wars' had settled, the uneasiness remained. It was possible to recognise the extraordinary advances in knowledge that science had given us and at the same time to regret some of the consequences of that knowledge. It was possible to appreciate the material benefits that science had delivered and at the same time to fear its power. It was possible to recoil from a scientized culture without mythologising the past. It was possible to accept there was no alternative to scientific industrialism and yet retain misgivings about its operational practices. It was possible to seek imaginative truths without rejecting the epistemology of science. And it was still possible to feel insignificant when confronted with laws of nature which turned out to be cold, impersonal and utterly devoid of human meaning.

In looking back over the gradual but relentless erosion of human significance by the progress of science, the physicist, Steven Weinberg, observed: 'We did not want it to come out this way, but it did'.[63] Behind the polemic, one senses that Raymond Tallis didn't want it come out this way either. But for Tallis, there was no point in looking for meaning in science, because that was to confuse science with religion. Science might behave as if it were a religion, but it was incapable of confronting the questions of meaning and purpose which religion addressed. Religion, however, had been comprehensively undermined by science and could no longer fulfil its old function unless we rejected the very truths which science had taught us to accept. For rationalists such as Tallis, this was, of course, impossible. But nevertheless, in Tallis's view, the spiritual impulses which lay behind the neo-Romantic critiques of science could, at least partially, still be satisfied in a secular world through the mediation of art and artists. Ironically, this is a claim with which the early Romantics would have undoubtedly concurred. Yet, as we shall see, in the postmodern world art, too, was at the centre of another narrative of decline.

Art

Tallis's claim that art could answer to at least some of the needs formerly met by religion arose from his view that, while science was confined to the 'Kingdom of Means', both religion and art inhabited the 'Kingdom of Ends'. Although people tended to live most of their lives in the former, pre-occupied as they were with the material problems of existence, there was still a powerful human need to enter the latter. The 'Kingdom of Ends' concerned itself not with the instrumental questions of 'how' (the province of the 'Kingdom of Means') but with the ultimate purposes of living. For Tallis, it represented that space where 'being', in itself, could be endowed with transcendent meaning and where the ceaseless experience of 'becoming' could be transformed into a sense of 'arrival'. Religion, of course, and the art from which it had been inseparable, had histori-cally fulfilled this function, but with the recession of religious feeling, at least in the West, art was left to take up the mantle. Art could not have the metaphysical content of religion – what Tallis called the 'transcendental cognitive', with its doctrines of both terror and comfort – but it could nevertheless generate subjective meanings of a unique intensity in an otherwise meaning-free universe. In a modern re-statement of Schillerian aesthetics,[64] Tallis argued that art possessed this power by virtue of its singular capacity to work at the most general level of ideas while at the same time rooted in the particularity of sense experience. This property, which was common to all of the arts, more than anything else accounted for that sense of connectedness, of heightened consciousness, which great art could produce in those who were receptive to it.[65]

Tallis's identification of art with the 'Kingdom of Ends', and of art's assumption of the mantle of religion, found support in the work of Roger Scruton, who argued that it was through the sacred, and the aura of meaning which surrounded the sacred, that we gained access to the 'Kingdom of Ends'. Scruton's 'Kingdom', like Tallis's, offered consoling visions of meaning in a world where meaning had been relentlessly denied by science. Art had its roots in the sacred, once the province of religion, and it was now through the mediation of art that we could apprehend the profound mysteries and ineffable meanings which religion used to supply. Scruton believed that access to this transcendental world was intimately associated with the education of feelings, particularly the feeling for beauty, and that, in a secular world, it was only through art that this education could be now acquired. The aesthetic was thus elevated to the highest spiritual position, and, Scruton maintained, through the experience of the aesthetic, our lives could be 'redeemed of their arbitrariness, their contingency and littleness'.[66]

While both Tallis and Scruton shared a vision of art as a redemptive power, their analysis of why such redemption might be necessary was very different. For Tallis, the sense of incompleteness, to which both religion and art answered, had its roots in the biological history of human consciousness itself. While he did not go so far as Dostoyevsky, who suggested that human consciousness was a 'mistake', he did argue that it had served no evolutionary purpose, could actually have been maladaptive and certainly could not be explained by orthodox Darwinian metabiology. The most plausible explanation was that human consciousness was an evolutionary accident, but which, having come into existence, was compelled by its own properties to search for a meaning for itself. From such accidents of biology arose the entire superstructure of human culture, religion and art. Tallis saw this as neither tragic nor (as Samuel Beckett did) funny. On the contrary, the free creation of meaning, through art liberated from religion, was, for Tallis, 'the dance of human consciousness celebrating existence for its own sake'.[67]

Scruton's historical perspective was rather shorter than Tallis's, but nevertheless art was left with the task of constructing meaning on equally precarious foundations. In Scruton's account, the standard distinction was drawn between high culture in the Arnoldian sense and culture, as understood by anthropologists, as a way of life. Scruton called the latter 'common culture' and, following T. S. Eliot, argued that common culture had always been the 'incarnation of religion'. It had been the particular achievement of religion, not only of Christianity but of all religions, to impart to culture the 'ethical vision of life'. For Scruton, this vision involved, above all, a deep knowledge of how to 'feel', in the light of an external standard of judgement that could not be escaped. When in possession of this vision, our smallest actions could be imbued with significance, both our own lives and the lives of those around us dignified with meaning, and our world enriched by a powerful sense of shared community.

According to Scruton, the 'ethical vision' and the common culture which sustained it were one of the chief casualties of the Enlightenment. The enlightened individual found himself cut off from a common culture, without a source of authority and, in the final analysis, utterly alone. This was the down-side, to use Kant's famous phrase, of liberating oneself from man's self-imposed minority. There was no going back, and the yearning for community, which the consolations of the sacred had been able to assuage, would not die away. This was a problem with which the modern world had still fully to come to terms – as the experiences of Communism and Nazism, both of which were inspired by quasi-religious political philosophies, served as a potent reminder. The Enlightenment had left us with a spiritual void, and one way or another it demanded to be filled.

Scruton's account of the development of modern culture is the story of how art attempted to answer to this demand. Central to his thesis was the contention that the high culture of the Enlightenment had been an attempt to rescue the 'ethical vision' which had flourished spontaneously in the old religious culture. 'When religion dies', wrote Scruton, 'and the common culture evaporates like a mist beneath the sun of reason . . . imagination acquires its modern role – the role of ennobling, spiritualising, re-presenting humanity as something higher than itself'.[68] It was after the publication of A. G. Baumgarten's *Aesthetica* in 1750, which could be seen as an early response to the decline of faith, that art, music and literature ceased to be merely recreational and began to take on this role, thus acquiring the enormous significance in intellectual life that they have retained to this day. Kant was a decisive influence, maintaining in his *Critique of Judgement* (1790) that it was through aesthetic contemplation, and particularly through the feeling for beauty which it inspired, that we received intimations of the divine. Thus, for Scruton, the work of the great Romantic artists of the late eighteenth and early nineteenth centuries – Goethe, Schiller, Wordsworth, Beethoven, Schubert and Keats – could be seen as an attempt to reconnect with the sacred, to recreate in the imagination the old culture, rooted in mystery, which the Enlightenment had destroyed. In the same vein, modernism, far from being a reaction against Romanticism, could be seen as a desperate continuation of the Romantic attempt to recover the sacred in a world from which all traces of mystery were steadily being erased. From this perspective, the transfiguration of the commonplace becomes the 'Eucharist of modern art', as modernism, 'standing vigil at the grave of the old religion . . . maintains its unearthly dignity year after year'.[69] The grave might be visited less and less, but, for Scruton, when a community had outlived its gods, the path of high culture remained the only way of learning how to live as if our lives mattered eternally. The alternatives were stark: to fake the higher emotions or to collapse, as Edmund Burke put it, into the 'dust and powder of individuality'.[70]

Many readers will find all this preposterous. Not only does Scruton's 'as if' involve a 'faking' of its own, and on a very grand scale; it also accords art the power to bestow meaning and redemption in a manner which seems quite disproportionate to the actual capabilities of art as it is experienced by most people in the contemporary world. Nevertheless, if we are going to claim that art possesses more than the capacity merely to entertain or to distract, then it will be necessary to draw on the kind of meaning-making theories of art outlined here, of which Tallis and Scruton provide just two examples.[71] So why, as both Tallis and Scruton readily concede, are such theories difficult to accept?

Scruton himself provided part of the answer with an extensive and excoriating attack on contemporary art and culture, which he believed to be in such a terminal condition that we were effectively living in a new dark age, with only the work of a few 'undaunted monks' keeping the flame of high culture alive.[72] Scruton's account was but one of many, from both left and right perspectives, which contributed to a growing literature on the theme of artistic decline and the 'dumbing down' of Western culture. In a 'dumbed-down' culture, the idea of an art which might be 'ennobling and spiritualising' was destined to be mocked.

There were two key elements to this narrative of artistic decline. On the one hand, there was a conviction that the 'modernist impulse', which lay behind the greatest artistic achievements of the twentieth century, had finally exhausted itself, culminating in the cul-de-sac of a weary and cynical postmodernism. On the other, a corrosive relativism was seen to be at work within the general culture, which denied judgements of value, degraded the conditions for the reception of art and led to a 'dumbing down' of both cultural institutions and intellectual life. It is worth looking more closely at each of these elements in turn.

Before examining the demise of artistic modernism, it is necessary first of all to try and clarify when modernism 'happened' and what it was that made a work of art 'modern'. Neither question could be easily answered. Raymond Williams, for example, argued that literary modernism could just as plausibly be said to have begun in the 1840s with Gogol, Flaubert and Dickens as in the 1900s with the conventionally modernist names of Proust, Kafka or Joyce.[73] David Harvey, in contrast, believed the first quintessentaially modern poet to have been Charles Baudelaire (1821–67).[74] For Malcolm Bradbury and James McFarlane, it was the geography that was critical, with a modernism viewed from Berlin, Vienna or St Petersburg looking very different from that viewed from the New York-London-Paris axis.[75] Nevertheless, despite these differences, the years from around 1890 to 1950 became the most widely accepted 'periodisation' of modernism, after which there was a brief hiatus before the 'post-modern' emerged, 'somewhere between 1968 and 1972'.[76]

The defining characteristics of modernism were also difficult to pin down. What could such a diverse range of artistic practices, from Cubism in painting to Serialism in music, from Expressionist drama to the Symbolist novel, possibly have in common to justify the all-embracing term of 'modernism'? Again, a consensus amongst cultural historians emerged, which suggested that the one characteristic which all the modernisms could be said to have shared was a commitment to the ceaseless experimentation with form. Modernism was thus seen by David Harvey as a ferment of 'creative destruction', by Bradbury and McFarlane as 'less a style than a search for style', and by Williams as a series of (often competitive) 'breaks in form'. It was this restless searching for the new, which mirrored the titanic forces of change that were transforming the material world, that imparted to modernism the extraordinary energy and originality that brought about an unprecedented revolution in all of the arts within the space of a few decades. As the historian, Alan Bullock, observed, this cataclysmic upheaval of culture marked a change in consciousness and sensibility that could be compared to that produced by the Renaissance, the scientific revolution of the seventeenth century, or the Romantic movement of the late eighteenth and early nineteenth century.[77] However, it could not, and did not, last.

The story of modernism's decline, which was effectively the story of the decline of the high art of our times, was told by many cultural critics, whose scale of values and political perspectives were often sharply contrasted.[78] What was striking was the degree of common ground that they shared. Three clear themes emerged. First, the driving force of modernism, the perpetual search for the new, found itself with nowhere left to go. The jarring, abrasive quality of modernism which, at its most effective, shocked us in all of the arts into experiencing the world in new ways, depended for its effect upon the existence of conventions which it consciously transgressed. But, once those conventions had receded, and the overturning of convention had itself become the new convention, modernism began to lose its point. However, there was no going back to earlier forms, unless to borrow or pillage with the ironic stance of postmodernism; and yet to go forward led only to what Scruton described as 'the cliché of the unexpected'. Marcel Duchamp's urinal (1917), which turned art into whatever the artist chose to tell us was art, had become the longest-running joke in art history. But, as Suzi Gablik pointed out, if

130

everything could become art then art became nothing; and artists could enjoy only the 'freedom of the insane'.[79]

Secondly, the oppositional quality of modernism, the standing for something other than the dominant cultural values of the day, gave way after the Second World War to what Raymond Williams described as 'a comfortable integration into the new international capitalism'.[70] Modernism was thus seen to lose its 'heroic' status, but, of course, for very different reasons: by conservatives such as Scruton, for its retreat from the high ground and descent into what he saw as 'institutionalised flippancy'; by radicals such as Williams and Harvey, for its new association with the dominant centres of power. Both sides saw the irony of the eventual transformation of what had begun as a fiercely anti-bourgeois movement (of both the left and the right) into the establishment arts and, in the case of the visual arts, a multi-million dollar art market. Modernism had lost its historic autonomy and was now as orientated towards production and profit as any other business. 'Why do people think artists are special?', Andy Warhol had asked. 'It's just another job'.[81] For Hobsbawm, the avant-garde had become 'a subdepartment of marketing',[82] while Williams noted that the great stylistic innovations of modernism now formed the working language of advertising. Art and commerce had become indistinguishable.[83]

Thirdly, it followed from this that high art was no longer capable of providing that profound sense of meaning which Tallis, Scruton, Gablik and others demanded of it, let alone the experience of redemption which had formerly been supplied by religion. Such a role required a high seriousness which was quite at odds with the dominant mood of the art of the postmodern world, an art which many saw as celebrating trivia and capitulating to the logic of consumption. For Hilton Kramer, postmodernism was 'a creation of modernism at the end of its tether', a set of practices shut off from any sense of a higher reality, unable to move beyond the ultimately sterile world of the ironic and the facetious.[84] For Suzi Gablik, the arts had lost all connection with the transcendental realm and, indeed, so ingrained had the cynicism of postmodernity become that it appeared naïve to suggest that such a realm might even exist. In Gablik's view, the arts had suffered a complete loss of moral authority, and there were now very few people who even had any idea of what they were for.[85] As for meaning, it was more accurate to suggest that advertising, rather than art, had succeeded religion as the dominant meaning-making system in the modern world.[86]

The 'internal' decline of modern art was, as mentioned earlier, only one part of a broader narrative of artistic decline, which included within it an account of a widespread relativism within the general culture that had had the effect of reducing art to little more than just another component of the leisure industry. This relativism had been nurtured in two main ways. First, those responsible for what Scruton described as 'keeping the flame of high culture alive', that is, the directors of cultural institutions, university teachers, broadcasters and so on, began to question whether the status of the arts they were promoting was derived exclusively from their intrinsic properties, or whether in fact some other, non-artistic considerations might be at work. What if those arts owed their status not to some universally understood scale of values but instead to the operation of a highly selective tradition, inflected by the unquestioned assumptions of class, race or gender? If this were the case, the upholders of the tradition, whilst no doubt acting from the best of motives, would turn out to have been promoting a highly ideological view of what constituted high culture. Raymond Williams referred to this as the 'Fabian tone in culture', that is, the practice of 'leading the enlightened to the particular kind of light which the leaders find satisfactory for themselves'.[87] Once this possibility had been admitted, anyone attempting to make judgements about which works of art did or did not represent the highest pinnacles of cultural achievement found themselves on very unstable ground. This sense of instability was, of course, not confined to the arts, and was only one reflection of a much broader position of radical uncertainty which had been promoted by various forms of postmodern theory. Whilst such theory, in challenging the universalist claims of the Enlightenment, had undoubtedly helped to open up spaces for previously marginalised or silenced voices, the relativism which it introduced had a logic of its own which had far-reaching implications. If all valuations of art (or of anything else for that matter) were in the final analysis determined by ideology, then a disinterested judgement was impossible to make. As Richard Hoggart found out, relativism worked like dry rot: when you tried to stand on a floor board, it gave way under you.[88]

Secondly, a climate of cultural relativism both reinforced and was reinforced by the growing power of the cultural industries. What David Harvey described as an ' "anything goes" market eclecticism'[89] was perfectly suited to the economic logic of the increasingly globalised industries of film, broadcasting, recording and publishing. Writing in 1936, Walter Benjamin had been the first to understand the implications of this for the 'work of art', when he predicted that art would lose its 'aura' and that its nature would be irrevocably changed once sounds and images could be brought into people's houses like gas, water and electricity.[90] From the perspective of the 1990s, Eric Hobsbawm paid tribute to Benjamin's foresight, illustrating just how enormous this change had turned out to be. Not only had we witnessed the universal triumph of the society of mass entertainment, where distinctions between what was good and what was bad were cast more and more in terms of market appeal, but also the 'work of art' itself had disappeared in the process. 'The novelty', Hobsbawm wrote,

> was that technology had drenched everyday life in private as well as public with art. Never had it been harder to avoid aesthetic experience. The 'work of art' was lost in the flow of words, of sounds, of images, in the universal environment of what once would have been called art.[91]

Although Hobsbawm could not under any circumstances be described as a 'postmodernist', here his vision of an almost total aestheticisation of reality came close to that of one of the most renowned of postmodern theorists, Jean Baudrillard. Baudrillard, who was best understood as dealing in imaginative rather than literal truths, argued, like Hobsbawm, that art was everywhere, since artifice had penetrated the heart of reality. But, he went on, art was dead, not because its critical transcendence had gone, but because there was nothing left for it to transcend. The world had become so saturated with reproductions of itself, that reality had become confused with its own image; it had become its own simulation.[92]

Why should this rise in relativism be seen as a manifestation of decline? Surely the collapse of old forms of cultural authority should be celebrated as a liberation from repressive forms of cultural domination? Was this not a proposition on which both the radical left and populist conservatives might agree? Indeed it was, and it was precisely this 'unholy alliance' which so dismayed those who stood outside the new consensus, believing the field had now been cleared for the total ascendancy of a commercial culture which embodied forms of domination more insidious and pervasive than those which it had replaced. According to Alain Finkielkraut, for example, the collapse of belief in the superiority of Western culture, which had been a necessary and inevitable consequence of the anti-colonial struggle, had led to a relativising of values within Western culture. The idea of 'cultivation', with its connotation of self-improvement, had been one of the chief casualties. It was replaced by an anthropological notion of 'the cultural', in which distinctions of value were dissolved and everyday activities, however banal, elevated to the status of 'culture'. With the same logic, what had once been perceived as the greatest achievements of art turned out to be just another manifestation of 'the cultural'. This, of course, played straight into the hands of the advertising industry, whose ceaseless hyperbole attempted, in the interest of sales, to bestow the status of 'culture' on even the most banal and mediocre of products.[93] In Richard Hoggart's view, this was turning the landscape of art into 'a flat and featureless plain', while the devaluation of language, brought about by the ubiquitous influence of marketing, made it more and more difficult to find the words with which to make critical distinctions.[94] George Steiner might have believed that the coming in our culture of another Michelangelo, Shakespeare or Mozart was unlikely;[95] the question for Finkielkraut and Hoggart was whether or not anyone would notice.

For Finkielkraut, the distinction between culture and entertainment had been completely blotted out, with the result that we now inhabited a kind of cultural Disneyland, where adolescence had become the universal condition. In this final triumph of 'babydom', we found ourselves living through the first period of European history when 'non-thought' had been elevated to the same status as thought itself.[96] This notion of cultural regression, fuelled by the demand for the instant gratification of desire, was echoed by Scruton, who believed that youth culture ('Yoofanasia') was now the official culture of Britain, where 'adverts stand in for aesthetic objects; fantasy for imagination and kitsch for feeling'.[97] For Hoggart, the relentless trivialisation of culture, which had been the chief consequence of the rise of relativism, was far worse than 'paternalism', in that it reflected a barely concealed contempt on the part of cultural producers towards the people whose interests they claimed to serve. It was only people in the mass media, the press baron Cecil King had once said, who had any idea 'quite how indifferent, quite how stupid, quite how uninterested . . . the great bulk of the British public are'.[98] In Hoggart's view, this was the mindset which characterised many of those in the cultural industries, a near-hatred of the audience, wrapped up in a consumer flattery which celebrated ignorance with a kind of 'stay-as-sweet-as-you-are' philosophy that was in reality deeply patronising.[99] The complicity of many intellectuals in these processes, which they not only failed to resist but actually legitimised

in the name of emancipatory cultural politics, was seen by Finkielkraut as a new *trahison des clercs*.[100] Angela McRobbie, one of the
leading figures in Cultural Studies, the discipline that had done most
to legitimise popular culture as a serious focus of academic study,
came close to endorsing this view when she pointed out that the
unpopular questions of relative value were 'simply no longer
asked'.[101]

Narratives of artistic decline, and of the deleterious effects on art of
tendencies within the general culture, were not, of course, unique to
the era of postmodernity. In the English context, for example,
Wordsworth had complained in the 1800s that unprecedented social
forces 'were acting . . . to blunt the discriminating powers of the
mind and . . . to reduce it to a state of almost savage torpor'.[102] The
great works of literature, he went on to say, 'were being driven into
neglect by frantic novels, sickly and stupid German Tragedies, and
deluges of idle and extravagant stories in verse'. In the 1860s,
Matthew Arnold had objected to a publishing industry which conceptualised the working class as 'the masses' and then 'reached down'
to it with a specially prepared and adapted 'intellectual food'.[103] This
was the industry which, thirty years later, became the subject of
George Gissing's novel *New Grub Street*, where literature had become
a trade and whose most successful practitioners 'thought first and
foremost of the markets';[104] it was an industry which trampled on the
sensitive and which, in Oscar Wilde's words, 'justified its own existence by the great Darwinian principle of the survival of the
vulgarest'.[105] As publishing was augmented in the 1920s and 1930s
by the new industries of film, broadcasting and recording, the
critique of mass culture took on a much darker tone, most notably
in the work of the German sociologists, Adorno and Horkheimer.
Their experiences of the media, first in Nazi Germany and then, after
they had been forced to leave Germany, in the United States,
combined with their fatalistic vision of capitalism to produce a
depiction of the culture industry as a predatory, inescapable and
deeply repressive force. In their account, the ubiquitous products of
the culture industry colonised the deepest structures of the mind,
promoting a cultural conformity which eroded human potential and
cast people in a servitude of which they were only dimly aware. For
Adorno, this kind of servitude could be compared to that of the
prisoner who loved his cell because he had been left 'nothing else to
love'. The only antidote was the negating power of aesthetic modernism, which denied the 'false universality' of the culture industry

with an emphatic assertion of its own autonomy. But the price of this denial was an exclusivity, which left high art and mass culture forever separated, the torn halves of an integral freedom which could never add up. In this division, the truth was at least expressed.[106] This kind of pessimism could also be found amongst cultural conservatives, such as T. S. Eliot, who wrote in 1948:

> We can assert with some confidence that our own period is one of decline; that the standards of culture are lower than they were fifty years ago; and that the evidences of this decline are visible in every department of human activity. I see no reason why the decay of culture should not proceed much further, and why we may not even anticipate a period, of some duration, of which it is possible to say that it will have *no* culture.[107]

Eliot also deplored the advance of mass culture, but not, as in Adorno and Horkheimer, because it affirmed and consolidated repressive forms of social control; but, on the contrary, because it formed part of the levelling process that destroyed the traditions and distinctions on which, in his view, a healthy and variegated culture depended. As we have seen, the decline of art could become a rallying cry for those with diametrically opposed world-views.

The fact that narratives of artistic decline could be found in virtually every historical period suggested to some critics that the narratives of their own era reflected nothing more than a conservative nostalgia and an inability to come to terms with change. In short, they were just the latest manifestation of those 'ageless mythologies of historical decline' that were discussed in Chapter 2. Moreover, from this perspective, the relentlessly negative view of both contemporary art and commercial culture reflected a crude and 'totalising' form of theory, which, by failing to make qualitative distinctions, expressed precisely the relativism that it purported to attack. The entire world of the contemporary arts could not just be written off as aesthetically and intellectually bankrupt any more than the total output of the film and broadcasting industries could be dismissed as banal. Furthermore, what such theories failed to acknowledge were the complex ways in which cultural artefacts of all kinds were received and experienced. The 'hypodermic' model of cultural consumption, through which cultural junk somehow bypassed all resistances and injected itself straight into the centre of consciousness, was replaced by a more subtle model in which the cultural consumer, far from being a passive recipient of predetermined meanings, constructed his or her own meanings in creative and unpredictable ways. The culture industry, therefore, was not only cleared of exercising ideological hegemony, but was seen to represent new forms of cultural democracy.[108] In contrast, the old idea of a superior high culture, distanced from both the market place and popular consumption, was, despite Adorno, seen as a historical relic, intimately associated with outdated forms of power, privilege and patronage.[109]

None of this was going to be of much comfort to those who were still looking for art to provide the transcendent meanings which science had destroyed. It made no difference whether one saw popular culture as replete with possibilities for self-enrichment; whether one saw only a sea of dross, which occasionally threw up the exceptional; or whether one saw an Adornoesque world of deception and exploitation; from all of these perspectives, the work of art, as a source of those profound and sacramental experiences that stood in for the religious, had disappeared from view. In this respect, it was logical to conclude that, just as our 'scientized culture' had destroyed religion, it had gone on to remove the mystery from art. In other words, the absence of meaning which lay at the heart of the scientific project could no more be remedied by art than it could be by science: the 'consoling vision' had gone for good. This was a source of profound pessimism to those who both felt the need for this vision and who believed it to have a fundamental human importance; and it was a pessimism that was intensified by the realisation that few people shared it. As Tallis had observed, 'few seem haunted by an insufficiency of meaning'.[110] We were thus left with the memory of Scruton's 'undaunted monks', the reincarnation of Matthew Arnold's 'aliens', desperately trying to keep alive a flame that was destined to be extinguished from a world which simply did not care. Did it matter? Not if an 'insufficiency of meaning' could be accommodated indefinitely. But if it couldn't, then it seemed logical to expect that something else would have to emerge to provide meaning in a scientized culture that was becoming progressively global. The growth of virulent new forms of identity politics could, at least partly, be understood as one such answer. The conditions for this had been exacerbated, as we shall see in the next chapter, by the emergence in the postmodern world of an uncontrollable and more aggressive phase of global capitalism.

Notes

1. Roszak, *Where the Wasteland Ends: Politics and Transcendence in Postindustrial Society*, p. 31.
2. Appleyard, *Understanding the Present*, p. 4.
3. Fukuyama, *The End of History and the Last Man*, pp. 71–81.
4. Sinsheimer, 'The presumptions of science'.
5. See Davies, *Are We Alone?*, pp. 59–90.
6. Steiner, *A Festival Overture*. In relation to Steiner's point, it is worth noting that the nature of the scientific mind has become a popular theme amongst contemporary novelists. See, for example, Martin Amis's *Night Train* and Ian McEwan's *Enduring Love*.
7. Isaiah Berlin, *The Crooked Timber of Humanity*, p. 1.
8. For a comprehensive discussion of counter-Enlightenment traditions, see Berlin's collection of essays in *Against the Current* and *The Crooked Timber of Humanity* .
9. Ravetz, *Scientific Knowledge and Its Problems*, pp. 31–68 and p. 409.
10. Shils, 'Faith, utility, and the legitimacy of science'.
11. Etzioni and Nunn, 'The public appreciation of science in contemporary America'.
12. Dollery, *The End of an Age of Optimism*, p. 2, and Garrett, *The Coming Plague* pp. 30–3.
13. Woolger, *Science*.
14. Lyotard, *The Postmodern Condition*.
15. Harré, 'Narrative in scientific discourse'.
16. Jacob, 'Hubris about 'science', p. 64. In Jacob's account, Thomas Kuhn's influential *Structure of Scientific Revolutions* (1962), which casts doubt on the claims of science to objective truth, is a symptom not a cause of the collapse of what she calls 'hubristic science'.
17. Jacob, *The Politics of Western Science*, p. 5.
18. Roszak, *The Making of a Counter Culture; Where the Wasteland Ends;* and 'The monster and the titan'.
19. Roszak, *Where the Wasteland Ends*, p. xxviii.
20. Ibid. p. 168.
21. Ibid. pp. 257–8.
22. Ibid. pp. 236–7.
23. Ibid. p. xxxi.
24. Ibid. p. 64.
25. Ibid. p. 196.
26. Appleyard, *Understanding the Present*. Jacob appeared unaware of both Roszak's and Appleyard's work, declaring that 'the loss of faith [in science] has yet to receive any systematic study by historians', 'Hubris about science', p 64.
27. Appleyard, *Understanding the Present*, p. 9.

28. Davies, *Are We Alone?*, p. 85.
29. Capra, *The Tao of Physics*. See also Zohar and Marshall, *The Quantum Society*.
30. Dawkins, *River out of Eden*, p. 17.
31. Appleyard, *Understanding the Present*, p. 16.
32. Roszak, *Where the Wasteland Ends*, p. 458.
33. Appleyard, *Understanding the Present*, pp. 108 and 232.
34. Blake, 'Letter to Thomas Butts', p. 818.
35. Carlyle, 'Signs of the times', pp. 61–85.
36. Shelley, 'A defence of poetry', p. 293.
37. Wordsworth, 'Preface to the Lyrical Ballads', pp. 734–43.
38. Whitehead, *Science and the Modern World*, p. 138.
39. Tallis, *Newton's Sleep*, pp. 11–28.
40. L. Marx, 'Reflections on the neo-romantic critique of science', p. 61.
41. Appleyard, *Understanding the Present*, p. 4.
42. Hobsbawm, *Age of Extremes*, p. 528.
43. McKie, 'Antimatter set to blast scientists to other side of the cosmos'.
44. Hobsbawm, *Age of Extremes*, p. 538.
45. Roszak, *Where the Wasteland Ends*, p. 53.
46. Jacob, 'Hubris about science', pp. 64–5.
47. Rousseau, 'A discourse on the moral effects of the arts and sciences', p. 13.
48. Sinsheimer, 'The Presumptions of Science', pp. 34–5.
49. Leslie, *The End of the World*, pp. 90–122.
50. Drexler, *Unbounding the Future*.
51. Quoted in Leslie, *The End of the World*, p. 104.
52. Leslie, *The End of the World*, pp. 103–6.
53. Ibid. p. 110.
54. Jacob, 'Hubris about science', pp. 66–7.
55. Hobsbawm, *Age of Extremes*, p. 547.
56. Relman, 'What market values are doing to medicine'.
57. Berlan and Lewontin, 'It's business as usual'.
58. See Woolger, *Science*, for an illuminating account of the sociology of science, the sociology of scientific knowledge and (his own particular perspective) the social study of science.
59. Gross and Levitt, *Higher Superstition*.
60. Tallis, *Newton's Sleep* and *Enemies of Hope*.
61. Tallis, *Newton's Sleep*, p. 43.
62. See, for example, Aronowitz, *Science as Power*, and Harding, *The Science Question in Feminism*.
63. Weinberg, 'Reflections of a Working Scientist', p. 43.
64. See Schiller, *On the Aesthetic Education of Man*.
65. Tallis, *Newton's Sleep*, pp. 111–208.
66. Scruton, *An Intelligent Person's Guide to Modern Culture*, pp. 28–43.

67. Tallis, *Newton's Sleep*, p. 125.
68. Scruton, *An Intelligent Person's Guide to Modern Culture*, p. 57.
69. Ibid. p. 77.
70. Ibid. p. 14
71. See also Gablik, *Has Modernism Failed?*
72. Scruton, *An Intelligent Person's Guide to Modern Culture*, p. 136.
73. Williams, *The Politics of Modernism*, p. 32.
74. Harvey, *The Condition of Postmodernity*, pp. 10–38.
75. Bradbury and McFarlane, 'The name and nature of modernism', p. 36.
76. Harvey, *The Condition of Postmodernity*, p. 38.
77. Bullock, 'The double image', p. 68.
78. For this account, I have drawn mainly on the following: Finkielkraut, *The Undoing of Thought*; Gablik, *Has Modernism Failed?*; Hobsbawm, *Behind the Times*; Kramer, *The Revenge of the Philistines*; Scruton, *An Intelligent Person's Guide to Modern Culture*; Washburn and Thornton, *Dumbing Down*; Williams, *The Politics of Modernism*.
79. Gablik, *Has Modernism Failed?*, p. 31.
80. Williams, *The Politics of Modernism*, p. 35.
81. Quoted in Gablik, *Has Modernism Failed?*, p. 61.
82. Hobsbawm, *Behind the Times*, p. 7.
83. Williams, *The Politics of Modernism*, p. 62.
84. Kramer, *The Revenge of the Philistines*, pp. 4–8.
85. Gablik, *Has Modernism Failed?*, pp. 73–87.
86. Twitchell, ' "But first, a word from our sponsor" ', p. 201.
87. Williams, *Culture and Society*, p. 234.
88. Hoggart, *The Way We Live Now*, p. 305.
89. Harvey, *The Condition of Postmodernity*, p. 42.
90. Benjamin, 'The work of art in the age of mechanical reproduction', pp. 221–4.
91. Hobsbawm, *Age of Extremes*, pp. 513–21 (520).
92. Baudrillard, *Simulations*, p. 146.
93. Finkielkraut, *The Undoing of Thought*, pp. 111–18.
94. Hoggart, *The Way We Live Now*, pp. 72 and 139.
95. Steiner, *A Festival Overture*, p. 13.
96. Finkielkraut, *The Undoing of Thought*, pp. 111–30.
97. Scruton, *An Intelligent Person's Guide to Modern Culture*, p. 104.
98. Quoted in Shaw, Elitism versus Populism in the Arts, pp. 7–8.
99. Hoggart, *The Way We Live Now*, p. 335.
100. Finkielkraut, *The Undoing of Thought*, p. 120.
101. Quoted in Hoggart, *The Way We Live Now*, p. 172.
102. Wordsworth, 'Preface to the Lyrical Ballads', p. 735. See also Wordsworth, 'Essay, supplementary to the Preface', p. 751.
103. Arnold, *Culture and Anarchy*, pp. 69–70.

104. Gissing, *New Grub Street*, pp. 38–9.
105. Wilde, 'The critic as artist', p. 1015.
106. See Adorno and Horkheimer, *Dialectic of Enlightenment*, and Adorno, *The Culture Industry*.
107. Eliot, *Notes towards the Definition of Culture*, p. 19.
108. See Ang, *Desperately Seeking the Audience*; Fiske, *Television Culture*; and Seiter, *Remote Control*.
109. See Lewis, *Art, Culture and Enterprise*.
110. Tallis, *Newton's Sleep*, p. 201.

4

Political Decline: The 'New' Capitalism

> What I predict is the imminent disintegration of the global capitalist
> system
>> (George Soros, *The Crisis of Capitalism: Open Society Endangered*)

Introduction

N ARRATIVES OF POLITICAL AND economic decline have arisen
from a distinctive new phase of capitalism, which emerged in
the United States in the 1970s and subsequently spread to other parts
of the advanced industrialised world. This phase was characterised by
the transition from 'Fordism' to more aggressive forms of capital
accumulation and by the emergence of a new kind of global economy. Seen by some observers as the defining 'moment' of postmodernity, it involved organisational, economic and political changes
that were unprecedented in the history of capitalism.

In these narratives, the 'new' capitalism, whilst arguably the most
productive system ever devised, was at the same time producing
intolerable social, psychological and environmental impacts. Moreover, one of its distinguishing features was its capacity not only to
evade political control but also to give rise to a political consensus
which saw its further advance as both essential and inevitable. Whilst
resistance was offered by some states, notably those in Europe and
Asia with highly developed social market economies, this resistance
was increasingly difficult to maintain in the face of the competitive
pressures which the 'new' capitalism had generated. In the absence
of any effective framework for international regulation, and with little

prospect of this being introduced, social and environmental instability was expected to intensify. Capitalism in its latest manifestation could not remain a viable way of organising social and economic relations. However, this would not become widely accepted until after a period of prolonged and intense crisis.

These quasi-apocalyptic intimations recalled Marx, in whose intellectual legacy had appeared a sharp dichotomy. On the one hand, his account of the dynamic yet self-destructive powers of capitalism had acquired an extraordinary new resonance; on the other, his utopian visions of a post-capitalist world could hardly have seemed more remote or more incredible. The dichotomy in this legacy to some extent explained the de-coupling of critiques of capitalism from any idea of what might conceivably succeed it. We were offered a vision of capitalism moving stubbornly towards its own collapse; but a post-capitalist world could not even be imagined.

Exporting the end of history

Within just a few years of the collapse of Communism in the former Soviet Union and its satellite states, the American historian Francis Fukuyama was declaring that the end of history was in sight.[1] This rather startling claim was based on the view that the world was finally coming to understand that there was no better way of managing its affairs than through the institution of liberal, capitalist democracy. The terrible experiences of Nazism and Communism had eroded all belief in a directional history, but, in the closing years of the twentieth century, Fukuyama thought it was possible to see that history did, after all, have a direction and that it was once again moving towards its democratic destination. Capitalism could, of course, exist without democracy, and indeed could produce faster growth without it, as the many examples of the market economy combined with the authoritarian state had shown;[2] but, in the fullness of time, liberal democracy would prevail, because it was only this which could provide a satisfactory balance between the human desire for security and material comforts on the one hand and for the recognition of one's individual freedom and dignity (*thymos*) on the other. For Fukuyama, these were the twin pillars of a universal historical process, the evidence for which could be found in the steady if interrupted growth in the number of liberal democratic states from three in 1790 to sixty-one in 1990. The lessons of the years 1970 to 1990 had been critical, demonstrating that authoritarian regimes, whether of the Right as in Greece and Spain, or of the Left as in the Soviet Union and eastern Europe, would eventually and inevitably be undermined by their own illegitimacy. Furthermore, as liberal democracies in the modern world were extremely reluctant to go to war with one another, life at the end of history would be generally peaceful and secure, even if a little boring. The fashion for cultural and political relativism, which paradoxically had acquired the status of a universal truth in the postmodern world, would seem increasingly out of date, as more and more of the world's governmental systems converged on the liberal democratic model. Indeed, as this process gathered pace, the very idea of relativism would cease to have any meaning. With a quintessentially American conceit, Fukuyama concluded his thesis by likening the development of mankind not to the flowering of a thousand different shoots but to a long wagon train heading for the same town. Some of the wagons would get there quickly; some would veer off in the wrong direction; others would be strung out across the desert. But in the end, the vast majority would complete the journey, even if there were some casualties along the way.

Fukuyama's quasi-utopian vision was, as one might have expected, fiercely contested. As we saw in Chapter 2, the collapse of Communism, far from being seen as one more milestone on the evolutionary path to democracy and a conflict-free world, was instead seen by many historians as the prelude to a new world of instability and incipient anarchy, from which no state was immune. According to John Gray, Professor of European Thought at the London School of Economics, Fukuyama could only have reached his idiosyncratic conclusions by over-estimating the importance of ideology as a source of political and military conflict, thus grossly inflating the long-term historical implications of Communism's collapse.[3] His mistake had been to see an almost timeless and universal relationship between ideological rivalry and war, rather than to see this relationship as the product of a particular historical and cultural context. Political ideologies had, it was true, been a major cause of conflict in the twentieth century and, arguably, since the French Revolution. But to postulate the end of history and the resolution of all major struggles on the basis of the disintegration of Communism was to make an extraordinary generalisation from a very brief historical period. It ignored the fact that throughout human history wars had been fought for other than ideological reasons – for territory, for resources, for religious or ethnic reasons; and it ignored the fact that such wars had continued to break out, even during those periods when the world's major conflicts were ideologically driven. Above all, Gray argued, in claiming that the defeat of Communism represented 'the triumph of the Western idea', Fukuyama had failed to recognise that Communism and democracy had both sprung from the European Enlightenment; in short, the conflict between the two was not a clash between the West and the rest but 'a family quarrel among Western ideologies'.

Fukuyama's anticipation of a universal civilisation, modelled on the Western conjunction of capitalism and liberal democracy, was provocative and, to say the least, premature. Gray, who believed that Fukuyama had made the basic error of conflating modernisation with Westernisation, noted that the claims which Fukuyama had advanced had been generally treated in Europe and Asia with 'incredulous contempt'. Nevertheless, Fukuyama had been right to suggest that there were universalising tendencies at work, even though in his analysis of these tendencies he had appeared to misjudge the relative importance of capitalism and democracy. For a number of other historians, there were indeed universalising processes at work, but the driving force was not democracy but more ruthless forms of capital accumulation. Whether represented as 'turbo-capitalism' (Edward Luttwak), 'market fundamentalism' (George Soros), 'casino-capitalism' (Richard Longworth), the 'cancer stage of capitalism' (John McMurtry), or simply as 'McWorld' (Benjamin Barber), they all referred to broadly the same thing: the emergence of a distinctive new phase of global capitalism which was penetrating every corner of the world. But while Fukuyama had celebrated the dynamic and wealth-producing powers of this new global economy, and saw no conflict with the worldwide democratic revolution which he believed to be unfolding at the same time, others saw the unleashing of dangerously destabilising forces, which wrecked the lives of large numbers of people and actually threatened rather than promoted the conditions for democratic government. Furthermore, the new capitalism was not 'universal' in the sense that it had arisen spontaneously throughout the world, but was a product of the United States which was being vigorously exported to all who could be persuaded or compelled to adopt it. By the end of the 1990s, only Britain, Mexico and New Zealand could be said to have fully done so, but, according to Edward Luttwak, it was 'advancing on every continent'. In John Gray's view, the political and economic leadership of the United States was engaged 'in a revolutionary make-over of the world economy' and consumed by a 'messianic fantasy'.[4] Both Luttwak and

Gray suggested that this project had much in common with the Soviet version of Communism: it offered a single economic model to every country in the world, regardless of society and culture; it attempted to mould human consciousness to the demands of a social and economic system; and allegiance to it was called for on the grounds of historical inevitability. According to the international investment manager, George Soros, 'market fundamentalism' was 'a greater threat to open society than any totalitarian ideology'.[5] In all of these accounts, the emergence of this new phase of capitalism was represented as a narrative of political decline.

The 'new' capitalism: operational practices

The degree to which turbo-capitalism, market fundamentalism (or whatever epithet we choose to use) *was* actually establishing itself as the dominant economic system in the world will be discussed later in this chapter; but, first, it is necessary to consider how the 'new' capitalism differed from the 'old', what its operational practices were and what kind of social impacts it produced. One of the most lucid accounts of the transition to the 'new' capitalism could be found in David Harvey's *Condition of Postmodernity*.[6] Harvey, along with Soros, Luttwak, and Hobsbawm, saw the early 1970s, and 1973 in particular, as the decisive period, when the West experienced a sharp recession, which was compounded by the decision of the oil-producing companies to band together as the Organization of Petroleum Exporting Countries (OPEC) and to raise oil prices by over 500 per cent. At the same time, the Bretton Woods agreement, which had been devised in 1944 by the United States and its allies to help stabilise the world economy through a framework of fixed exchange rates, finally collapsed, ushering in the era of floating currencies. Thus began the move from the highly controlled forms of capitalism that had been put in place at the end of the Second World War towards the more anarchic versions which came to be associated with the new global economy. In Harvey's view, this transition could be seen as a shift from Fordist-Keynesian practices to what might be called 'a regime of flexible accumulation'.[7] From this perspective, the long post-war boom, which had lasted from 1945 to 1973, was seen to have depended upon a stable, although at times uneasy, balance of power between organised labour, large corporate capital and the nation state. Labour had had to rein in its radicalism and take on new responsibilities in terms of production and performance; corporate capital had to take a long-term view in its search for profit; and the state had to follow Keynesian models of economic and institutional intervention. This tripartite compromise was reproduced in the United States, Europe and Japan, and, although the precise conditions varied from country to country, it resulted in unparalleled levels of industrial growth and the wholescale reconstruction of economies which had been devastated during World War II. Mass production was matched by mass consumption – a key 'Fordist' idea – producing rising living standards for the majority of the population and a relatively stable environment for corporate profits. There were losers in all this, of course, and the protectionist activities of some unions provoked resentment amongst those they excluded – often minorities, women and the underprivileged. But most governments were also creating strong welfare states, which did at least provide basic levels of support through social security, health care and housing.[8] Hobsbawm called this period the 'Golden Age', an age which went some way to achieving 'the most dramatic, rapid and profound revolution in human affairs of which history has record'.[9]

What happened after 1973? In Harvey's account, the capitalist world, after the phenomenal twenty-year boom which the Fordist-Keynesian regime had produced, found itself stuck in the rut of 'stagflation', that is, stagnant output of goods combined with high inflation of prices. This, of course, had not happened suddenly, but had been building up in the preceding years as a result of what Harvey called 'rigidities' in the system. There were the rigidities of long-term and large-scale fixed capital investments, which did not allow for much flexibility of design and which assumed stable and unchanging consumer markets; there were rigidities in employment practices, which any attempts to modify could provoke strikes and other forms of labour disruption; and there were rigidities in expanding state commitments to welfare programmes, which were not matched by levels of economic growth that could finance increasing state expenditures. All of the OECD countries showed significantly lower rates of economic growth after 1973. Fenced in by all these constraints, states could only resort to printing more and more money in order to keep their economies stable. The price paid was massive inflation. What had begun as a productive alliance of big capital, big labour and big government turned into what Harvey characterised as 'a dysfunctional embrace of such narrowly defined vested interests as to undermine rather than secure capital accumulation'.[10] Under the combined pressures of a major recession, the first since the end of World War II, the staggering rise in oil prices and soaring inflation, the Fordist-Keynesian compromise finally fell apart, leading to economic restructuring, political readjustment and radical new approaches to capital accumulation.

This 'regime of flexible accumulation', as Harvey described it, contained in embryonic form most of the key features which subsequently appeared in Luttwak's 'turbo-capitalism', Soros's 'market fundamentalism', Barber's 'McWorld' and many of the other attempts to capture the nature and dynamics of the new global economy. What all these accounts illustrated was how the 'rigidities' of the 'Fordist-Keynesian' regime – from labour markets to production processes, from welfare payments to consumption patterns – were systematically broken down. Thus, the roll-back of trade union power became a key objective of corporate policy, in order that more flexibility could be introduced into labour practices, and higher rates of productivity and growth achieved. This was accompanied by a sharp reduction in 'regular' employment, and a far greater reliance on the use of temporary, part-time and sub-contracted employees. Harvey noted, for example, that between 1981 and 1985 'flexible workers' in Britain increased by 16 per cent to 8.1m while permanent jobs decreased by 6 per cent to 15.6m. Over roughly the same period, nearly one-third of the 10m new jobs created in the USA were thought to be in the 'temporary' category.[11] Longworth pointed out that, until the 1980s, American 'temps' were virtually unknown beyond the level of receptionists or secretaries, whom they were called in to support at busy periods or to replace during vacations; but by the 1990s, in those same offices, anyone below the level of Chief Executive Officer could be a 'temp'.[12] These workers, of course, enjoyed little security and did not have the same kind of pension rights, promotion prospects and fringe benefits enjoyed by those in regular employment. But from a company point of view, 'flexible' workers who could be taken on and laid off at short notice, depending on market conditions, were less expensive to maintain than a large core staff and could be crucial in giving a company its competitive edge. Sweeping reductions in the workforce produced high levels of 'structural' unemployment, thus ensuring that there was always a pool of available labour and that wage claims remained depressed. Under these conditions, and with a labour force increasingly dispersed through sub-contracting and out-sourcing, trades unions had little chance of deploying the traditional forms of working class organisation or of regaining the influence they had had in the

'Fordist' years. Indeed, Harvey noted the revival of older forms of labour organisation, such as sweatshops and extended families, which were once banished to the fringes but were now taking on a more central role in the production system.

'Flexible' labour systems were needed in order to develop 'flexible' production processes. Under 'Fordism', production had been geared towards the steady supply of a relatively limited range of standardised products. Neither the choice nor the flow of goods and services could be rapidly adapted to the changing rhythms of the market. In Harvey's view, it was only going to be a matter of time before capitalism experienced one of its periodic crises of overaccumulation and the limitations of inflexible 'Fordist' production were exposed. The early 1970s turned out to be one of those periods, when, in conditions of overproduction, excess capital found itself standing side by side with excess labour and 'no apparent way to bring these . . . resources together to accomplish socially useful tasks'.[13] The way out of this impasse was to break up the rigidities of the 'Fordist' production system, and to replace it with mechanisms that were much more finely tuned to increasingly competitive and unpredictable market conditions. Thus began the move away from standardised products for a mass market to a proliferating array of diverse products, designed to meet or create a multitude of smaller scale market niches. 'Fordist' production systems, with their long set-up times, large inventories and economies of scale, were too unwieldy to cope with the new conditions. In their place came more agile forms of organisation, characterised by small batch production, smaller inventories, just-in-time delivery systems, greater use of automation and higher turn-over times. For an accelerated pace of production to be effective – to resolve rather than exacerbate problems of oversupply – it had, of course, to be matched by an even greater acceleration in the pace of consumption. Planned obsolescence was intensified. This was achieved either by inbuilt product deterioration or, more often, by highly effective marketing strategies which mobilised the power of fashion to promote an endless cycle of dissatisfaction and desire for the new. Harvey reckoned that the need to speed up consumption at least partially explained the phenomenal growth in supply of cultural products and events, many of which, such as films and sporting events, had an almost instantaneous turnover time; and it also explained why attempts were made to endow even the most mundane of products with the status of fashion or 'culture'.[14]

These transformations of labour practices and production processes, involving confrontation with union power, falling wages and radical changes to the working conditions of millions of people, could not have been achieved without the active engagement of government. However, what began as an economic necessity in the crisis of the early 1970s had, in Britain and the United States, mutated into a political mission by the beginning of the 1980s. The irony was that all the power of the state was being deployed to remove the state as far as possible from anything that might interfere with the free play of market forces. Public ownership, central planning, administrative direction, regulatory control – one after another, these key planks of the 'Fordist-Keynesian' regime were undermined, scaled down, or removed altogether. Industries which could no longer compete in the market place, but which had been kept alive through government subsidies, were either forced to close or drastically reduce themselves in size. Increases in efficiency, made possible by rapid advances in computer technology and automation, together with the changes in employment practices outlined above, could produce economic growth, but only by slashing labour costs. For example, up until the early 1980s, automobile assembly plants required an average of 70 hours of labour to assemble a car; by the late 1990s, this had been more than halved to roughly 35 hours, with an expected further reduction to only 15 hours. In the heavy engineering sector, labour saving had been even greater, so that over the same period the time required to produce a diesel-electric locomotive, for example, had declined from 12,000 labour hours to only 4000.[15] All these changes had brought about a fundamental shift in the structure of employment in the advanced capitalist countries, with a huge growth in service employment, as the numbers of people needed in agriculture and manufacturing industry declined (see Table 4.1). But there was a limit to how much surplus labour the service industries could soak up, as they too were facing competitive pressures of their own and shedding labour as technology advanced. For example, the US long-distance phone company AT&T handled more phone calls in the late 1990s than it did in 1984, yet because of automated systems, it employed only 12,000 operators instead of 44,000. Similarly, because of computerised office systems, the number of US commercial bank employees declined from roughly 480,000 in 1984 to less than 300,000 in 1997.[16] The stark truth was that in its pursuit of economic growth a regime of flexible accumulation found people increasingly redundant. Under these circumstances, governments found it neces- sary, with varying degrees of enthusiasm, to cut back on welfare payments, in order to minimise the tax burden, and thus avoid alienating both the business community and the majority of the electorate, on whose support they depended. This explained why a Democratic President of the United States, Bill Clinton, could become a leading advocate of 'welfare reform', a euphemism for the reduction of support to mothers with dependent children; why New Labour's Tony Blair attempted to cut off assistance to the long-term unemployed; and why Italy's Ulivo coalition made cuts in government pensions one of its highest priorities.[17] As John Gray observed, the new capitalism 'set the terms within which oppositional parties were compelled to operate'.[18]

Table 4.1 Structure of civilian employment in selected advanced capitalist countries, 1973–97, illustrating the rise of the service economy

| Country | Percentage of employed population in: | | | | | | | | | | | |
| | Agriculture | | | | Industry | | | | Services | | | |
	1973	1981	1987	1997	1973	1981	1987	1997	1973	1981	1987	1997
Australia	7.3	6.5	5.7	4.9	35.4	30.3	26.2	22.1	57.3	63.2	68.1	73.0
Canada	6.5	5.4	4.7	3.7	30.6	28.3	25.3	22.3	62.8	66.3	70.0	74.0
France	11.2	8.4	6.9	4.5	39.5	35.0	30.8	25.6	49.3	56.0	62.5	69.9
Germany	7.3	5.2	4.2	2.9	47.5	43.0	40.4	34.8	45.2	51.9	55.4	62.3
Italy	18.3	13.4	10.5	6.8	39.2	37.6	32.6	32.0	42.5	49.0	56.8	61.2
Japan	13.4	10.0	8.3	5.3	37.2	35.3	33.8	33.1	49.4	54.7	57.9	61.6
Spain	24.3	18.8	15.1	8.4	36.7	35.3	32.3	30.0	38.9	45.9	52.5	61.7
Sweden	7.1	5.6	3.9	2.8	36.8	31.3	29.7	26.0	56.1	63.1	66.3	71.3
UK	3.0	2.7	2.3	1.8	42.3	35.8	32.9	26.7	54.7	61.6	64.8	70.7
USA	4.2	3.5	3.0	2.7	33.2	30.1	27.1	23.9	62.6	66.4	69.9	73.4

Source: OECD (1989) *Labour Force Statistics, 1967–1987*, Paris: OECD, pp. 40–2; OECD (1999), *Labour Force Statistics, 1978–1998*, Paris: OECD, pp. 32–4

These trends were greatly exacerbated by the emergence of the global economy. In its 'purest' form, a global economy would allow money to be raised, businesses set up, people employed and products sold, anywhere in the world and in whatever configuration best suited the market conditions. If such an economy were fully realised, money, jobs, goods, services and people would all be able to move as easily from one country to another as they could now from, say, New York to California. It was still a long way off, but a revolution had begun which had nevertheless created a world economy that was already quite unlike anything that had existed before. The distinguishing feature of this revolution was the free movement of capital. Although small-scale trading in currencies had, of course, existed for centuries, the explosive growth in international financial markets only really began after the final collapse of the Bretton Woods agreement in 1973. This agreement, named after the New Hampshire hotel in which the parties to the agreement had met in 1944, had been designed to avoid a repeat of the economic catastrophes that had been such a major factor in the outbreak of war. Central to the agreement, which was imposed by the Western powers, was a framework of fixed exchange rates, with the dollar pegged to gold (at $35 per ounce), and all other major currencies pegged to the dollar. This effectively made the dollar a universal currency, which guaranteed the value of all other currencies. Of course, currencies could be adjusted from time to time if conditions changed and the pegged rates proved to be unrealistic; but, for the most part, exchange rates remained the same and there was therefore no great scope for a money market which might speculate on currency fluctuations.

This all began to change in the 1960s. In order to help Europe and Japan recover from World War II, the United States had opened up its market to their exports, thus enabling them to earn dollars and finance their own expansion. It was a brilliantly successful strategy, to which the extraordinary recovery of the war-torn economies testified, but it depended upon the willingness of the United States to run up trade and fiscal deficits in order to finance it. As Longworth pointed out, this willingness was both the strength of the system and its downfall. Deficits could not be run forever. Gradually, other nations began to accumulate more dollars than they needed, which had the effect of exerting a downward pressure on their value. After a further era of deficit spending, brought about by America's involvement in Vietnam, the US finally succumbed to the inevitability of devaluation, devaluing the dollar in 1971 and detaching it from the gold standard early in 1973. From that point on, the world's currencies were freely traded on the world's money markets, which determined at any given moment what a nation's currency was worth, and which set up the opportunity for big money to be made by guessing correctly which way one currency might move against another. The growth of these markets was phenomenal, boosted both by rapid advances in computerised telecommunications and by the ideological commitment of Thatcher and Reagan to detach the state as far as possible from market mechanisms. Trading on the foreign exchanges grew from a relatively modest $10b a day in 1973 to an estimated $1.5 trillion in 1997 – over fifty times the level of daily world trade, more than the annual Gross Domestic Product (GDP) of France and greater than the total foreign currency reserves of the all the world's central banks put together.[19] Almost all of this trading was speculative, much of it based on new forms of 'derivatives', such as futures and options. It was meant to fuel the world's economy but, according to Longworth, it was 'as far removed from the "real economy" as a game of poker, and had taken on a life of its own.'[20] In addition to this was the global bond market, which allowed traders to take advantage of differing prices for both corporate and government bonds that were available around the world. This market, together with the secondary market of unmatured bonds, was given a huge boost during the Reagan years, when the US government used the global bond market to finance its growing budget and trade deficits. By the end of the 1990s, trading on the global bond market stood at around $200b each day. In comparison, the global equity market, trading at around $25b a day, was relatively small, because most investors still preferred to buy shares in their own countries. But this was changing, with more people investing in shares across national borders and the global equity market growing by around 25 per cent a year.[21] All these components combined to create for the first time a single world market for investment, money and credit supply. With a bewildering diversification of new financial instruments, involving discounting, hedging, debt futures and so on, the new global financial system had become so complex that, in Harvey's view, 'it surpasse[d] most people's understanding'. But one thing was clear: it was an increasingly independent force, operating according to its own laws.

The new global economy was also characterised by a huge expansion of world trade. By 1998, world trade in goods and services, already valued at more than $6.3 trillion a year, was expected to grow at 8 per cent a year, and around three times as fast as the world economy itself.[22] In nearly all countries, imports and exports constituted a far greater proportion of economic activity than ever before. A survey in 1994, for example, showed that, in the United States, even small companies which had traditionally confined their activities to the American market, were having to move into foreign markets, with a fifth of those employing less than 500 people now exporting their goods or services. Gray concluded that by the 1980s the ratio of world trade to gross domestic product had exceeded that at any other historical period.[23] A key factor in this was the massive growth in multinational corporations, which by the 1990s accounted for about one-third of world output and two-thirds of world trade.[24] These giant companies found that they could cut costs and increase profits by splitting up their production processes and relocating them in different parts of the world. This allowed them to take advantage of the labour markets, tax regimes and regulatory frameworks which gave them the greatest competitive advantage. Caterpillar, for example, produced winches in Brazil, engines in Japan, axles in Germany and transmission systems in the Unites States; it shipped the whole lot to a factory in Toronto for its parts to be assembled; and then exported the finished product to countries around the world, including Brazil, Japan, Belgium and the United States. With global communications, any problems could be dealt with instantaneously; and with global freight carriers (air, sea, road and rail), the costs of transportation did not begin to outweigh the savings in wages, raw materials and taxes that could be gained from global manufacturing.[25] Whilst manufacturing industry had taken the lead in the globalisation of these operational practices, service industries were not far behind. Major airlines, for example, used cheaper labour in Jamaica to process tickets and reservations; the insurance company Metropolitan Life 'outsourced' the processing of medical claims to employees in County Cork, Ireland.[26] The growth in multinational corporations of all kinds was such that by the end of the 1990s between 40 per cent and 50 per cent of world trade was conducted not between different countries but between the different parts of global companies. According to a United Nations survey, the combined output of multinationals was by 1993 roughly equivalent to that of the United States as a whole.[27] If the GDP of nation states was compared with the annual sales of the biggest companies, it was possible to conclude that by 1995 only 49 of the world's 100 biggest economies were actually nation states. General Motors, ranked at number 26, was bigger than Denmark or Thailand; Wal-Mart, at 42 was bigger than Poland, the Ukraine or Portugal; and Hitachi, at 46, was bigger than Israel, Greece or Malaysia.[28]

From these narratives of the 'new' capitalism, an outline of both its origins and its key characteristics begins to emerge, which can be summarised as follows: first, under the twin pressures of the first major post-war recession and the massive rise in oil prices of 1973, growth stagnated in all of the advanced industrialised countries. Secondly, due to its inherent 'rigidities', the 'Fordist-Keynesian' system, which had been largely responsible for the economic 'miracle' of the 1950s and 1960s, could not provide solutions to the new conditions. Thirdly, more ruthless forms of capital accumulation were adopted, resulting in the transformation of labour markets, production processes and consumption patterns. Fourthly, with the

154

phenomenal growth of new information and communication technologies, these trends were intensified by the free movement of capital, the expansion of world trade and the growth of multinational corporations – in other words, 'globalisation'. Finally, all of these processes, which were vigorously promoted by American (and British) governments, eventually came to exercise a decisive influence on the parameters within which the government of any capitalist state was able to operate.

This account is, of necessity, simplified, and cannot do full justice to the complex and variegated process of economic transformation which took place across the advanced industrialised world. It should not be construed, for example, that the practices associated with 'Fordism' could always be so clearly distinguished from those of 'flexible accumulation'; nor that 'Fordism' somehow 'stopped' in 1973, to be replaced by an entirely new and unrelated form of productive enterprise. Different forms of accumulation could, and did, co-exist side by side; elements of the 'old' could be found in the 'new', and vice-versa; and, as we shall see, there were important geopolitical variations. Nevertheless, despite these reservations, the narratives outlined here clearly signalled an interconnected series of tendencies – organisational, economic and political – which could be discerned around the world. Furthermore, although these tendencies were directly linked to the underlying logic of capitalist accumulation, and could therefore be represented as variations on an old theme, the shifts which were taking place were of such scale and speed that they also amounted to an industrial revolution of a quite different order from anything that had been experienced before. It might be argued, as Paul Hirst and Graham Thompson did, that the 'globalisation' which emerged in the 1970s and 1980s signified no more than a return to the international economy that had flourished under British leadership from the 1870s up until 1914;[29] and, as Soros reminded us, that the antecedents of the global capitalist system went back even further to the Hanseatic league and Italian city-states, where autonomous territories were linked by commercial and financial ties. But, as Soros went on to say, the free movement of capital, together with the speed of communications and the volume of world trade, had by the 1980s produced in the global system a degree of economic integration that marked it out from any previous period in history.[30] Even David Harvey, who argued that the underlying logic and crisis tendencies of capitalism remained the same, conceded that we were entering uncharted waters, and that the autonomy of the global finance system was 'unprecedented in the history of capitalism'.[31] It is to signify this sense of the new, yet at the same time to recognise continuities, that I have used 'new' in inverted commas to describe the phase of capitalism that is the subject of this chapter.

The 'new' capitalism: social impacts

Few would dissent from Richard Longworth's assessment that market capitalism was 'by far the most productive and liberating channel for the realisation of human ambitions and needs'.[32] Most (though some reluctantly) would probably also accept Edward Luttwak's view that capitalism, 'unobstructed by public ownership, government regulations, cartels, monopolies, effective trade unions, cultural inhibitions or kinship obligations', was 'by the far the most productive system ever devised on this earth'.[33] It was certainly a view endorsed by Brian Moore, director-general of the World Trade Organisation, who pointed out that in the global economy, more of us were getting richer, living longer, staying healthier and enjoying greater political freedoms than ever before.[34] So why, even after the communist alternatives had disintegrated in such spectacular fashion, was the 'new' capitalism, which embodied so much of what Luttwak described, represented as a narrative of decline that wrecked the lives of millions and threatened the conditions of democratic government?

First, the search for profits in an increasingly competitive environment demanded more ruthless approaches to business management. Employed to deliver maximum returns to their shareholders (and often to themselves as well through share ownership or stock option schemes), company chief executives sought lower costs, higher productivity and bigger margins, in their efforts to produce efficiency gains wherever they could be found. As we have seen, in the pursuit of these gains, described in management jargon as 'best practice', labour was required to be increasingly 'flexible'; that is, employees could be fired at will, with minimal severance payments and with little that their weakened unions could do about it. There was often a clear and direct relationship between a company's willingness to make savage cuts to its workforce and the value of its shares on the stock market. Thus, when Philip Conduit, chief executive of Boeing, announced in 1997 that 12,000 jobs would be eliminated (despite the fact that the company had a huge backlog of overdue deliveries), the stock market reacted immediately by adding 3 per cent to the value of its shares.[35] Similarly, takeover bids, such as the struggle for control of the NatWest bank in Britain in 1999, could result in an unseemly public auction of the number of jobs to be cut, in the attempt of each bidder to convince shareholders of where their best interests lay. The growth of 'shareholder rights' was pursued to its logical conclusion in the United States, where, under American law, chief executives and boards of directors could be sued if they did not maximise shareholder value in every possible way. Despite the fact that the commitment of shareholders to a company was minimal in comparison with that of its employees, and could be terminated by just a telephone call to a broker, it was shareholder interests which led to the slash-and-burn restructuring strategies that were becoming such a feature of the corporate landscape and which were placing such immense pressures on the workforce. In these circumstances, to protect the interests of employees who were either replaceable by cheaper alternatives or simply no longer needed – in other words, to be a 'good' employer – was seen as 'soft' management and sympto-matic of a badly managed business. From the same perspective, incurring extra costs to reduce environmental degradation (see Chapter 1) was equally inefficient. Efficiency was exalted above all else, and the 'new' capitalism was indisputably more efficient than any of its previous incarnations. A return to the inefficiencies of 'Fordism' was neither possible nor desirable. But, the ruthless logic of what followed, as it played itself out in environmental disasters, redundant communities and the psyches of discarded individuals, left many people convinced that the economy had become un-coupled from those who lived within it: society increasingly appeared to exist for the economy rather than the other way round.[36]

Secondly, while some got richer, many more got poorer. The move to a 'flexible' regime of accumulation had certainly succeeded in producing faster growth; and, although it had been produced at the expense of massive job losses, according to neo-liberal economic orthodoxy greater profits would lead to new investment and new jobs, replacing those which had been lost. However, this failed to take account of the fact that the link between investment and jobs had been broken, on the one hand, by the technological revolution which business itself was driving and, on the other, by the global market economy. Expanding or new businesses looked more to technology and less to people for the most cost-effective fulfilment of tasks; and from the 1980s this applied as much to white-collar office workers as to blue collar workers in manufacturing industry. Both groups now had direct experience of the impact of a technology which appeared to destroy far more jobs than it created. Where people *were* still needed, they could often find themselves facing intense global competition from workers in low wage economies. This could take the form either of cheap imports or, more directly, of a 'cheaper' workforce willing and able to deliver greater profits to its employers. Under these conditions, labour had the option of making its costs competitive or pricing itself out of the market. If it chose the former, which it would eventually have to do, then it conformed to what economists referred to as 'factor-price equalisation'; that is, if goods could be made equally well in two different places, one paying high wages and the other low wages, then the wages in the two places would converge over time. This is what economists meant when they suggested that the level of many people's wages were now set in Peking.[37]

As a result of these pressures, a growing proportion of the work-force in the advanced industrialised world was confronted with either unemployment or declining rates of pay. Conditions varied from country to country, but, as a broad generalisation, Europe protected the status of its workers at the cost of high unemployment, while the United States brought unemployment down at the cost of lower wages and the insecurity of maximum 'flexibility'. Only Japan managed the trick of keeping both unemployment low and the workforce relatively stable. It had been able to do this by using income from trade surpluses which it had accumulated over the years (mainly at the expense of the United States) to employ all those workers who, if the criteria of 'best practice' and 'shareholder value' had been applied, would have been made redundant long ago. In Europe, unemployment had remained low from the post-war years through to the mid-1970s, rarely rising above 3 per cent. But from then on, the rate went up, the average for the European Union reaching over 10 per cent (more than 17m people) in 1997.[38] Even this was probably a conservative figure, excluding both those who had given up looking for jobs and had dropped out of the statistics and those on short-term government-sponsored training schemes, who were training for jobs which didn't actually exist. In the United States, unemployment began to drop from its post-war peak of around 7 per cent in the early 1990s, falling to under 5 per cent and staying there from 1997 onwards. This relatively low level of unemployment was achieved at the cost of declining or stagnant rates of pay for 70 per cent of American employees, whose wages were well below those of their

European counterparts.[39] Median wages had begun to fall in the US in the mid-1970s, first of all amongst manual workers, then amongst high school graduates and finally, by the late 1980s, amongst male college graduates as well. By the mid-1990s, the only broad category for whom wages were still rising was female college graduates, and this was only because they had started from a much lower base. For most people, the norm was longer hours for less money. Indeed, by the 1990s, the majority of families found that it was necessary for both partners to find paid work if they were to have any chance of earning what a family would have received from one partner's income in the early 1970s. Even then, according to one authoritative estimate, for 60 per cent of two-income families, the addition of the second partner's earnings failed to make up for the decline in income of the first.[40] In Luttwak's view, the theory of 'factor-price equalisation' was proving itself in practice in the US, with the wages of the workforce slowly converging with those of the Third World.[41]

It could thus be seen that, whilst rates of unemployment in the US compared favourably to those in most parts of Europe, they were bought at the cost of a general process of downward mobility for the majority of the population. These rates also disguised the fact that by the late 1990s around 12 per cent of the workforce, or roughly 17m people, were paid so little that they remained below the official poverty line, despite being fully employed, working forty hours a week for fifty weeks a year.[42] This, of course, had a knock-on effect on the poverty levels of entire families. Of those with children, the number living in poverty rose from 11.4 per cent in 1973 to 18.5 per cent – nearly one-fifth – in 1995.[42] US unemployment rates were further disguised by a massive incarceration programme, which kept between 1.5 and 2.0 per cent of the potential workforce in jail, amounting in 1998 to 1 in every 150 adult Americans.[44] All this took place against the background of steady economic growth which, if not reaching the heady levels of the 1950s and 1960s, had picked up from the low point of the 1970s, consistently outperforming Europe and sustaining itself at around 3 per cent a year throughout the 1990s.[45] But, as we have seen, the benefits of this did not 'trickle down' to the majority of Americans, who struggled to maintain their livelihoods against the pressures of 'shareholder value', 'flexible' labour and all that that entailed; instead, there was a phenomenal increase in the inequality of wealth distribution, as almost all the benefits of the growing economy accrued to the top 20 per cent of wage earners.[46] Within this 20 per cent, the top 5 per cent of households were in a league of their own, their share of total household income rising from 16.6 per cent in 1968 to 21.2 per cent in 1994. In contrast, the share of the bottom 40 per cent declined. This meant that while, in 1968, the total income going to the bottom 40 per cent had exceeded that going to the top 5 per cent, by 1994 the share of the top 5 per cent was almost twice that of the bottom 40 per cent.[47] There were many different methods of measuring inequality, but, whichever method one chose, the conclusion was always the same: greater inequality was an integral feature of the 'new' capitalism. Longworth believed that the United States had indisputably become the most unequal nation in the First World. For Zygmunt Bauman, the new rich had finally succeeded in severing their connection with the poor. 'The old rich', he argued,

> needed the poor to make and keep them rich. That dependency at all times mitigated the conflict of interest and prompted some effort, however tenuous, to care. The new rich do not need the poor any more. At long last the bliss of ultimate freedom is nigh.[48]

The third reason for the association of the 'new' capitalism with decline arose from the social disruption which came in its wake. The unpredictable nature of capitalism, with its crisis tendencies and its propensity for 'creative destruction', had, of course, been long understood; the compromises of 'Fordism' could be seen as one attempt to control it. But when these compromises were abandoned in favour of global laissez-faire, a seemingly unstoppable process of accelerating structural change was unleashed. Every day of the week, companies merged, downsized, closed down, opened up or relocated, in what seemed to be an almost ceaseless revolution. Factory workers were the first to feel the full force of this, seeing their livelihoods and their communities destroyed, as the old manufacturing industries were either drastically scaled down or closed altogether. But they were soon joined by large numbers of the middle class, once prosperous employees in secure jobs, now having to compete with blue-collar workers for whatever jobs they could find. Together, they formed the new (sometimes university-educated) proletariat, picking up low-paid and insecure work as new businesses came and went. In Gray's view, they resembled the classic proletariat of nineteenth-century Europe, dependent upon increasingly uncertain jobs, and with minimal welfare support to fall back on in hard times. The downward mobility of the middle class thus represented a reversal of the process of *embourgeoisement*, the very opposite of the social and economic progress which political advocates of the 'new' capitalism had held up as the prospect for all.[49] As more and more people were subjected to the forces of perpetual change, uncertainty and competition, so greater strains were placed on the connective ties of families, friendships and communities. At the same time, as we saw in Chapter 2, there was evidence of a growing social disintegration throughout the First World, particularly in Britain and the United States, which manifested itself in soaring rates of crime, divorce and family breakdown. Although the link between these changes in the economy and social life was not something that could be conclusively proved, it was difficult to believe that they were not intimately connected.

Fourthly, and this can also be related to the disintegrating forces described above, market values appeared to be penetrating the very texture of social life. The 'trickle down' theory might not have worked as far as economic benefits were concerned, but the values of the 'new' capitalism had certainly begun to trickle down. Just as employers found that social responsibilities got in the way of the single-minded search for profit, so it was that others learnt to understand that altruistic concerns were an obstacle to advancement. There was, of course, nothing new in this, but what worried those such as George Soros, who had an intimate understanding of the dynamics of global capitalism, was the extent to which untrammelled individualism was becoming the prevailing social norm. Soros called this market fundamentalism. It produced 'transactional societies', in which long-term co-operative relationships were replaced by short-term market transactions, governed only by considerations of expediency. In such societies, the pursuit of self-interest was elevated into a moral principle and the acquisition of wealth celebrated as the highest form of achievement. Indeed, in Soros's view, principles based on anything other than self-interest, and achievements which were not rewarded by wealth, were increasingly disregarded or denigrated. This went hand-in-hand with the extension of market values into formerly non-market activities, such as medicine, education and sport, whose practices were distorted and ethical boundaries blurred. Soros believed that the growth of transactional societies was an on-going historical process, which, if taken to its logical conclusion, would result in the final collapse of any notion of common interest, leaving only battlegrounds of competing self-interest, mediated by market mechanisms. Ideas of civic virtue would disappear, with the goal of civilisation reduced to a vulgar social Darwinism. Furthermore, there seemed little prospect of these trends being reversed. If the pursuit of self-interest, unhindered by the obligation to consider others, was the prevailing social norm, then what was there to stop these values reproducing themselves in perpetuity? There was no moral imperative, derived from the workings of abstract reason, which would break the cycle; social values reflected the societies which produced them; and if societies continued to organise more and more of their functions around the logic of the market, it was difficult to see how alternative values could make much headway. A transactional market society had never existed in its purest form; nor did Soros believe that it could without tearing itself apart. But, he suggested, we were 'closer to it than at any time in history'.[50]

Fifthly, the 'new' capitalism mobilised all its resources to promote in the individual a profound sense of insufficiency, which could only be relieved, and then only temporarily, in the act of consumption. As we saw earlier, accelerated production could only deliver greater profits and growth if it was matched by accelerated consumption. For some products, this could be achieved by increasing the pace of product deterioration, thus shortening replacement time; but for most products and services it could only be brought about by engendering a perpetual state of dissatisfaction in the psyche of the consumer. The gratification yielded by one consumption experience had to give way in the shortest possible time to the desire for another. Indeed, the ideal consumer would forego satisfaction altogether – and desire only desire. For Zygmunt Bauman, the consumer in the postmodern world was a different kind of consumer to that of any other historical period. Human beings had always 'consumed', but it was only under the conditions of the 'new' capitalism that consumption took on a greater importance than production in the social roles ascribed by society to its members. Both roles were still required, of course, but while production now only needed the few, satisfactory levels of consumption required the increasingly frenetic activity of the many.[51] As Bauman argued, 'consumers must never be allowed to rest. They need to be kept forever awake and on the alert, constantly . . . in a state of never wilting excitation'.[52] Behind the rhetoric of consumer sovereignty ran the subtle logic of consumer discontent. Without it, the 'new' capitalism could not function.

Sixthly, and perhaps most importantly, the emergence of a global market economy was widely perceived to have undermined the processes of democratic government. The free movement of capital meant that investors in the money, bond and stock markets acquired an unprecedented degree of influence over the direction of national economic policies; and the interests of these investors did not coincide, indeed would often work against, those of elected governments and of the people who voted for them. This conflict of interest could be most clearly seen in the issue of public expenditure. Whatever political importance might be attached to the expansion of health care programmes or to the maintainance of social security systems, and however popular these measures might be with the electorate, when it came to implementing them governments found themselves increasingly boxed in with little room for manoeuvre. If they tried to increase their spending through greater taxation, the biggest taxpayers – corporations and the wealthiest citizens – simply moved their capital to a more tax-friendly environment; there was never a shortage of countries competing to attract it. The end result was thus a 'bidding down' of corporate taxation, which, in the United States, for example, saw the corporate share of the total tax burden fall from around one-third in the years before World War II to just 12 per cent in the late 1990s.[53] This was partially offset by a rise in both income tax and sales taxes (the latter, of course, having a disproportionate impact on the less well off), which, in Europe as well as the US, produced a general shift in the burden of taxation from capital to citizens. However, there was clearly a limit to how much money could be raised in this way, and, when that limit was reached, governments were pushed into heavier and heavier borrowing commitments and huge budget deficits. While this could create some room for manoeuvre in the short-term, in the long-term it placed governments in even further thrall to the markets. During the 1980s, for example, the Reagan and Bush administrations financed their growing budget deficits through the bond markets, issuing billions of dollars worth of government bonds, which were largely bought up by the Japanese. But in 1987, amidst fears about the value of the US dollar, these bonds were sold off, prompting the government to raise interest rates in an attempt to stem the flow. Fearing higher inflation, higher costs for industry and the possibility of recession, investors stampeded out of the market, causing the 'Black Monday' stockmarket crash of 19 October. The legacy of all this, picked up by the Clinton administration, was a budget deficit which the markets would no longer allow to be financed through either increasing taxation or further borrowing. The only option was to cut spending. This was a lesson learnt four years earlier in France by Mitterand's socialist government, whose whole programme of economic and social policies had been built on the basis of deficit-led expansion. The reaction of the markets was to put pressure on the franc, forcing interest rates up, thus increasing the costs not only of financing new expenditure but of refinancing old debts. After just two years, the French government, no longer able to withstand this sustained assault from the markets, was forced to devalue its currency, abandon its expansionist economic policy and introduce austerity measures, albeit 'with a human face'. It was the same throughout Western Europe – Tories and Labour in Britain, Christian Democrats and Social Democrats in Germany, Right and Left in Italy – every political party found the scope of its economic and social policies severely restricted by the demands of the global economy. Whether through taxation, deficit spending or regulation, any government attempting to work outside the limits acceptable to corporate and financial interests was liable to be severely punished by the markets, thus making matters worse.

None of this was to suggest that there was now some new form of invisible world government, led by multinational corporations and currency speculators, which had somehow appropriated to itself the powers of the nation state. It was widely acknowledged that the nation state had, indeed, lost control of key aspects of its economic and, by extension, social policies; but the threat to democracy came not from an alternative source of government but from the impossibility of governing. Democratic governments had, of course, always been subject to forces beyond their control, but what distinguished the political context of the 'new' capitalism was the sheer unpredictability of these forces and the speed with which unpredictable events would unfold. Soros, who understood as well as anyone how unstable the international financial markets were, believed that the 'new' capitalism had moved into 'dynamic disequilibrium', a state where events moved 'too rapidly for people's understanding, causing a gap between thinking and reality to appear'.[54] In Gray's view, the global market had become anarchic, in both its operation and effects, and was now 'ungovernable by either sovereign states or multinational corporations'.[55] For Zygmunt Bauman, the anarchic forces of the 'new' capitalism had, at least partially, been concealed from view during the tensions of the Cold War, but, after 1989, had fully revealed themselves. 'The world does not look like a totality anymore', he had argued.

> It looks rather like a field of scattered and disparate forces, congealing in places difficult to predict and gathering momentum which no one really

knows how to arrest . . . To put it in a nutshell: *no one seems now to be in control* [Bauman's italics]. Worse still – it is not clear what 'being in control' could, under the circumstances, be like.[56]

These, then, were the key elements in the representation of the 'new' capitalism as a narrative of decline: the ruthless pursuit of shareholder value, whatever its human or environmental costs; the growth of inequality and the legitimisation of poverty; social disruption and the promotion of insecurity; the marketisation of social life; consumerism and its discontents; the power of the financial markets and the undermining of democratic government. The question of whether the practices which gave rise to these narratives could actually be classified as 'new' was considered earlier in this chapter (pp. 156–6); how far the narratives of decline themselves could be seen as 'new' must also be addressed. But, first, it is necessary to return to the question of how far the 'new' capitalism was mutating from an essentially Anglo-American speciality into a global phenomenon.

The 'new' capitalism: a global phenomenon?

During the Cold War, the opposition of capitalism to Communism was of such magnitude that it both eclipsed and subordinated the diversity of economic practices which existed within the capitalist world itself. With the collapse of Communism, which disintegrated just as the 'new' capitalism was manifesting itself as a powerful global force, the differences between capitalisms were thrown into sharp relief. In particular, the 'new' capitalism, which, as we have seen, first took root in Britain and the United States, displayed expansionist tendencies which brought it into conflict with those forms of capitalism that reflected less individualistic traditions. In the First World, for example, France, Germany and Japan had all developed alternative models of a capitalist economy which, in their separate ways, placed a higher valuation on collective interests and the importance of social cohesion. France, in keeping with its strong centralist traditions, had retained extensive public ownership of both industry and services, with the state making heavy investments in the maintenance and renewal of infrastructure. The state had also maintained a generous welfare system, providing comprehensive medical care, free university education and extensive social security. Retirement provision had been particularly generous, with blue-collar workers permitted to retire at fifty-five on pensions of up to 70 per cent of their final salary, and white-collar workers at sixty on up to 80 per cent.[57] In exchange for these benefits, French workers had accepted wages which were, on average, lower than their European counterparts, but it was a price they had been prepared to pay as part of a guaranteed social contract. Jacques Chirac referred to this as 'the European social model, where the state is the guardian of unity'.[58]

Germany too had maintained its social contract, delivering its economic 'miracle' and at the same time attempting to create social stability and cohesion. Like France, it had also constructed a comprehensive welfare state, but, while France's economy had been directed by a centralist élite, Germany had relied upon an elaborate system of institutionalised co-operation. In what became the classic model of a social market economy, a broad range of 'stake-holders' were locked into the processes of corporate governance, involving not only employers and employees but also bankers, local communities, suppliers and even customers. Under the system of *Mitbestimmung* (co-determination), workers in large companies were guaranteed places on the board, where they joined shareholders and other interested parties in taking key management decisions. Industry-wide collective bargaining over wages was common practice and there was a high degree of job security. The processes of consultation could be cumbersome and time-consuming, but they helped to establish openness and trust, giving the 'Rhine' model of capitalism the best record of labour relations in the West.

Japan had developed yet another model of capitalism, so different from that of the United States that for some analysts it barely even qualified for the term 'capitalism'.[59] Japanese companies had sought profits, certainly, but the return on capital for investors was only one of a much broader range of corporate objectives. These had included the goal of global advantage in key industries, through the pursuit of maximum market share, and the maintenance of full employment at home. Such objectives were determined and pursued through the interwoven interests of an extremely powerful bureaucracy, centred on the Ministry of Finance, and gigantic industrial groupings, known as *keiretsu*, which linked together manufacturers, suppliers, distributors and banks in self-protective networks. The control which these networks could exert over all aspects of industrial and commercial activity had enabled Japan to erect 'invisible' trade barriers, which had kept cheap imports out whilst Japan had built up its manufacturing base in key strategic industries. With the highest rates of corporate and personal saving in the world on which to draw, and an investment culture which favoured the long term over the short term, Japan had been able to finance the expansion of these industries from its own resources, keeping foreign investment at minimal levels and avoiding the pressures of 'shareholder value'. It was thus that Japan had been able to acquire its world monopoly in the production of high-technology goods, slashing its prices on exports when necessary, driving out competition and dominating world markets. By restricting cheap imports at home, the 'invisible' trade barriers operated by the *keiretsu* had allowed prices to remain high within Japan, thereby protecting workers in enterprises which would otherwise either have had to close or reduce their workforce. Whilst the widely reported phenomenon of 'lifetime employment' was often exaggerated, applying as it did to no more than 30 per cent to 40 per cent of employees (usually those in senior or middle management), it was true that unemployment in Japan, which had remained at between 2 per cent and 4 per cent throughout the 1980s, had been consistently lower than anywhere else in the industrialised world.[60] This had been achieved through a system of 'planned inefficiency', whereby many more people were employed, particularly in the retail and distribution sectors, than were actually needed. It all amounted to a sort of private welfare state, made possible by government-business co-operation, and financed by Japan's massive trade surpluses; or, to turn it round, as one American expert on Japan had put it, 'this is a welfare state that has largely been financed by foreigners'.[61]

These brief observations on some of the distinguishing features of French, German and Japanese capitalisms, as they had appeared at the end of the Cold War, illustrate how capitalism had not evolved across the First World as a homogeneous enterprise, but had been moulded into different forms by differing historical circumstances and cultural traditions. In Longworth's view, these three capitalisms, together with that of the United States, were so distinctive that they could be considered 'paradigms', the four basic models of capitalism which made up the advanced industrialised world.[62] If one looked further, one could construct further paradigms: 'familial' capitalism in Asia (though, of course there was no more a generic 'Asian' capitalism than there was a 'Western' capitalism); 'anarcho' capitalism in the Russian Federation, driven forward by the mafia and other agencies of organised crime; 'market-Leninism' in China, where a market economy was grafted on to a totalitarian state; and so on.

Luttwak suggested a typography of capitalisms, in which the differentiating factor was the degree of privatisation/deregulation which could be observed in selected countries over the period 1985 to 1998. In this schema, there was a four-fold division into: residual state-capitalist ('communist') economies, such as Belarus, Vietnam and Cuba; ex-state capitalist ('communist') countries being privatised, such as China, the Russian Federation and the countries of eastern Europe; controlled economies being privatised/deregulated, such as Argentina, India and Italy; and fully 'turbo-capitalist' economies, such as the United States and the United Kingdom.[63]

Given these diverse practices, there was clearly a long way to go before it could be said that the 'new' capitalism had become the capitalism of the entire world. *Pace* Fukuyama, the end of economic history was not yet nigh. Nevertheless, as we have seen, the free movement of capital was allowing the markets to exercise a 'discipline' over both political and corporate life, from which no economy was immune. In Germany, for example, the home of 'stake-holder capitalism', the carefully constructed balance of power between big business, big government and big labour was being gradually undermined by the pressures of global competition. More and more companies were seeking to escape the 'rigidities' of the social market economy, by moving some of their production outside Germany, particularly to post-communist eastern Europe, where labour was cheaper and social and environmental regulation less demanding.[64] Furthermore, if German companies were to maintain and strengthen their market position, they could no longer rely only on their banks for investment, as they had been accustomed to do, but now had to turn to the international capital markets as well. Whilst the banks had traditionally held a long-term stake in their clients' growth, international investors brought with them expectations of 'shareholder value' and all the profit pressures that this implied. There were huge job losses, with Germany losing 1.1m jobs in the 1990s alone, a growth in part-time employment and the beginnings of a breakdown in the tradition of consensual negotiation between employers' federations and trade unions. At the same time, the scope of the welfare state was reduced for the first time since World War II.[65] Whilst these familiar symptoms of the 'new' capitalism at work were nothing like as pronounced as those produced in the United States and the United Kingdom, they were enough to convince Longworth that 'the prized Social Market Economy ha[d] begun to unravel'.

It was the same with Sweden's 'classic' model of the welfare state, which had not only provided cradle-to-the-grave protection for every citizen but had also attempted to maintain full employment by using the government as the employer of last resort. When these policies resulted in a debt crisis in 1994, producing an accumulated government deficit of nearly 95 per cent of GDP, international bond-purchasers responded by refusing to buy Swedish government bonds. With the economy already deeply depressed, and unemployment soaring, the price demanded by bond-purchasers for their return to the marketplace was a massive increase in interest rates and savage spending cuts. This, of course, produced even more unemployment. The signals sent out by this episode were very clear: bondmarkets would not allow governments to pursue policies which they considered to be fiscally imprudent. It was of no matter whether those policies might promote social cohesion in the longterm and thus reduce costs to both society and the state.[66] In other words, even in those states with the strongest social democratic traditions, the post-war objectives of full employment and welfare for all could no longer be realistically pursued.

If the old social market economies of Europe and Scandinavia were threatened by the 'new' capitalism, so also were the complex and connective ties which bound together different interests in Japan. Japan's version of controlled capitalism still held together, but at the end of the 1990s some analysts believed that a new consensus was forming which would 'liberate' the Japanese economy from the burdens of bureaucracy, tradition and restraint. This consensus was being led by a new breed of corporate executive which admired and envied the freedoms enjoyed by their counterparts in the United States and other seemingly more dynamic economies. According to Luttwak, it would 'abolish most market rules and restrictions, formal and informal, demote the already partly discredited bureaucrats, stop the protection of all weak industries and weak firms, and release competition in all its forms'.[67] Disillusioned by corruption within the government bureaucracy, frustrated by years of economic stagnation, and mindful of the growing resentment towards high prices in Japan relative to just about everywhere else, these advocates of the 'new' capitalism were 'making rapid progress in persuading their fellow Japanese to accept turbo-capitalist reforms'.[68] Throughout Asia as well, Luttwak saw the breakdown of 'familial' capitalism, as old loyalties and long-established commercial linkages were replaced by contractual agreements and the temporary relationships that these implied. 'Everywhere', wrote Luttwak, 'familial capitalism is rapidly retreating, and turbo-capitalism is rapidly advancing.' This was borne out by a survey, conducted by Luttwak, which compared key indicators of 'turbo-capitalism' in thirty selected countries between 1985 and 1998.[69] These indicators included: the privatisation of industry, services and banks; the withdrawal of public authorities from the economy; the removal of barriers to both international commerce and internal competition; and other forms of deregulation. Classifying the thirty countries into four types (mentioned on p. 168), Luttwak showed that in every case except North Korea, there was some movement during this period towards the practices associated with the 'new' capitalism. There was absolutely no movement the other way. There was, of course, an inescapable logic to this: in a globalised world, national economies were in competition with one another; and, in such a competition, the social market economies of Europe and Asia were bound to come off worse against those economies where lean business and lean government had pared the cost of their social obligations to the minimum. The pressures of downwards harmonisation were enormous. For Gray, it was simply a variation of Gresham's Law: bad capitalism drove out the good.[70]

Global pessimism

How did this narrative end? Was the 'new' capitalism destined to carry all before it? And, if so, with what consequences? Or would it be resisted and forced to reform? There seemed little doubt that the logic of the 'new' capitalism would both demand and ensure its continued geopolitical advance; at the same time, for the reasons that have been outlined, it would become increasingly necessary to moderate the adverse social effects which came in its wake. But, as we have seen, one of the essential attributes of the 'new' capitalism was its capacity to evade national attempts to control or regulate it. What was needed, therefore, was a framework for international regulation, which would tame the excesses of the markets and bring some stability to the global capitalist system. Only then might it be possible to introduce and administer ameliorative measures, such as the global tax on currency speculation – the so-called 'Tobin tax' – proposed by the Nobel prize-winning economist, James Tobin, as far back as 1978. However, the creation of international financial institutions, such as an international regulatory authority and an international central bank, with comparable powers to those which existed at national levels, would have required a relinquishing of national sovereignty in key fiscal areas that was simply inconceivable.

This inability to control or reform a seemingly unstoppable force accounted for the undercurrent of deep pessimism which ran through these narratives of political and economic decline. Luttwak believed that those in the advanced industrialised world were now confronted with an impossible choice: resisting the 'new' capitalism or embracing it. To resist it meant dropping out of the competitive world economy and accepting a progressive impoverishment; yet to embrace it meant accelerating the processes of social disintegration. No government appeared to have found a way out of this impasse, with most doing little more than 'allowing turbo-capitalism to advance without limit, while hoping that faster growth [would] remedy all its shortcomings'.[71] In other words, the answer to the problems created by turbo-capitalism was more turbo-capitalism. Longworth, who questioned how long societies could be kept going in this way, saw 'no solution . . . in sight'.[72] For Hobsbawm, this latest phase of capitalism had reached 'a point of historic crisis', where the very structure of human societies was threatened. Without being able to offer prescriptions for change, Hobsbawm argued only that humanity could not have a recognisable future 'by prolonging the past or the present'. To build the third millennium on that basis would result in failure – and the price of failure would be 'darkness'.[73] Soros predicted 'the imminent disintegration of the global capitalist system'.[74] As he acknowledged, predicting the future was 'more like alchemy than science', but he believed that the instabilities and defects in the system had now become so pronounced that we could expect a 'bust' in capitalism's 'boom/bust' cycle of such magnitude that it would turn global recession into depression.[75] This breakdown could be prevented by the intervention of international financial authorities, but, for the reasons which have already been considered, the prospects of this happening were dim.[76] In *Jihad vs. McWorld*, Benjamin Barber represented the 'new' capitalism as a form of 'economic totalism' (*McWorld*), locked into a dialectical relationship with the 'tribalism' that its universalising tendencies provoked. *Jihad* was a metaphor for this 'tribalism', an identity politics turned cancerous, which Barber saw crystallising around the globe in response to the relentless advance of *McWorld*. Both *Jihad* and *McWorld* gnawed away at the foundations of democracy, and unless an alternative to the struggle between the two could be found, the epoch on whose threshold we stood – 'postcommunist, postindustrial, postnational, yet sectarian, fearful and bigoted' – was 'likely also to be terminally postdemocratic'.[77] Like Barber, Gray also believed that the 'new' capitalism would meet powerful cultural resistance, and predicted that the current attempt to establish a universal economic order would be no more successful than that of the late nineteenth century, which collapsed into the trenches of the Great War. But resistance alone would not turn the tide: the lessons would be learned only after a prolonged period of crisis. 'As a result', wrote Gray,

> we stand on the brink not of the era of plenty . . . but a tragic epoch in which anarchic forces and shrinking natural resources drag sovereign states into ever more dangerous rivalries . . . The likelihood must be that the *laissez-faire* regime will not be reformed. Instead, it will fracture and fragment, as mounting scarcities of resources and conflicts of interest among the world's great powers make international cooperation ever more difficult. A deepening international anarchy is the human prospect.[78]

It was clear from this quasi-apocalyptic apprehension that the pessimism of these narratives went beyond the question of political and economic decline in the advanced industrialised world; it could not be construed as just an inflated and parochial response to a sense of economic beleaguerment in the West. To be sure, not everyone shared this pessimism, and from the perspective of an industrialising poor country, the 'new' capitalism could offer relief from impoverishment and hold out real prospects of material advancement.[79] This, as we have seen, was one consequence of 'factor-price equalisation', where workers in low-wage economies could benefit at the expense of those in high-wage economies. But for how long? When would the cost of their labour also begin to appear unacceptably high, relative either to technological alternatives or to regions of the world where labour costs were even lower? The pressures of downwards harmonisation would not disappear and, already, the movement of jobs from the First World was not just one-way. In 1997, for example, two companies – one Korean and one British – transferred their production from Korea, a newly industrialising country, to Wales, a First World European region, where substantial savings on labour costs could be made.[80] In the same year, the widespread loss of job security in Korea provoked mass demonstrations in Seoul. Some analysts, mostly free trade liberals, hung on to the idea that higher skills protected high-wage economies from low-wage competition. This was certainly true in the short term, but, in the longer-term what was to protect higher wage economies from competition which was both low wage and high skill? The world's labour force amounted to 1.5b workers in 1950; by 1995 it had grown to 2b. By 2025, it was expected to have grown by another 2b, as more Third World countries – especially China and India – became full participants in the global economy.[81] It was reasonable to suppose that a proportion of these workers would, with technological support and faster communications, be able to carry out a broad range of jobs at a fraction of their cost in the United States or Europe. But nobody knew whether there would be jobs to employ all these new workers, or how the global economy would cope with this massive expansion of the labour pool. The logic of the 'new' capitalism suggested a further and dramatic phase of downwards harmonisation, provoking political tensions and social disruption on a scale that lent credence to Gray's anticipation of 'deepening international anarchy'. There was always the possibility that this logic would turn out to be false, that the 'new' capitalism, like so many versions of the 'old', would perform another economic 'miracle' and spread its material benefits widely enough to avert the anticipated crisis. But this scenario, which implied the gradual extension of the consumption levels enjoyed in the First World to everywhere else, offered equally alarming prospects: the rapid exhaustion of the planet's natural resources and a fast track to environmental collapse.[82] Either way, in the narratives we have considered here, the 'new' capitalism prompted a pessimism which, if originating in the West, was global in its reach.

In reading these narratives, it was difficult not to experience a profound sense of déja vu, which could be traced back through 150 years of Marxian literature to *The Communist Manifesto* itself. A massively globalised capitalism, constant revolutions in production, instability and recurrent crises, increasingly commodified labour, the collapse of the family, persistent social disruption, all of this was foreseen by Marx and Engels in their famous vision of a world where 'all that is solid melts into air'.[83] As Hobsbawm observed, it was remarkable that they should have been able to write in 1848 an account of capitalism not as it was then but of how it was destined to transform the world: at the end of the twentieth century, this transformation had taken place more or less as predicted.[84] The irony, of course, was that just as Marx's apocalyptic warnings seemed so apposite to the 'new' capitalism of our own time, the political regimes which had claimed Marx as their inspiration, having been comprehensively discredited, were now finally disintegrating. It was difficult to think of any other intellectual of modern times (with the possible exception of Freud) who had got it both so right and so wrong, and on such a grand scale, at the same time; right, because his analysis of the underlying logic and dynamic of capitalism had never been bettered; wrong, because capitalism did not 'produce its own grave-diggers' – at least, not in the way in which he foresaw. This explained the sharp dichotomy in Marx's intellectual legacy: on the one hand, his account of capitalism's dynamic yet self-destructive powers continued to have an extraordinary resonance, echoing, as we have seen, through the writings of an otherwise politically diverse group of contemporary analysts; on the other, his utopian visions of communism as 'the solution to the riddle of history' had, in the postmodern world, at best been met with incredulity and at worst held responsible for some of the most terrible crimes against humanity. The real significance of this dichotomy lay in the subsequent decoupling of critiques of capitalism from any idea of what could conceivably replace it. Capitalism, like its predecessors, would turn out to be another temporary phase in humanity's history; who, apart from Fukuyama, could confidently predict otherwise? But no one could suggest what the next phase could possibly be like: the post-capitalist world could not even be imagined, let alone planned for. In these narratives, we were left with Marx's sense of incipient crisis, amplified and recast for our own times, but without the capacity to see beyond it. The intimations of apocalypse remained; but all glimpses of new Jerusalem had vanished from sight.

Notes

1. Fukuyama, *The End of History and the Last Man.*
2. For example, Chile under Pinochet, Taiwan, South Korea and Thailand in the 1960s, etc.
3. Gray, *False Dawn,* pp. 119–21.
4. Luttwak, *Turbo-Capitalism: Winners and Losers in the Global Economy,* pp. 27–8, and Gray, *False Dawn,* p. 141.
5. Soros, *The Crisis of Capitalism,* p. xxii.
6. Harvey, *The Condition of Postmodernity,* pp. 121–97.
7. Ibid. p. 147.
8. Ibid. pp. 125–40.
9. Hobsbawm, *Age of Extremes,* p. 286.
10. Harvey, *The Condition of Postmodernity,* p. 142.
11. Ibid. p. 152.
12. Longworth, *Global Squeeze,* p. 85.
13. Harvey, *The Condition of Postmodernity,* p. 180.

14. Ibid. p. 156.
15. Luttwak, *Turbo-Capitalism*, p. 110.
16. Ibid. p. 110.
17. Ibid. p. 235.
18. Gray, *False Dawn*, p. 54.
19. Ibid. p. 62.
20. Longworth, *Global Squeeze*, p. 46.
21. Ibid. p. 49.
22. Ibid. p. 8.
23. Gray, *False Dawn*, p. 61.
24. Ibid. p. 62.
25. Longworth, *Global Squeeze*, p. 31.
26. Ibid. p. 31.
27. Quoted in Gray, *False Dawn*, p. 62.
28. Longworth, *Global Squeeze*, pp. 32–3.
29. Hirst and Thompson, *Globalization in Question*.
30. Soros, *The Crisis of Capitalism*, pp. 103–8.
31. Harvey, *The Condition of Postmodernity*, p. 194.
32. Longworth, *Global Squeeze*, p. 6.
33. Luttwak, *Turbo-Capitalism*, p. 36.
34. Bunting, 'Stop. I want to get off'.
35. Luttwak, *Turbo-Capitalism*, p. 58.
36. See Gray, *False Dawn*, p. 82; Soros, *The Crisis of Capitalism*, p. 208; Luttwak, *Turbo-Capitalism*, p. 61; Longworth, *Global Squeeze*, p. 24.
37. Gray, *False Dawn*, p. 85.
38. OECD, *Labour Force Statistics: 1977–1997*, pp. 32–3.
39. Luttwak, *Turbo-Capitalism*, pp. 62–3. Measured in constant 1982 dollars, the average earnings of all non-supervisory American employees (except in agriculture or government) peaked in 1978 at $8.40 per hour. In 1997 it was $7.66 and equivalent to 1966 levels (Luttwak, *Turbo-Capitalism*, p. 96).
40. Longworth, *Global Squeeze*, pp. 199–200.
41. Luttwak, *Turbo-Capitalism*, p. 62.
42. Ibid. p. 67.
43. Longworth, *Global Squeeze*, p. 75.
44. Edward Walsh, 'Prison population still rising, but more slowly'.
45. OECD, 'Frequently requested statistics'.
46. Longworth, *Global Squeeze*, p. 197.
47. Weinberg, *A Brief Look at Postwar U.S. Income Inequality*. See also the State Fiscal Project, *Pulling Apart*.
48. Bauman, *Globalization*, p. 72.
49. Gray, *False Dawn*, pp. 111–12.
50. Soros, *The Crisis of Capitalism*, p. 75.
51. Bauman, *Globalization*, p. 80.

52. Ibid. p. 83.
53. Longworth, *Global Squeeze*, p. 61.
54. Soros, *The Crisis of Capitalism*, p. 71.
55. Gray, *False Dawn*, p. 70.
56. Bauman, *Globalization*, p. 58.
57. Longworth, *Global Squeeze*, p. 232.
58. Quoted ibid. p. 232.
59. Alan Blinder and Eisuke Sakikabara, quoted ibid. p. 135.
60. OECD, *Labour Force Statistics: 1977–1997*, pp. 32–3.
61. Robert M. Orr, jnr., quoted in Longworth, *Global Squeeze*, p. 153.
62. Longworth, *Global Squeeze*, p. 15.
63. Luttwak, *Turbo-Capitalism*, p. 247.
64. A 1996 survey of 10,000 medium-sized companies found that one-third of them were planning to move part of their production abroad. See Hildyard, Hines and Lang, 'Who competes? Changing landscapes of corporate control', *The Ecologist*, vol. 26, No. 4, July/August 1996, pp. 125–44 (135), referred to in Gray, *False Dawn*, p. 86.
65. Longworth, *Global Squeeze*, p. 19.
66. Gray, *False Dawn*, p. 92.
67. Luttwak, *Turbo-Capitalism*, p. 126.
68. Ibid. pp. 125–6.
69. Ibid. pp. 247–79. The selected countries were:
ex-state capitalist ('communist') countries being privatized – China, Czech Republic (process complete), Hungary, Poland, Romania, Russian Federation, Slovenia and Ukraine (process only started); residual state-capitalist ('communist') economies – Belarus, Cuba, North Korea and Vietnam; controlled economies being privatized/deregulated – Argentina, Australia, Chile, France, India, Italy, Japan, Korea (South), Mexico, Peru, Spain and Turkey; and fully 'turbo-capitalist' economies – Hong Kong, New Zealand, Singapore, Taiwan, United Kingdom and United States.

The key indicators which Luttwak used to measure the advance of 'turbo-capitalism' were: (1) role of the state, regional and/or local, authorities in the economy – ownership of industry: privatization underway? ownership of services: privatization underway? ownership of agricultural land: privatization underway? (2) barriers to international commerce – tarriffs, licences required? quotas, vexatious non-tariff barriers, investment restrictions and limits on service imports; (3) barriers to internal competition – bank ownership public, bank ownership private, bank privatization underway? restrictions on bank activities, stock-market activities, central planning of the economy, degree of regulation by: bureaucratic controls and licensing.
70. Gray, *False Dawn*, p. 78.
71. Luttwak, *Turbo-Capitalism*, pp. 236–7.

72. Longworth, *Global Squeeze*, p. 100.
73. Hobsbawm, *Age of Extremes*, pp. 584–5.
74. Soros, *The Crisis of Capitalism*, p. 103.
75. Ibid. pp. 170–1.
76. Ibid. p. 174.
77. Barber, *Jihad vs. McWorld*, p. 20.
78. Gray, *False Dawn*, p. 207.
79. This was poignantly illustrated in *Mange Tout*, a documentary film shown on the UK's Channel 4 in October 1996. The film recorded the gratitude shown by agricultural workers in Kenya to the Tesco supermarket chain, to which they supplied mangetout peas. It was reported that these workers were paid 1p for every 150 gms of mangetout picked. When Tesco buyers visited the farm to discuss the possibility of a future order of peas, they were treated to a 'royal' welcoming ceremony in the village, which involved the flying of the Tesco's flag, the offering of gifts, and performances of traditional dance and songs, with words adapted to praise 'Tesco'. Some of the workers believed that 'Tesco' was a European country.
80. The companies were Lucky Goldstar and Ronson. *Independent*, 13 January 1997, referred to in Gray, *False Dawn*, pp. 84–5.
81. Longworth, *Global Squeeze*, p. 96.
82. Barber calculated, for example, that if China really did succeed in its policy of cars for everyone, as it promised to do in 1994, and if the Chinese were to drive as many per capita passenger miles as the Americans did, it would take only five years to use up all the earth's known energy reserves. See Barber, *Jihad vs. McWorld*, pp. 37–8.
83. K. Marx and F. Engels, *The Communist Manifesto*, p. 83. This phrase was taken by Marshall Berman for the title of his own exploration of modernity.
84. Hobsbawm, '23 pages that shook the world', p. 5.

5

Cultural Pessimism

I see that what you feel leads to how you think; that it drafts out your conclusions in advance

(Tim Lott, *The Scent of Dried Roses*)

RAYMOND WILLIAMS'S OBSERVATION THAT 'culture' is 'one of the two or three most complicated words in the English language' must be one of the two or three most frequently used quotations in the collective writings on culture.[1] It is not necessary to give a reprise of his history of the word here, only to reiterate that 'culture' can be conceived of as on a continuum, from 'culture' in its narrowest sense as a set of intellectual and artistic practices, through 'culture' as a 'signifying system', to 'culture' in its broadest sense as a 'whole way of life'. It is 'culture' in this last sense to which the cultural pessimism that is the subject of this book primarily refers.

If the narratives examined in the previous chapters are taken together, we can see how they might coalesce to produce a representation of decline that was not only pessimistic but also reflected so many different aspects of the postmodern world that the pessimism generated could justifiably be described as cultural. As acknowledged in the Introduction, a representation of the cultural in this broad sense was always going to be partial, given the impossibility of representing 'a whole way of life', and particularly when that 'whole way of life' was defined by a period, rather than a specific civilisation, nation or group. Nevertheless, the configuration used here – of the environmental, the moral, the intellectual and the political – at least provides some form of matrix through which the viewing of the

178

culture of a period can be attempted. Of course, the matrix could be constructed in alternative ways, as could each element within it, and it must therefore also be acknowledged that, in charting and juxtaposing these particular narratives, we are at the same time creating our own narrative: this book has been a story of stories.

While the logic behind this construction of the cultural will be readily understood, the representation which it produces will be strongly resisted by some readers. In the first instance, there will be those who simply do not accept the validity of the arguments which one or more of the narratives present. This might be due to a rejection of the evidence, alternative interpretations of the same evidence, adherence to a different set of values or a combination of these factors. References to these 'oppositional' perspectives, such as those of Raymond Tallis in Chapter 3 and Francis Fukuyama in Chapter 4, have been made throughout the book. If our representation of decline can only be seen as cultural with the acceptance of all its different narratives; if our idea of the cultural is contingent upon the sum of all the different parts, then it takes the rejection of only one of these parts for the whole notion of cultural decline, and the cultural pessimism that comes with it, to fall away.

Secondly, although convinced by the individual narratives of decline, some readers will either consider that, in their totality, they do not cover enough ground to produce a representation that can justifiably be called cultural; or, that representing the culture of the 'postmodern world', as opposed to that of a specific people or group, involves a level of generalisation that is just not sustainable. Indeed, given, as we have noted, that any representation of the cultural will always be inadequate, there will be those who prefer to reject the idea altogether, seeing it as too nebulous and imprecise to have any value in analytical discourse.

Thirdly, although accepting the arguments of the narratives, and willing to go along with the synecdochic quality of cultural representation, some readers will consider that more positive and optimistic narratives have been wilfully excluded, resulting in an excessively negative representation that is in fact highly partial; or, to put it another way, it is not just a question of whether the glass has been seen as half full or half empty: there appears to be almost nothing in the glass at all.

Finally, there will be those who resist the notion of cultural decline on the grounds that knowledge in the postmodern world has become so specialised and so complex that it is no longer possible for anyone other than specialists, who will often disagree amongst themselves, to make judgements on the formidable and often abstruse issues that the various narratives raise.[2] The experience of intellectual uncertainly that this can generate is exacerbated by two further factors: the sheer impossibility of assimilating the huge volume of information that is increasing in virtually every department of knowledge; and the consciousness that the 'purity' of knowledge cannot be taken for granted, that it is a valuable commodity whose creation and exploitation is increasingly governed by commercial interests. All this can reduce the student of culture to the status of observer, intellectually disempowered, and certain of nothing except his own uncertainty.

If our representation of cultural decline can be rejected or resisted on any of these grounds, then it follows that the cultural pessimism which stems from it will only be experienced when all of the following conditions are met: (1) when the narratives of decline, together with their different pessimisms, are broadly accepted *in toto*; (2) when these narratives, although synecdochic, are collectively considered to be an adequate representation of the culture of the postmodern world; (3) when there is no attachment to more positive or optimistic narratives; and (4), despite the difficulties involved, when judgements have been made over a broad range of specialised, complex and often highly technical issues.

Whether or not these conditions are met will, of course, to some extent depend upon intellectual judgement, which in turn is intimately associated with the values that an individual holds. However, in arriving at a position of cultural pessimism as we have conceptualised it here, intellectual judgement may not be the only factor involved; or at least, not in the sense that it operates as an autonomous sphere, independent of that interacting complex of cognition, affection and motivation which makes up the psychological system. Indeed, it is questionable whether any intellectual activity can exist in such an autonomous state, but that is beyond the scope of our discussion here. What we can say, in looking at the intellectual judgements which lead to the formation of cultural pessimism, is that the cognitive processes behind these judgements may be closely bound up with other psychological factors; and that these factors may produce a disposition towards forms of reasoning which can result in cultural pessimism. If we refer back to the 'conditions' set out in the previous paragraph, we can identify three distinct aspects of this reasoning: first, the tendency to generalise, which, as we have seen, is a sine qua non of attempting to take a view of the cultural; secondly, an attachment to the negative, with a corresponding *de*tachment from the positive; and thirdly, an attachment to certainty, despite the formidable problems of finding certainty on a canvas as large as the cultural. In short, cultural pessimism is characterised by generalised negative certainty.

If we want to understand this condition further, we can usefully turn to studies in cognitive psychology and, in particular, the work of Aaron Beck, where we find some interesting parallels between the mode of reasoning identified above and some of the cognitive tendencies which are associated with depression and anxiety disorders.[3] In brief, Beck's research, which has been subsequently endorsed by a number of other researchers within both cognitive and social psychology, has led him to conclude that all depressive disorders and many anxiety disorders are accompanied by what he calls the 'negative cognitive shift'.[4] This refers to a shift in the cognitive apparatus, which produces an endless cycle of 'automatic' negative thoughts, resulting in an incapacity to see the self, the world or the future in anything other than negative terms. Although the subject will be painfully aware of the thoughts themselves, he is usually no more conscious of the biased cognitive processes that produce them than of 'the functioning of the internal organs'.[5] Beck is careful not to suggest that these thoughts cause depression or anxiety (this would be analogous to suggesting that delusions cause schizophrenia), but he does propose that they can 'shape' the feelings which characterise these conditions.[6] At the same time, since the cognitive and the affective are so obviously linked within the psychological system as a whole, depressive and anxious feelings can themselves produce the negative thinking that is characteristic of the 'negative cognitive shift'. Indeed, Lewis Wolpert, a distinguished biologist who, having suffered from depression himself, has reviewed the current state of knowledge about it, leans towards the idea that changes in feeling precede changes in cognition and that the 'cognitive shift' is brought about by the malignant invasion by emotion of cognitive processes.[7] In this view, individuals adjust their thinking to fit in with the emotions they feel, and negative thinking becomes a type of rationalisation of that individual's own fear or sadness. However, whether cognition precedes emotion or whether emotion precedes cognition, there is little disagreement that automatic negative thoughts feature strongly in depression and many anxiety disorders. Negative thinking and negative feeling are closely entwined, producing, at their worst, a feedback loop, with negative thoughts generating negative feelings which generate more negative thoughts ad infinitum.

What are the nature of these negative thoughts? On the basis of the observation of depressed and anxious patients over a period of many years, Beck and others have built up an 'inventory' of the cognitive tendencies which these patients repeatedly exhibit.[8] They include, for example, the propensity to make negative 'overgeneralisations' on the basis of limited evidence which are then extrapolated out into predictions of the future. Thus, a localised and contingent incident becomes symptomatic of an eternal and unchanging verity. This process is often facilitated by what Beck calls 'cognitive blockade', or 'selective abstraction', that is, the tendency to screen out positive information and to admit only the negative. Alternatively, the positive is given minimal significance, while the implications of the negative are magnified. This can reflect another tendency, that of 'dichotomous thinking', in which the individual thinks in polar opposites, seeing things as either all good or all bad, unable to tolerate ambiguity or uncertainty. As things are rarely all good, they are invariably perceived as all bad. Both depressed and anxious people persistently 'catastrophise', that is to say, dwell on the worst possible outcome of any situation in which dangers or threats present themselves. The probability of such an outcome and the possible consequences of its occurrence are both exaggerated. Moreover, danger will always be detected somewhere, because the anxious person maintains a hypersensitive alarm system, constantly scanning the environment for signs of impending disaster or personal harm. As Beck puts it, cognitive processes become 'usurped' by the primal mode of anxiety response.[9]

What all these negative modes of thinking have in common is the conviction that not only can matters not improve but also they are destined to get worse. Those who live with severe depression live without the possibility of hope; those who suffer from anxiety believe that catastrophe awaits them. Terrible as these conditions are, it is evident that they develop in many cases as a defence or a protection against something that is perceived to be even worse. Tim Lott, who has attempted to understand the nature of the depressive illness that devastated his own family (including himself), has observed that depressives believe in the absolute certainty of their own bleak vision.[10] The reason, he argues, why they cling to this vision, is because it serves as a bulwark against doubt; and doubt, or uncertainty, is what human beings fear more than anything else. Thus, 'depression is engineered by the depressive to serve their own – usually hidden or unconscious – purposes, and to bolster their own myths against a frightening, incomprehensible world'.[11] Similarly, 'catastrophising', although it actually intensifies the anxiety it is designed to avoid, is practised by the anxious to 'prepare' them for the worst if and when it arrives. None of this is to suggest that those who suffer from these disorders are somehow 'to blame' for their condition. These defence mechanisms, as we have noted, are largely involuntary, triggered by factors which are beyond the control of the individuals concerned.

From this brief account, we can see that the 'negative cognitive shift' which Beck and others have observed in depressive and anxiety disorders has striking similarities with the 'negative generalised certainty' that we have identified with the formation of cultural pessimism. Of course, there is one crucial distinction, and that is that in depression and anxiety it is towards the self that negativity is primarily directed, whilst in cultural pessimism it is directed towards the external world (culture). But even this distinction is not as clear-cut as it might seem, given the symbiotic relationship between perceptions of the self and of the world: just as the depressed and anxious extend their negative cognitions to the world around them, so do the culturally pessimistic find that their cognitions about the world affect their own selves. It is perhaps useful to think of the distinction as one of degree rather than of kind, with the turn 'inward' and the turn 'outward' inextricably linked, both manifesting forms of psychological defence, and both resting on negatively 'contaminated' cognitive processes. Cultural pessimism might even be seen as a defence against depression or anxiety itself, a projection on to the external world of a negativity which would otherwise be directed towards the self. There are also degrees of 'contamination', which can be seen on a continuum from the severe to the mild, and, as we shall see, the extent to which intellectual judgement might be considered impaired will depend upon the degree of 'contamination' experienced.[12] But, first, it is necessary to look at the causes of this cognitive 'contamination'. What produces this disposition towards negative thinking which cultural pessimism, depression and many forms of anxiety all seem to have in common?

A good place to start is by looking at how thinking and emotions affect the chemistry of the brain and how the chemistry of the brain affects our thinking and feeling. Although we are still a long way from fully understanding these processes, we do now know that specific affective disorders can be shown to correspond with specific changes in the biological functioning of the brain. This is an enormously complex subject, and I have neither the space nor the competence to give anything other than the barest outline of what I understand to be some of the key developments.[13] Perhaps the most widely-known of these is the discovery, which goes back to the 1950s, of the relationship between depressive disorders and levels of serotonin (also known as 5–HT) in the brain. Serotonin is a chemical neurotransmitter, which is believed to play a crucial role in controlling negative feelings, such as sadness, fear and anger, and maintaining adaptive behaviour in the face of threatening or stressful situations. No one is quite certain how it plays this role, but it is now broadly accepted that low serotonin levels feature in a significant proportion of affective disorders and that, when these levels are raised through drugs such as Prozac, the condition of many of those who suffer from these disorders can be greatly improved.[14] However, serotonin is not the only neurotransmitter whose levels can affect emotion and cognition. Noradrenaline, which is both a neurotransmitter and a hormone, has long been implicated in the cause of depression and, indeed, the first generation of antidepressants, Tricyclics, although acting on a number of brain chemicals, were thought to be effective specifically because they succeeded in producing higher concentrations of noradrenaline. Another neurotransmitter, known as substance P because of its involvement with pain, has also been found to play a major role in depression. This is a completely different chemical compound from noradrenaline or serotonin, with a much slower action, but when drugs have been used to raise its level in the brain, they too have been found to reduce the symptoms of depression.

Another group of chemical signals thought to be significant in the biology of depression are hormones. Hormones circulate throughout the body via the bloodstream and are capable of causing major changes in bodily and brain function. It is through the action of hormones, and in particular that of cortisol, that clear links have been established between stress and depression. Cortisol is one of the steroid hormones known as glucocorticoids, which are released into the bloodstream when stressful events are experienced. Abnormally high levels of cortisol can not only induce depression, but there is evidence to suggest that they can also damage that part of the brain, known as the hippocampus, which is involved in the making of memories. It is significant that memory impairment is itself often one of the symptoms of depression. Cortisol is also linked to serotonin, in that serotonin can affect the mechanism which regulates cortisol levels, and the presence of high cortisol can reduce the function of serotonin.

The way in which the brain is structured throws further light on the biological basis of depressive and anxiety disorders. According to Wolpert, the brain has a number of discrete structures, each of which is associated with specific brain functions. For example, the cortex, which is the outer layer of the brain, is particularly involved in cognitive processes; the amygdala, of similar size and shape to a walnut and lying near the roof of the mouth, plays a crucial role in emotion; close to the amygdala is the hippocampus, which, as mentioned above is associated with memory; and at the base of the brain are the two structures which release hormones, the pituitary and the hippothalmus.[15] The behaviour of these and all the other brain regions are dependent upon neurotransmitters, the chemical mechanism through which the billions of neurons (nerve cells) that make up the brain communicate. The important point to grasp is that, although the different parts of the brain have their specific functions, it is an interdependent system, and activity in one part of the system will impact upon activity in another. Wolpert is particularly interested in how the amygdala, whose functions are associated with emotion, affects other elements of the system, particularly those involved in cognition, and even speculates that the amygdala might be the 'site of origin of malignant sadness' – his term for depressive disorders.[16] There is still much more to be learnt about these processes, but it is clear that the idea of the negative 'contamination' of cognitive processes, which we have taken from cognitive psychology, is consistent with what is already known about the structure and functioning of the brain.

However, to know that specific affective disorders can correlate with specific changes in the functioning of the brain does not necessarily take us much further in understanding the causes of these disorders and of the negative thinking that they exhibit. Low serotonin, for example, might be a physical cause of depression, but what causes low serotonin? Does it represent no more than a physiological malfunction, the explanation for which can be found solely in terms of a breakdown in the organism's operating system? Or can it be related in some way to environmental factors? Or, to use clinical terminology, are there both endogenous and exogenous conditions, that is to say, those which have a mainly biological origin and those which result from 'life events'? Lott traces this distinction right back to Ancient Greece, where Imhotep, Homer and the Greek temple doctors believed 'melancholy' to be one of the four kinds of madness, rooted in physical disease, whilst the Greek dramatists saw it as the result of inner conflicts. Ever since, Lott suggests, 'a dirty war has been going on over the real meaning of depression, with the battlefield divided between these two camps'.[17] One camp is now inhabited by the psychiatrists, who see depression and other disorders as dysfunctions of the brain, to be treated by drugs and other medical interventions; the other is inhabited by psychologists, therapists and analysts, who see it as a psychological dysfunction, which can be addressed through a variety of 'talking' cures.

Although these two camps undoubtedly still exist, the divisions between them have become increasingly blurred. As we have seen in the case of stress-related depression, for example, many affective disorders can be traced both to changes in brain chemistry and to 'life events'. Nevertheless, there is evidence to suggest that in a significant proportion of cases either the disorder itself, or the vulnerability to the disorder (which could be triggered by a 'life event'), is genetically determined. Take anxiety, for example. Anxiety is a normal response to a threatening situation and fulfils a constructive role by keeping us alert when we encounter these threats and dangers. It is only when anxiety becomes overactive, when threats are exaggerated, 'catastrophised' or constantly imagined, that it becomes dysfunctional. Studies of infants and young children, with supporting evidence from studies of infant rhesus monkeys, have suggested that levels of 'reactivity' are influenced by our genetic inheritance.[18] This does not, of course, mean that environmental factors can be discounted, but it may explain why similar environmental conditions can produce such differing levels of anxiety within different people. Studies of identical twins have shown that genes also play an important part in the disposition towards major depressive illnesses. These suggest that the heritability for such illnesses, that is, the extent to which an individual's susceptibility to the illness can be attributed to genetic factors, is as much as 50 per cent or 60 per cent.[19] The position is different, however, with minor depression, where heritability is reckoned to be no more than 10 per cent.[20]

If genetic inheritance is only partially responsible for an individual's vulnerability to depression and anxiety, and if, in the case of minor depression, it plays only a minimal role, then what are the other factors involved? This is, of course, a very large subject which cannot be examined in its entirety here, but it is nevertheless still possible to make some general observations which will throw light on the matters with which we are primarily concerned. A particularly useful concept is that of 'learned helplessness'. This was first postulated by Martin Seligman, following laboratory experiments in which dogs were repeatedly given moderately painful electric shocks from which there was initially no possibility of escape. The dogs soon became listless and helpless, giving up all attempts to escape, even when the possibility was subsequently introduced. Studies on humans in experimental situations showed that they also became passive and 'helpless' if, when confronted with unpleasant experiences, they found that whatever they did they could not reduce either the incidence or the intensity of these experiences. Seligman believed that the symptoms of experimentally helpless humans and animals were almost identical to those of depressed people.[21] The common factor was a loss of control over external events and a conviction that nothing could be done to regain it. This loss of control is characteristic of many of the 'life events', such as bereavement, poverty and chronic illness, that are known to be linked with depression.

Further insights into the environmental causes of depression can be found in 'rank theory' and the notion of 'ritualised submission'. This theory connects with evolutionary explanations of depression, which suggest that depressive behaviour is integral to the establishment of the status hierarchies that are common to most groups of mammals. The emergence of these hierarchies is usually accompanied by a physical struggle for dominance amongst members of the group. Following such a struggle, it has been observed that those who have been defeated display the submissive and 'helpless' behaviour that is characteristic of depression in humans. The defeated animal stops taking initiatives, appears to lose confidence and becomes withdrawn, passive and inhibited. However, this only happens if the animal is unable to escape and forced to remain within the group. Amongst vervet monkeys, there is also evidence that low status correlates with low serotonin levels which, as we have seen, is a biological indicator of depression. The submissive behaviour displayed is said to have served an adaptive function, in that it signals to those at the top of the hierarchy that those beneath do not constitute a threat. Through 'ritualised submission' – also referred to as 'depressive strategy' – the subordinated thus decrease the likelihood of attack by dominant members of the group. In this way, depression evolves as a psychobiological mechanism which contributes to survival. However, as the clinical psychologist, Oliver James, points out, whilst depression might serve a useful evolutionary function amongst primates and other mammals, 'in humans it is a pathological hangover from our primordial past'.[22] There is evidence to suggest, as we shall see, that the social conditions under which humans feel subordinate or inferior may be increasing, and that these conditions continue to promote depressive feelings; but as it is no longer necessary to display these feelings to avoid physical attack (at least, not usually), 'ritualised submission' has long since ceased to confer evolutionary advantage.

Of course, many people experience low social status and the sense that they have little control over their lives, without succumbing to the negativity of depression or hyperanxiety. As we have seen, genetic disposition is one determining factor in this, but another, for adults, is the legacy of their childhood experiences. The influence of Freud in this respect has been enormous, and although Freud's methods have been ferociously attacked in recent years,[23] and his account of the child's progress through the Oedipus complex largely discredited, it is still largely due to Freud that childhood experiences are today seen to be so emotionally formulative. But whereas Freud focused on an imagined sexual obstacle course which every child had to negotiate before it could emerge as an emotionally stable adult, modern psycho-analytical theorists tend to focus on the quality of the relationships that the young child is able to form with those around him. Influential amongst these are the so-called 'object-relations theorists', in particular, John Bowlby, whose theory of attachment places great importance on the patterns of attachment that a young child develops with its parents or carers, especially between the ages of six months and three years.[24] If a young child experiences secure parental care, then he is likely to 'internalise' this, develop a strong sense of self-esteem and enter into satisfactory relationships of his own as he gets older. If, on the other hand, he forms 'anxious' attachments, that is to say, becomes fearful of rejection or abandonment, he is more likely to develop a sense of inadequacy and insecurity in later life. This can lead to further difficulties in relationships with others, including those with his own children, when the time comes. The legacy of all this can be a pervasive sense of low self-esteem, itself both a symptom and a cause of depression, and a lack of resilience towards those other depressogenic influences, namely low status and lack of control, which we have considered above.

From this brief survey, we can see that depression and anxiety, and the cognitive and affective negativity that comes with them, can be explained with reference to biological mechanisms, 'life events', psychological tendencies formed in childhood and the interaction of all these different factors within the individual. But they also need to be seen in a historical and social context. Are there particular periods of history or types of society in which depression and anxiety are more prevalent than in others? This is an extremely difficult question to answer, both because the medical concepts of these conditions have varied greatly over time and because the precise data is simply not available. There is the further problem that depression and anxiety, although universal across all cultures, can be expressed in very different ways. In Peru, India, Turkey and Iraq, for example, they are often somatised, that is, emotional pain is expressed as bodily pain. This was also true of communist regimes, where depression, as it was understood in the West, was dismissed as a bourgeois construct. So cross-cultural and long-term historical comparisons can at best be no more than speculative. However, as data has accumulated, and as organisations such as the World Health Organisation have developed international classifications of diseases, it has been possible to get a clearer idea of trends in more recent times; and these trends show a significant increase in depression and anxiety, across many different countries, during the second half of the twentieth century.[25] Today, in the USA and Europe, the percentage of the population that is at any one time severely depressed (see n. 12 for definition) is now reckoned to be about 3 per cent, and over a period of one year, around 7 per cent. The percentage that will experience a major depressive episode in their lifetime is anything between 10 per cent and 15 per cent.[26] Given that the definitions of severe depression are so strict, the number of people that experience some form of depressive or anxiety disorder is obviously much greater. One study, published in 1992, found that three-quarters of the US population suffered from 'one or more unreasonable fears, spells of panic or general nervousness'.[27] In the developing world, according to the World Health Organisation, depression had become the fourth most important health problem by 1990 and is now expected to become the number one health problem by 2020.[28] In James's view, it is for once 'no exaggeration to use the word "epidemic" in describing a social trend'.[29]

Why should this be so? Why should the postmodern world exhibit such trends? Genetic factors can obviously be ruled out, as changes in the genetic pool could not possibly take place over such a short period of time. If an explanation is to be found, it will therefore lie in changes to the social environment, which can be specifically linked to the affective conditions we have discussed. But can such links be made? Can an increase in 'learned helplessness', for example, be traced back to specific forms of social organisation? 'Learned helplessness', it will be recalled, describes a depressive condition, which can arise when the individual feels trapped in a negative situation over which he has no control and from which he feels there is no escape. The incidence of some of the factors associated with this condition, such as bereavement and chronic illness, will have obviously remained fairly constant over the last few decades, or, in the case of illness, even decreased due to medical advances. But during the same period, as we saw in the last chapter, there was evidence that an increasingly aggressive global economy was promoting widespread insecurity, growing inequality and a powerful sense of instability in social life; in short, precisely those conditions under which people can feel they have less and less control over their own lives.

For Oliver James, these conditions are made even more 'emotionally toxic' by the pressures which lead to what he sees as a growing trend in 'maladaptive social comparison'. By this he means the tendency to compare oneself unfavourably with others, developing incessantly negative valuations of the self and internalising a sense of inferiority. In this way, self-esteem is eroded, and one's status is perpetually experienced as subordinate; in other words, 'maladaptive social comparison' becomes the modern form of 'ritualised submission' which, as we saw above, was conducive to both the biological and psychological symptoms of depression. Drawing on an extensive series of studies, James cites four main factors which he believes can explain this development. First, rampant individualism, which has become the dominant political and economic value of the West, has led to constant 'upward comparison' and a growing gap between expectation and reality. Secondly, the mass media fuels such comparisons, presenting an overwhelmingly idealised view of both men and women and establishing wholly unrealistic 'norms'. Thirdly, with the realisation by governments that education is crucial to economic growth, children throughout the developed world have been spending more time in the classroom and have been exposed to intensifying educational competition. The comparisons thus engendered can leave many children with lifelong feelings of intellectual inadequacy. Finally, the increased competitiveness of the global economy is reflected in the labour market, where employees must not only compete ever more fiercely with each other to gain employment, but are then subjected to an unprecedented level of competitive assessment once in employment.[30] All these factors can work together to produce a deep-rooted sense of failure, a conviction that, whatever one does, it will never actually be 'enough'.

However, in James's account, the increasing incidence of maladaptive social comparison, and the feelings of low status and low self-esteem which it generates, is not the only explanation for the spread, to use Tim Lott's phrase, of 'this modern plague'. A second factor, which can also be a contributory cause of the first, is the increasing incidence of 'anxious attachment'. James attributes much of this to the astronomical rise in divorce which has been taking place throughout the West since the 1950s. In this, his conclusions are consistent with those studies we referred to in Chapter 2, which found that the children of divorced parents were far more prone to depression and other psychological problems than the children of parents who had not separated. But James also reminds us of another and often overlooked aspect of Bowlby's attachment theory, namely, that it is not only stability that is important to young children but also responsiveness. If the main carer does not, or is not able to, respond consistently to the child's emotional demands, then there is a significantly higher risk of 'anxious attachment' as the child grows older. 'Unresponsiveness' has been found to be highest amongst both nonmaternal carers and mothers who themselves suffer from depression. According to James, the number of children looked after by both these groups has increased in recent years: the former because more and more mothers work full-time outside the home and need to leave their children with childminders or in daycare centres; the latter because mothers who stay with their infants feel increasingly under-valued and socially isolated.[31] This is the Scylla and Charybdis between which so many women, particularly single mothers and/or those with low-income, try to steer their children to emotional safety.

As James points out, when families disintegrate, the psychological consequences can be comparable to bereavement for those involved. Bearing this in mind, he calculates that the two and half million or so divorces which have taken place in Britain alone since 1950 may well have caused as much distress to relatives and friends as the 470,000 British people killed during World War II. Of course, he does not deny that there are many happily separated couples who in an earlier period would have been trapped in dismal relationships; but he speculates that there may well have been 'a great many more whose lives have been wrecked by the pursuit of "greener grass" which in the event turned to straw'.[32] Furthermore, the difficulties of finding happiness in personal relationships are exacerbated, on the one hand, by what he sees as increasingly unrealistic expectations placed upon them; and, on the other, by unprecedented levels of 'gender rancour' as men and women struggle to find a stable basis for relating to one another when all the old co-ordinates appear to be in a ceaseless state of flux. Add to this the increasing loneliness of the elderly as the atomisation of family and social life continues, and we begin to get some idea of the scale of what James refers to as this 'tidal wave of broken bonds'.[33]

We can now return to the subject of cultural pessimism and make some concluding comments. It was suggested earlier in the chapter that cultural pessimism was characterised by generalised negative certainty; and that there were some clear parallels between the modes of reasoning displayed and some of the cognitive tendencies associated with depression and anxiety disorders. These tendencies were described by Aaron Beck as representing a negative cognitive shift. In his model, which was consistent with what was known about the interconnectedness of different brain functions, negative thoughts produced negative emotions and vice-versa. Cultural pessimism, depression and many forms of anxiety disorder could therefore all be said to exhibit negatively 'contaminated' cognitive processes. From studies of depression and anxiety, a disposition towards negative cognitions could be attributed to one or more of four main factors: genetic inheritance, bio-chemical dysfunction, 'life-events', and psychological tendencies formed in childhood. Although long-term historical trends were impossible to establish, there was evidence to suggest that there had been a significant increase in the incidence of depressive and anxiety disorders during the second half of the twentieth century. In Oliver James's view, this was due to the social impacts of the 'new' capitalism, which was producing an epidemic of 'learned helplessness', 'maladaptive social comparison' and 'anxious attachment'.

If I am right in suggesting that cultural pessimism is another manifestation of Beck's negative cognitive shift; that, in other words, it is itself a form of minor depression, in which negative thoughts and negative feelings feed back on each other, then we can say that the intellectual judgements on which cultural pessimism rests are inflected by that same complex of biological, psychological and sociological factors that are linked to the incidence of some forms of depression and anxiety. Moreover, if James is right – which I believe he is – to suggest that over the last few decades these disorders have been exacerbated by the conditions of the 'new' capitalism, then we can say that the same is probably also true of cultural pessimism; that in the postmodern world cultural pessimism is thus not only a judgement about our culture, but also a structure of feeling that is increasingly produced by our culture. The idea that cultural pessimism is itself a form of mild depression raises the interesting question of whether the intellectual judgements that are integral to it might be affected by antidepressant drugs or even forms of therapy. Pertinent to this are the experiments conducted by James with a group of artists in 1995, during which they took Prozac to see how it affected their creative work. Two of these artists, whose work had reflected dark and melancholic preoccupations, found that having taken the drug the content of their work changed, taking on a lighter tone.[34] If SSRI antidepressants can affect artistic vision in this way, it seems logical to suppose that they might also affect judgements of the kind of world or culture we inhabit. Schopenhauer on Prozac would perhaps have produced a very different philosophical system.

So does this mean that we dismiss cultural pessimism, rejecting its generalisations, its negativity and its certainty as no more than the illusions of a 'contaminated' cognitive system? Or do we still remain attached to it, despite all the caveats, constructing a vision of the cultural out of the pessimistic narratives which surround us? If the argument of this chapter is valid – that cultural pessimism is as much a function of disposition as it is of disinterested intellectual judgement – then we may not have a great deal of control over how we answer these questions; at least, not without working on the complex set of factors which give rise to this disposition. But where does this leave 'truth'? Is one kind of disposition more likely to lead to error than another? Does negatively 'contaminated' cognition always produce, as we might expect, false representations of reality? This of course begs the philosophical question of whether reality can ever be known and whether a representation of it can therefore be said to be false. However, we can bypass this particular conundrum by turning again to studies in social psychology, where, under experimental conditions, reality can be functionally defined and the degree of distortion of an individual's perception of it accurately measured. Here, we come across the counter-intuitive finding that it is not negative 'contamination' which is most responsible for cognitive illusions, but what we might term positive 'contamination'; that positive illusions are not only widespread but are actually a fundamental characteristic of what is considered to be 'normal' human thought.[35]

What are these positive illusions? Numerous studies have now established that 'normal' (that is, non-depressed) people exhibit three main tendencies: first, they tend to maintain unrealistically positive views of themselves, persistently overestimating their strengths and discounting their weaknesses; secondly, they tend to have an exaggerated belief in their ability to control their environment; and, thirdly, they nurture a view of the future that is unrealistically optimistic, believing that it will bring what is personally or socially desirable rather than what is objectively likely.[36] These illusions are not only 'pervasive, enduring and systematic' but have been shown to fulfil an essential role in maintaining psychological well-being, particularly during times of adversity.[37] By keeping negative thinking and feeling at bay, they act as a bulwark against depression and anxiety, helping to maintain a sense of happiness or contentment. This in turn has been shown to enhance an individual's capacity both to develop rewarding relationships with others and to work productively or creatively. The mechanism through which the illusions are generated involves a kind of cognitive screening process, which filters incoming information and distorts it in positive ways. This is reinforced by a variety of social interaction norms which, as two of the leading researchers in this field put it, 'conspire to protect the individual from the harsher side of reality'.[38] Even if negative cognitions penetrate these defences, following painful and unpleasant events, their impact is often only temporary: positive illusions may be briefly dispersed, but after a period of time, they 'drift' back and gradually reconstitute themselves.[39] All this adds up to a system of information processing which bears out T. S. Eliot's famous observation in his *Four Quartets* that:

> humankind
> Cannot bear very much reality.[40]

And the reality it can bear the least, of course, is death, to which the impulse to create positive illusions can be so clearly traced and against which such illusions offer the last line of defence.

We should be wary, therefore, of assuming that a disposition towards cultural pessimism is any more likely to lead to error than a disposition towards more optimistic visions of the future; that negative 'contamination' necessarily produces more cognitive distortion than positive 'contamination'. Indeed, some studies have postulated the existence of 'depressive realism', on the basis of evidence which suggests that depressed people have a more realistic assessment of both their level of control over events and their likely future circumstances than the non-depressed.[41] These studies are not yet conclusive, but Aaron Beck has proposed a convincing model of cognitive bias, in which it is the degree of depression that is critical. In this model, cognitive bias is shown on a continuum, moving from positive bias in the non-depressed towards negative bias in the severely depressed. But at some point in the middle, as cognitive organisation 'shifts towards depression', the positive bias is neutralised.[42] If this model is accurate, then it means that it is those who are in a condition of mild depression that tend to see themselves and their world with the least amount of cognitive distortion.

It can be argued, of course, that these reflections on the relationship between feeling, cognition and the self have little bearing on the serious business of cultural analysis; that although one might harbour distorted visions of oneself and one's immediate environment, the transference of that distortion to a wider canvas is prevented by the rigorous demands of academic discipline. This is an important objection, which resists an over-deterministic view of intellectual endeavour and allows for at least some degree of autonomy. But it is hard to believe that the 'contamination' of some cognitive functions, whether positive or negative, can be 'quarantined' and sealed off, while others remain entirely unaffected. A disposition towards cultural pessimism may therefore be resisted and moderated, but it will be very difficult to shift.

Notes

1. Williams, *Keywords*, p. 76; see also, Williams, *Culture*, pp. 10–14.
2. At a seminar on advancing the public understanding of science, I heard the distinguished biologist Lewis Wolpert tell his audience that there were no more than six people in the world who were able to comment authoritatively on his research. He went on to say that he was therefore not interested in 'opinions' on his work, that science had nothing to do with 'opinion', that sociologists of science were the enemies of science and that attacks on science were no more than 'moral masturbation'. Culture Wars conference, seminar on 'Teaching science or fear of science', Sunday 7 March 1999, held at the Riverside Studios, London.
3. See Beck, 'Cognitive therapy'.
4. Ibid. p. 369.

5. Ibid. p. 373.

6. Ibid. p. 371.

7. Wolpert, *Malignant Sadness*, p. 101.

8. Beck, 'Cognitive therapy', p. 369.

9. Beck, *Anxiety Disorders and Phobia*, p. 24.

10. See Lott, *The Scent of Dried Roses* and 'Story of the Blues'.

11. Lott, 'Story of the Blues', p. 25.

12. As Wolpert points out, very severe depression bears little resemblance to its milder varieties, and should perhaps be considered in a class of its own (Wolpert, *Malignant Sadness*, p. 46). According to the *Diagnostic and Statistical Manual of Mental Disorders* (fourth edition), a major depressive illness can be said to exist when over a period of at least two weeks there is a 'depressed mood or loss of pleasure in nearly all activities'. In addition, five of the following symptoms must be present during that two week period: depressed mood most of the day; diminished interest or pleasure; significant gain or loss of weight; inability to sleep or sleeping too much; reduced control over bodily movements; fatigue; feelings of worthlessness or guilt; inability to think or concentrate; and thoughts of death or suicide (Wolpert, *Malignant Sadness*, p. 17). Wolpert describes his own experience of major depression as 'the worst experience of my life . . . More terrible even than watching my wife die of cancer' (Wolpert, *Malignant Sadness*, p. vii).

13. For a fuller account of this, see ibid. ch. 9, 'Biological explanations and the brain', pp. 102–28.

14. Prozac is only the most well-known of a number of drugs which are classified as SSRIs (Selective Serotonin Reuptake Inhibitors). Others include Faverin, Lustral and Seroxat. When depressed people are treated with these drugs, at least half are reckoned to become less depressed. See Oliver James, *Britain on the Couch*, p. 32.

15. Wolpert, *Malignant Sadness*, p. 105.

16. Ibid. p. 127.

17. Lott, *The Scent of Dried Roses*, p. 69.

18. Wolpert, *Malignant Sadness*, pp. 89 and 92.

19. James, *Britain on the Couch*, p. 33; Wolpert, *Malignant Sadness*, p. 43.

20. James, *Britain on the Couch*, p. 33.

21. Ibid. p. 51.

22. Ibid. p. 51.

23. See, for example, Crews, *Unauthorized Freud*.

24. James, *Britain on the Couch*, p. 142; Wolpert, *Malignant Sadness*, pp. 57–8, 87–92.

25. James, *Britain on the Couch*, pp. 344–5; Wolpert, *Malignant Sadness*, p. 47.

26. Wolpert, *Malignant Sadness*, p. 45.

27. James, *Britain on the Couch*, p. 31.
28. Wolpert, *Malignant Sadness*, pp. ix–x.
29. James, *Britain on the Couch*, p. 31.
30. Ibid. pp. 42–68.
31. Ibid. pp. 128–58.
32. Ibid. pp. 156–7.
33. Ibid. p. 158.
34. Ibid. pp. 244–5.
35. S. E. Taylor and J. D. Brown, 'Illusion and well-being' and 'Positive illusions and well-being revisited'.
36. Taylor and Brown, 'Illusion and Well-Being', p. 197. This article includes a clear account of the methodologies used to establish the existence of 'positive illusions'.
37. Ibid. p. 200.
38. Ibid. p. 201.
39. Ibid. p. 202.
40. Eliot, 'Burnt Norton', *Four Quartets*, p. 190, lines 22–3.
41. See, for example, Alloy and Abramson, 'Judgement of contingency in depressed and nondepressed students'.
42. Beck, 'Cognitive therapy', p. 372.

Bibliography

Adorno, Theodor [1966] (1990), *Negative Dialectics*, trans. E. B. Ashton, London: Routledge.

Adorno, Theodor (1991), *The Culture Industry: Selected Essays on Mass Culture*, ed. J. M. Bernstein, London: Routledge.

Adorno, Theodor and Max Horkheimer [1944] (1979), *Dialectic of Enlightenment*, trans. John Cumming, London: Verso.

Alloy, Lauren B. and Lyn Y. Abramson (1979), 'Judgement of contingency in depressed and nondepressed students: Sadder but wiser?', *Journal of Experimental Psychology: General*, 108: 4, pp. 441–85.

Amis, Martin (1997), *Night Train*, London: Jonathan Cape.

Amnesty (1962), *Amnesty Annual Report 1961/2*, London: Amnesty International.

Amnesty International (1963–97), *Amnesty International Annual Reports 1962/3–1997*, London: Amnesty International.

Amnesty International (1973), *Report on Torture*, London: Gerald Duckworth Ltd.

Amnesty International (1984), *Torture in the Eighties*, London: Amnesty International.

Amnesty International (1996), *International Conference on Torture: Final Report*, London: Amnesty International.

Ang, Ien (1991), *Desperately Seeking the Audience*, London: Routledge.

Appleyard, Brian (1992), *Understanding the Present*, Basingstoke: Pan Books.

Arnold, Matthew [1869] (1981), *Culture and Anarchy*, Cambridge: Cambridge University Press.

Aronowitz, Stanley (1989), *Science as Power: Discourse and Ideology in Modern Society*, Mineapolis: University of Minnesota Press.

Bailey, Joe (1988), *Pessimism*, London: Routledge.

Bibliography

Barber, Benjamin R. (1996), *Jihan vs. McWorld: How Globalism and Tribalism Are Shaping the World*, New York: Ballantine Books.

Baudrillard, Jean (1983), *Simulations*, New York: Semiotext(e).

Baudrillard, Jean (1992), *Selected Writings*, ed. Mark Poster, Oxford: Polity Press/Blackwell Publishers.

Bauman, Zygmunt (1998), *Globalization: The Human Consequences*, Cambridge: Polity Press.

Beck, Aaron T. (1985), *Anxiety Disorders and Phobia: A Cognitive Perspective*, New York: Basic Books.

Beck, Aaron T. (1991), 'Cognitive therapy: A 30–year retrospective', *American Psychologist*, 46:4, pp. 368–75.

Benjamin,Walter (1936), 'The work of art in the age of mechanical reproduction', in Walter Benjamin, *Illuminations*, ed. Hannah Arendt, trans. Harry Zohn, Glasgow: Fontana/Collins, pp. 219–53.

Benjamin, Walter [1950] (1977), 'Theses on the philosophy of history', in Walter Benjamin, *Illuminations*, ed. Hannah Arendt, trans. Harry Zohn, Glasgow: Fontana/Collins, pp. 255–69.

Berlan, Jean-Pierre and Richard C. Lewontin (1999), 'It's business as usual: Analysis special on genetically modified food', *The Guardian*, 22 February.

Berlin, Isaiah (1979), *Against the Current*, London: The Hogarth Press.

Berlin, Isaiah (1990), *The Crooked Timber of Humanity*, London: John Murray.

Berman, Marshall (1982), *All That Is Solid Melts into Air: The Experience of Modernity*, New York: Simon & Schuster.

Blair, B. G. and H. W. Kendall (1990), 'Accidental nuclear war', *Scientific American*, December, pp. 53–8.

Blake, William [1802] (1976), 'Letter to Thomas Butts', in William Blake, *Complete Writings*, ed. Geoffrey Keynes, London: Oxford University Press, pp. 816–19.

Blake, William [1804] (1976), 'Milton', in William Blake, *Complete Writings*, ed. Geoffrey Keynes, London: Oxford University Press, pp. 480–535.

Bradbury, Malcolm and James McFarlane (1991), 'The name and nature of Modernism', in Malcolm Bradbury and James McFarlane (eds), *Modernism: 1890–1930*, Harmondsworth: Penguin Books, pp. 19–55.

British Medical Association (1983), Board of Science and Education, *The Medical Effects of Nuclear War*, Chichester: John Wiley & Sons.

Brown, Paul (1997), 'Illegal trade in banned CFC gases exposed', *The Guardian*, 4 September.

Bullock, Allan (1991), 'The double image', in Malcolm Bradbury and James McFarlane (eds), *Modernism: 1890–1930*, Harmondsworth: Penguin Books, pp. 58–70.

Bunting, Madeleine (1999), 'Stop. I want to get off', *The Guardian*, 19 November.

Calder, Nigel (1980), *Nuclear Nightmares: An Investigation into Possible Wars*, Harmondsworth: Penguin Books.

Capra, Fritjof (1992), *The Tao of Physics: An Exploration of the Parallels between Modern Physics and Eastern Mysticism*, London: Flamingo.

Carey, John (1992), *The Intellectuals and the Masses: Pride and Prejudice among the Literary Intelligentsia, 1880–1939*, London: Faber and Faber.

Carlyle, Thomas [1829] (1986), 'Signs of the times', in Thomas Carlyle, *Selected Writings*, ed. Alan Shelston, Harmondsworth: Penguin Books, pp. 61–85.

Carson, Rachel [1962] (1991), *Silent Spring*, Harmondsworth: Penguin Books.

Cohen, Stanley (1973), *Folk Devils & Moral Panics*, St Albans: Paladin.

Cohen, Stanley (1996), 'Witnessing the truth', *Index on Censorship*, 1, pp. 36–45.

Colborn, Theo, Dianne Dumanoski and John Peterson Myers (1996), *Our Stolen Future*, London: Little Brown & Company.

Cole, Leonard A. (1996), 'The specter of biological weapons', *Scientific American*, December, pp. 30–5.

Coleman, Clive and Jenny Moynihan (1996), *Understanding Crime Data: Haunted by the dark figure*, Buckingham: Open University Press.

Cowen, Tyler (1998), *In Praise of Commercial Culture*, Massachusetts: Harvard University Press.

Crews, Frederick C., ed., (1998), *Unauthorized Freud: Doubters Confront a Legend*, Viking: New York.

Davies, Paul (1995), *Are We Alone?*, Harmondsworth: Penguin Books.

Dawkins, Richard (1995), *River out of Eden*, London: Wiedenfeld & Nicholson.

Dennis, Norman (1993), *Rising Crime and the Dismembered Family: How Conformist Intellectuals Have Campaigned Against Common Sense*, London: IEA Health and Welfare Unit.

Dollery, Colin (1978), *The End of an Age of Optimism: Medical Science in Retrospect and Prospect*, London: The Nuffield Provincial Hospitals Trust.

Drexler, K. Eric (1997), *Unbounding the Future: The Nanotechnology Revolution*, published on Internet, Foresight Institute, last updated 16 July 1997, *www.foresight.org/UTF/Unbound_LBW/*.

Ehrlich, Paul (1971), *The Population Bomb*, London: Ballantine/Friends of the Earth in association with Pan Books.

Ehrlich, Paul (1994), 'Too many rich people: Weighing relative burdens on the planet', paper given to the International Conference on Population and Development, Cairo, 5–13 September.

Ehrlich, Paul and Anne Ehrlich (1991), *The Population Explosion*, New York: Touchstone.

Electrical Association (1997), *Environmental Briefing: Protecting the Earth's Ozone Layer*, London: Electrical Association.

Eliot, T. S. [1936] (1983), 'Burnt Norton' (*Four Quarters*), in *Collected Poems: 1909–62*, London: Faber and Faber, pp. 189–95.

Eliot, T. S. [1948] (1983), *Notes towards the Definition of Culture*, London: Faber and Faber Limited.

Etzioni, Amitai and Clyde Nunn (1974), 'The Public appreciation of science in contemporary America', *Daedalus*, Summer, pp. 191–205.

Fairhall, David, Richard Norton-Taylor and Tim Radford (1998), 'Saddam's Deadly armoury', *The Guardian*, 11 February, p. 15.

Field, Sally (1990), *Trends in Crime and their Interpretation: A Study of Recorded Crime in Post-War England and Wales*, Home Office Research Study No. 119, London: HMSO.

Finkielkraut, Alain (1988), *The Undoing of Thought*, trans. Dennis O'Keefe, London: The Claridge Press.

Fiske, John (1989), *Television Culture*, London: Routledge.

Florida Conservation Foundation (1993), *The Guide to Florida Environmental Issues and Information*, Florida Internet Center for Understanding Sustainability, *www.ficus.usf.edu/docs/guide_issue/chap1/chap1–2.htm*.

Foster, Hal (1990), 'Postmodernism: A preface', in Hal Foster (ed), *Postmodern Culture*, London: Pluto Press, pp. vii–xv.

Freud, Sigmund (1991), 'Civilization and its Discontents', in *Sigmund Freud: Civilization, Society and Religion*, trans. James Strachey, ed. Albert Dickson, London: Penguin Books, pp. 251–340.

Fukuyama, Francis (1992), *The End of History and the Last Man*, London: Penguin Books.

Gablik, Suzi (1992), *Has Modernism Failed?*, London: Thames & Hudson.

Garrett, Leslie (1995), *The Coming Plague: Newly Emerging Diseases in a World out of Balance*, Harmondsworth: Penguin Books.

Gissing, George [1891] (1985), *New Grub Street*, Harmondsworth: Penguin Books.

Gray, John (1998), *False Dawn: The Delusions of Global Capitalism*, London: Granta Books.

Gross, Paul R. and Norman Levitt (1998), *Higher Superstition: The Academic Left and its Quarrels with Science*, Baltimore: Johns Hopkins University Press.

Habermas, Jürgen (1990), 'Modernity-an incomplete project', in Hal Foster (ed.), *Postmodern Culture*, London: Pluto Press, pp. 3–15.

Harding, Sandra (1986), *The Science Question in Feminism*, Ithaca: Cornell University Press.

Harff, Barbara (1996), 'Rescuing endangered peoples: Missed opportunities', in Albert J. Jongman (ed.), *Contemporary Genocides: Causes, Cases, Consequences*, Leiden: PIOOM, pp. 117–30.

Harff, Barbara and Ted Robert Gurr (1996), 'Victims of the state: Genocides, politicides and group repression from 1945 to 1995', in Albert J. Jongman (ed.), *Contemporary Genocides: Causes, Cases, Consequences*, Leiden: PIOOM, pp. 33–58.

Harré, Rom, (1990) 'Narrative in scientific discourse', in Christopher Nash (ed.), *Narrative in Culture: The Uses of Storytelling in the Sciences, Philosophy, and Literature*, London: Routledge, pp. 81–101.

Harvey, David, (1990), *The Condition of Postmodernity*, Oxford: Basil Blackwell.

Heilbroner, Robert (1975), *An Inquiry into the Human Prospect*, New York: W. W. Norton & Co.

Hildyard, Nicholas, Colin Hines and Tim Lang, 'Who competes? Changing landscapes of corporate control', *The Economist*, vol. 26, No. 4, July/August 1996.

Hirst, Paul and Grahame Thompson (1996), *Globalization in Question*, Cambridge: Polity Press.

Hobsbawm, Eric (1994), *Age of Extremes: The Short Twentieth Century 1914–1991*, London: Michael Joseph.

Hobsbawm, Eric (1998), '23 pages that shook the world', *The Guardian*, 28 February.

Hobsbawm, Eric (1998), B*ehind the Times: The Decline and Fall of the Twentieth-Century Avant-Gardes*, London: Thames & Hudson.

Hoggart, Richard (1995), *The Way We Live Now*, London: Chatto & Windus.

Home Office (1996), *The 1996 British Crime Survey*, London: HMSO.

Hough, M. and Pat Mayhew (1983), *The British Crime Survey: First Report*, London: HMSO.

Huntington, Samuel P. (1996), *The Clash of Civilizations and the Remaking of World Order*, New York: Simon & Schuster.

International Statistical Yearbook, 1999 (1999), Rheinberg: Data Service & Information (CDROM).

Jacob, Margaret C. (1993), 'Hubris about science: Available responses late in the twentieth century', *Contention*, 2: 3, Spring, pp. 61–71.

Jacob, Margaret C. (ed.) (1994), T*he Politics of Western Science*, New Jersey: Humanities Press.

James, Oliver (1997), *Britain on the Couch: Treating a Low Serotonin Society*, London: Century.

Jameson, Fredric (1991), *Postmodernism, or, The Cultural Logic of Late Capitalism*, London: Verso.

Justus, John R. and Wayne A. Morrissey (1997), *Congressional Research Service Issue Brief 89005: Global Climate Change*, Washington: Committee for the National Institute for the Environment.

Kaplan, Robert (1994), 'The coming anarchy', *Atlantic Monthly*, February, pp. 44–76.

Keegan, John (1994), *A Brief History of Warfare – Past, Present, Future: The Sixth Wellington Lecture*, Southampton: University of Southampton.

Keegan, John (1995), 'Who says a Hitler could never happen again?', *Daily Telegraph*, 23 March.

Kramer, Hilton (1986), *The Revenge of the Philistines: Art and Culture, 1972–1984*, London: Secker & Warburg.

Kuhn, Thomas S. (1962), *The Structure of Scientific Revolution*, Chicago: The University of Chicago Press.

Lea, John and Jock Young (1993), *What Is to Be Done about Law & Order: Crisis in the Nineties*, London: Pluto Press.

Leggett, Jeremy (1992), 'Running down to Rio', *New Scientist*, 2 May, pp. 38–42.

Leslie, John (1996), *The End of the World: The Science and Ethics of Human Extinction*, London: Routledge.

Lewis, Justin (1990), *Art, Culture and Enterprise: The Politics of Art and the Cultural Industries*, London: Routledge.

Longworth, Richard C. (1998), *Global Squeeze; The Coming Crisis for First-World Nations*, Chicago: Contemporary Books.

Lott, Tim (1997), *The Scent of Dried Roses*, London: Penguin Books.

Lott, Tim (1999), 'Story of the Blues', *The Observer*, 21 February.

Lovelock, James [1979] (1989), *Gaia*, New York: Oxford University Press.

Luttwak, Edward (1999), *Turbo Capitalism: Winners & Losers in the Global Economy*, London: Orion Business Books.

Lyotard, Jean-François [1979] (1991), *The Postmodern Condition: A Report on Knowledge*, trans. Geoff Bennington and Brian Massumi, Manchester: Manchester University Press.

McEwan, Ian (1997), *Enduring Love*, London: Jonathan Cape.

McKie, Robin (1999), 'Antimatter set to blast scientists to other side of the cosmos', *Observer*, 7 February.

McLanahan, Sarah (1988), 'The consequences of single parenthood for subsequent generations', *Focus*, Institute for Research on Poverty, vol. ii, No. 3, 1988, pp. 16–21.

McMurtry, John (1999), *The Cancer Stage of Capitalism*, London: Pluto Press.

Maguire, Mike (1994), 'Crime statistics, patterns, and trends: Changing perceptions and their implications', in Mike Maguire, Rod Morgan and Rob Reiner (eds), *The Oxford Handbook of Criminology*, Oxford: Clarendon Press.

Marx, Karl (1977), *Selected Writings*, ed. David McLellan, Oxford: Oxford University Press.

Marx, Karl and Friedrich Engels, [1846] (1989), *The German Ideology*, ed. C. J. Arthur, London: Lawrence & Wishart.

Marx, Karl and Friedrich Engels [1848] (1985), *The Communist Manifesto*, London: Penguin Books.

Marx, Leo (1978), 'Reflections on the neo-romantic critique of science', *Daedalus*, 107: 2, pp. 61–74.

Mayhew, Pat and Natalie Aye Maung (1992), *Surveying Crime: Findings from the 1992 British Crime Survey*, Home Office Research and Statistics Department, Research Findings No. 2, London: HMSO.

Mayhew, Pat, and Jan J. M. van Dijk (1997), *Criminal Victimisation in Eleven Industrialised Countries*, Leyden: Wetenschappelijk Onderzoek- en Documentatiecentrum.

Meadows, Donella H. Dennis L. Meadows and Jørgen Randers (1992), *Beyond the Limits*, Post Mills: Chelsea Green.

Morgan, Patricia (1995), *Farewell to the Family? Public Policy and Family Breakdown in Britain and the USA*, London: IEA Health and Welfare Unity.

Morris, William [1884] (1979), 'Art and socialism', in William Morris *Political Writings of William Morris*, ed. A. L. Morton, London: Lawrence & Wishart, pp. 109–33.

Morris, William [1884] (1979), 'Art under plutocracy', in William Morris *Political Writings of William Morris*, ed. A. L. Morton, London: Lawrence & Wishart, pp. 57–108.

Nash, Harry T. (1980), 'The bureaucratization of homicide', in E. P. Thompson and Dan Smith (eds), *Protest and Survive*, Harmondsworth: Penguin Books, pp. 62–74.

Nisbet, Robert (1994), *History of the Idea of Progress*, New Brunswick: Transaction Publishers.

Nuttall, Jeff (1979), *Bomb Culture*, London: Paladin.

OECD (1989), *Labour Force Statistics, 1967–1987*, Paris: OECD.

OECD (1998), *Labour Force Statistics, 1977–1997*, Paris: OECD.

OECD (1999), 'Frequently requested statistics', Internet article, September.

OECD (1999), *Labour Force Statistics, 1978–1998*, Paris: OECD.

Pearson, Geoffrey (1983), *Hooligan: A History of Respectable Fears*, Basingstoke: Macmillan.

Philips, Alan (1998), 'West moves warily to counter the threat of nuclear anarchy', *Daily Telegraph*, 23 April.

Pronk, Jan (1996), 'The UN after 50 years', in Albert J. Jongman (ed.), *Contemporary Genocides: Causes, Cases, Consequences*, Leiden: PIOOM, pp. iii–xvi.

Ravetz, Jerome R. (1971), *Scientific Knowledge and Its Problems*, Oxford: Clarendon Press.

Relman, Arnold S. (1992), 'What market values are doing to medicine', *Atlantic Monthly*, March, pp. 99–106.

Roszak, Theodore (1970), *The Making of a Counter Culture: Reflections on the Technocratic Society and its Youthful Opposition*, London: Faber & Faber.

Roszak, Theodore (1972), *Where the Wasteland Ends: Politics and Transcendence in Postindustrial Society*, New York: Doubleday & Company.

Roszak, Theodore (1974), 'The Monster and the titan: Science, knowledge, and gnosis', *Daedalus,* Summer, pp. 17–32.

Rousseau, Jean-Jacques [1750] (1973), 'Discourse on the moral effects of the arts and sciences', in Jean-Jacques Rousseau, *The Social Contract and Discourses*, trans. G. D. H. Cole, London: Dent, pp. 1–26.

Rousseau, Jean-Jacques [1755] (1973), 'Discourse on the origin of inequality', in Jean-Jacques Rousseau, *The Social Contract and Discourses*, trans. G. D. H. Cole, London: Dent, pp. 27–113.

Rummel, Rudolph J. (1996), 'The Holocaust in comparative and historical perspective', in Albert J. Jongman (ed.), *Contemporary Genocides: Causes, Cases, Consequences*, Leiden: PIOOM, pp. 16–31.

Schell, Jonathan (1982), *The Fate of the Earth*, London: Picador/Jonathan Cape.

Schiller, Friedrich [1795] (1989), *On the Aesthetic Education of Man: In a Series of Letters*, ed. & trans. Elizabeth M. Wilkinson and L. A. Willoughby, Oxford: Oxford University Press.

Schopenhauer, Arthur [1851] (1970), *Essays and Aphorisms*, trans. R. J. Hollingdale, London: Penguin Books.

Scruton, Roger (1998), *An Intelligent Person's Guide to Modern Culture*, London: Gerald Duckworth.

Seiter, Ellen (ed.) (1989), *Remote Control: Television, Audiences and Cultural Power*, London: Routledge.

Shaw, Roy (1978), *Elitism versus Populism in the Arts*, Eastbourne: John Offord.

Shelley, Percy Bysshe [1821] (1988), 'A defence of poetry', in Percy Bysshe Shelley, *Shelley's Prose*, ed. David Lee Clark, London: Fourth Estate, pp. 275–97.

Shils, Edward (1974), 'Faith, utility, and the legitimacy of science', *Daedalus*, Summer, pp. 1–13.

Simon, Julian (1981), *The Ultimate Resource*, Princeton: Princeton University Press.

Sinsheimer, Robert (1978), 'The Presumptions of Science', *Daedalus*, 107: 2, pp. 23–35.

Soros, George (1998), *The Crisis of Capitalism: Open Society Endangered*, London: Little, Brown & Company.

Spengler, Oswald (1926), *The Decline of the West, Form and Actuality*, trans. Charles Atkinson, New York: Knopf.

State Fiscal Project (1997), *Pulling Apart: A State-by-State Analysis of Income Trends*, Washington: Center on Budget and Policy Priorities.

Steiner, George (1996), *A Festival Overture: The University Festival Lecture*, Edinburgh: University of Edinburgh.

Storr, Anthony (1989), *Freud*, Oxford: Oxford University Press.

Tallis, Raymond (1995), *Newton's Sleep: Two Cultures and Two Kingdoms*, New York: St. Martin's Press.

Tallis, Raymond (1997), *Enemies of Hope: A Critique of Contemporary Pessimism*, New York: St. Martin's Press.

Taylor, Gordon Rattray (1970), *The Doomsday Book*, London: Thames & Hudson.

Taylor, Shelley E. and Jonathon D. Brown (1988), 'Illusion and well-being: A social psychological perspective on mental health', *Psychological Bulletin*, 103: 2, pp. 193–210.

Taylor, Shelley E. and Jonathon D. Brown (1994), 'Positive illusions and well-being revisted: Separating fact from fiction', *Psychological Bulletin*, 116: 1, pp. 21–7.

Tester, Keith (1997), *Moral Culture*, London: Sage Publications.

Thompson, Damian (1996), *The End of Time: Faith and Fear in the Shadow of the Millennium*, London: Sinclair-Stevenson.

Thompson, E. P. (1980), 'Protest and survive', in E. P. Thompson and Dan Smith (eds), *Protest and Survive*, Harmondsworth: Penguin Books, pp. 9–61.

Twitchell, James B. (1997), ' "But first, a word from our sponsor": Advertising and the carnivalization of culture', in Katharine Washburn and John Thornton (eds), *Dumbing Down: Essays on the Strip-Mining of American Culture*, New York: W. W. Norton & Company, pp. 197–208.

[United Nations] (1996), *1994 Demographic Yearbook*, New York: United Nations.

United Nations Population Division (UNPD) (1992), *Long-Range World Population Projections: Two Centuries of Population Growth, 1950–2150*, New York: United Nations Population Division.

van Creveld, Martin (1991), *On Future War*, London: Brasseys.

van Creveld, Martin (1991), *The Transformation of War*, Oxford: Maxwell Macmillan International.

van Creveld, Martin (1993), *Nuclear Proliferation and the Future of Conflict*, New York: Free Press.

Wakefield, Neville (1990), *Postmodernism: The Twilight of the Real*, London: Pluto Press.

Wallerstein, Judith and Sandra Blakeslee (1989), *Second Chances*, London: Bantam Press.

Walsh, Edward (1999), 'Prison population still rising, but more slowly', *Washington Post*, 15 March.

Washburn, Katharine and John Thornton (eds) (1997), *Dumbing Down: Essays on the Strip-Mining of American Culture*, New York: W. W. Norton & Company.

Weinberg, Daniel H. (1996), *A Brief Look at Postwar U.S. Income Inequality*, Washington: U.S. Bureau of the Census, Internet article, June 1996, *www.census.gov/hhes/www/img/p60–191.pdf*.

Weinberg, Steven (1974), 'Reflections of a working scientist', *Daedalus*, Summer, pp. 33–45.

Whitehead, Alfred North (1947), *Science and the Modern World*, New York: Macmillan.

Whitehead, Barbara Dafoe (1993), 'Dan Quayle was right', *Atlantic Monthly*, April, pp. 47–84.

Wilde, Oscar [1890] (1986), 'The critic as artist', in Oscar Wilde, *The Complete Works of Oscar Wilde*, London: Collins, pp. 1009–59.

Williams, Raymond (1975), *The Country and the City*, St Albans: Paladin.

Williams, Raymond (1975), *Keywords*, Glasgow: Fontana.

Williams, Raymond (1981), *Culture*, Glasgow: Fontana.

Williams, Raymond (1989), *The Politics of Modernism*, London: Verso.

Williams, Raymond [1958] (1979), *Culture and Society 1780–1950*, Harmondsworth: Penguin Books.

Wilson, Andrew (1983), *The Disarmer's Handbook of Military Technology and Organisation*, Harmondsworth: Penguin Books.

Wolpert, Lewis (1999), *Malignant Sadness*, London: Faber and Faber.

Woolger, Steve (1988), *Science: The Very Idea*, Chichester: Ellis Horwood Limited; London: Tavistock Publications Limited.

Wordsworth, William [1800] (1969), 'Preface to the Lyrical Ballads', in William Wordsworth, *Wordsworth: Poetical Works*, ed. Thomas Hutchinson, rev. Ernest de Selincourt, Oxford: Oxford University Press, pp. 734–43.

Wordsworth, William [1815] (1969), 'Essay, supplementary to the Preface', in William Wordsworth, *Wordsworth: Poetical Works*, ed. Thomas Hutchinson, rev. Ernest de Selincourt, Oxford: Oxford University Press, pp. 743–51.

World Conservation Monitoring Centre (1995), *Biodiversity: An Overview*, Cambridge: World Conservation Monitoring Centre.

World Resources Institute (1989), 'Biodiversity: A History of Extinction', Internet Article, *www.wri.org/wri/biodiv/b03-koa.html#rates*.

Worldwatch Institute (1997), *State of the World 1997*, London: Earthscan Publications.

Wulf, Herbert (ed.) (1993), *Arms Industry Limited*, Oxford: SIPRI/Oxford University Press.

Young, Jock (1998), Letter to *The Guardian*, 8 January.

Zill, Nicholas, James L. Peterson, Kristin A. Moore and Frank F. Furstenberg, Jr. (1988), *1976–1987 National Survey of Children Waves 1, 2 and 3*, Los Altos, California: The Sociometrics Corporation.

Zohar, Danar and Ian Marshall (1994), *The Quantum Society: Mind, Physics and a New Social Vision*, London: Flamingo.

Index

Adams, Brooks, 1
Adams, Henry, 1
Adorno, Theodor, 3, 5, 135–6
Amnesty International, 67–72, 77, 95, 96
Angola
  'tribal' conflict in, 65
Antarctic
  destruction of ozone layer above, 27–8, 71n
apocalypse, 10–11
Appleyard, Brian, 104, 109–11, 113, 118
Arctic
  discovery of synthetic chemicals in, 24
Argentina
  'death squads' in, 70
Arnold, Matthew, 127, 135, 137
art
  and cultural industries, 132–3, 134–7
  and cultural relativism, 132–5
  and the evolution of consciousness, 127
  and meaning, 126–9, 131, 137
  modernism: characteristics of, 130; and cultural pessimism, 3–4; decline of, 130–1; negating power of, 135; periodisation of, 129; and postmodernism, 130; and Romanticism, 128
  and religion, 126, 128, 131, 137
  Romanticism, 112, 128
  and science, 103, 125

Bacon, Francis, 9, 105
Bailey, Joe, 61
Bangladesh
  effects of global warming on, 32
  population growth in, 43
Barber, Benjamin, 145, 148, 171–2, 177n
Baudrillard, Jean, 13, 133
Bauman, Zygmunt, 160, 162, 164–5
Beck, Aaron, 181–2, 192, 195
Beckett, Samuel, 4, 127
Belarus
  relinquishing of nuclear weapons, 63
Benjamin, Walter, 3, 132–3
Berlin, Isaiah, 105, 138n
Berman, Marshall, 177
biodiversity, loss of
  case for biodiversity conservation, 35
  extinction rates, 34–5
  measurement of biodiversity, 33–4
Blair, Tony, 151
Blake, William, 7, 49, 112, 113
Bosnia
  'tribal' conflict in, 65
Bowlby, John, 188, 191
Bradbury, Malcolm, 129, 130
Brazil
  grain deficit in, 39
Britain *see also* England; Scotland
  adoption of 'new' capitalism in, 145, 150
  banning of DDT in, 23

CULTURAL PESSIMISM

OLIVER BENNETT

Cultural pessimism arises with the conviction that the culture of a nation, a civilisation or of humanity itself is in a process of irreversible decline. In an incisive and wide-ranging analysis, *Cultural Pessimism: Narratives of Decline in the Postmodern World* charts the growth of pessimism in the West during the last decades of the twentieth century.

Drawing on studies from within a very broad range of fields, which include ecology, human rights, military history, international relations, criminology, history of science, cultural criticism and political economy, the author shows how cultural pessimism in the postmodern world can be related to the cumulative effect of four key narratives of decline:

- Environmental decline
- Moral decline
- Intellectual decline
- Political decline

After a review of pessimism in other historical periods, each of these narratives is explored in depth. The book attempts to answer a number of questions: how are the narratives constituted and what are the conditions to which they refer? To what extent are those conditions historically unprecedented? To which cultures do the narratives relate? What values do they reflect? To what extent are the identified processes of decline seen as irreversible? Concluding that cultural pessimism is as much a matter of psychological and biological disposition as of intellectual judgement, Oliver Bennett's challenging book offers valuable new insights into how we view the prospects of the twenty-first century.

FEATURES
- Provides an authoritative account of how the postmodern world has been represented as one of decline
- Brings together different perspectives kept apart by professional and academic specialisation
- Views culture in its broadest sense as 'a whole way of life'
- Provides an historical overview of cultural pessimism, tracing its various manifestations from the modern period back to its existence in early religions
- Examines the biological, psychological and sociological factors that can produce a disposition towards cultural pessimism
- Written in a clear, readable style, whilst maintaining academic integrity

OLIVER BENNETT is the Director of the Centre for Cultural Policy Studies at the University of Warwick. He has published widely on the subject of cultural policy and is the founding editor of the *International Journal of Cultural Policy*. He is the co-editor of a forthcoming book series in Cultural Policy Studies.

Edinburgh University Press
22 George Square, Edinburgh
0 7486 0936 9
Visit our web site on www.eup.ed.ac.uk

Cover design: Fionna Robson

ISBN 0-7486-0936-9

9 780748 609369